BEYOND THE REBEL GIRL

T0345062

Beyond the Rebel Girl

WOMEN AND THE INDUSTRIAL WORKERS OF THE WORLD IN THE PACIFIC NORTHWEST, 1905–1924

Heather Mayer, PhD

Oregon State University Press   Corvallis

Library of Congress Cataloging-in-Publication Data

Names: Mayer, Heather, author.
Title: Beyond the rebel girl : women and the industrial workers of the world in the Pacific
    Northwest, 1905–1924 / Heather Mayer.
Description: Corvallis : Oregon State University Press, 2018. | Includes bibliographical
    references and index.
Identifiers: LCCN 2018024436 | ISBN 9780870719394 (paperback)
Subjects: LCSH: Women—Northwest, Pacific—History—20th century. | Women—
    Political activity—Northwest, Pacific—History—20th century. | Industrial Workers
    of the World—History—20th century. | BISAC: POLITICAL SCIENCE / Labor &
    Industrial Relations. | SOCIAL SCIENCE / Women's Studies. | HISTORY / United
    States / State & Local / Pacific Northwest (OR, WA).
Classification: LCC HQ1438.A19 M39 2018 | DDC 320.082/09795—dc23

LC record available at https://lccn.loc.gov/2018024436

♾ This paper meets the requirements of ANSI/NISO Z39.48-1992
(Permanence of Paper).

© 2018 Heather Mayer
All rights reserved
First published in 2018 by Oregon State University Press
Printed in the United States of America

Oregon State University
OSU Press

Oregon State University Press
121 The Valley Library
Corvallis OR 97331-4501
541-737-3166 • fax 541-737-3170
www.osupress.oregonstate.edu

For Cameron and Maya—
May you be inspired by the rebels of the past
to create a more just and equitable future

"The Rebel Girl"
by Joe Hill, 1915

There are women of many descriptions
In this queer world, as everyone knows.
Some are living in beautiful mansions,
And are wearing the finest of clothes.
There are blue blooded queens and princesses,
Who have charms made of diamonds and pearl;

But the only and thoroughbred lady
Is the Rebel Girl

Chorus
That's the Rebel Girl! That's the Rebel Girl!
To the Working class she's a precious pearl.
She brings courage, pride, and joy
To the fighting Rebel Boy.
We've had girls before, but we need some more
In the Industrial Workers of the World.
For it's great to fight for freedom
With a Rebel Girl.

Yes, her hands may be hardened from labor,
And her dress may not be very fine;
But a heart in her bosom is beating
That is true to her class and her kind.
And the grafters in terror are trembling
When her spite and defiance she'll hurl;
For the only and thoroughbred lady
Is the Rebel Girl.

Contents

Introduction

On a warm July afternoon in 1910, two men hopped off a freight train in the Palouse agricultural region of eastern Washington State. Dirty and hungry, they petitioned the local farmers for some food. They were offered a small loaf of bread for the steep price of fifteen cents, and decided to visit the chicken coop and rid the farmer of one of his chickens instead. They then hiked to a hobo jungle where several itinerant men had camped out and were waiting for work on the harvest to begin that next week. They helped themselves to a few more chickens from the surrounding farms and spent the next few days in the jungle, likely singing songs from the first edition of the *Little Red Songbook* and discussing the emancipation of the laboring class. They were soon directed to a poor farm for some food, and updated the readers of the *Industrial Worker*, their union newspaper, on the possibility of work in the region.[1]

On a sunny July morning seven years later, a lively group of four hundred men, women, and children gathered for a monster picnic. They started the day by eating breakfast at a fully unionized restaurant in Aberdeen, a logging town on the coast of Washington. After breakfast, they congregated on the nearby dock and were entertained by a twenty-piece band while waiting for their excursion boats. The boats took the festive group to a picnic area on the mouth of the Chehalis River, where they were joined by four hundred more of their friends and Fellow Workers (a term of endearment used to denote fellow union members). Upon arrival, they feasted on two hundred dollars' worth of food, again served by unionized waitresses. Games with prizes entertained the children. The satisfied and jolly bunch ended the day with songs and a lecture on industrial unionism.[2]

Both events happened in the same region in the early twentieth century, and both featured members of the Industrial Workers of the World, a radical labor union. But the first scene is the familiar image of

A snapshot of IWW members on a Sunday picnic outing, location unknown, ca. 1910s. Walter P. Reuther Library, Archives of Labor and Urban Affairs, Wayne State University, 5176.

Wobblies (as members of the IWW were called) in the Pacific Northwest. The image of the disreputable hobo agitator was used by newspapers, state and local governments, and law enforcement to emphasize union members' outsider status and disregard for the law. But the second scene also represents a very important part of Wobbly life and culture in the Northwest: the more family-friendly radical community in cities and towns.

Today, a century after its heyday, the Industrial Workers of the World remains a popular subject for discussion and celebration. Its members are easy to love, with their songs and cartoons, general irreverent attitude, and courage in the face of the persecution they confronted from vigilantes, law enforcement, and government officials. But the popular narrative told about the Wobblies is well-worn. Neither academics nor activists have challenged the tale that has been around for the last century. And the story that has been told is a predominantly male and masculine one. But there is more to the story: Women appear in photographs of union events. They are mentioned in newspaper accounts. They were arrested in major conflicts. But they rarely appear in the history books.

This book takes a new look at that well-worn narrative of Wobblies in the Pacific Northwest as young, single, male, itinerant workers. Although those workers did form a large portion of the membership and were involved in important strikes in extractive industries, such as the 1917 lumber strike, they are only part of the picture. In small towns across the Northwest, and in the larger cities of Seattle, Portland, and Spokane, women played an integral role in Wobbly life. Not only single women, but also families—husband and wife Wobbly teams—were often present during some of the biggest fights for free speech or in defense of jailed members.

In most histories of the IWW, discussion of women's roles is usually limited to Elizabeth Gurley Flynn, the IWW's well-known female national organizer, and the roles of rank and file women in the famous textile strikes of Paterson, New Jersey, and Lawrence, Massachusetts. While Flynn and the textile workers are no doubt deserving of study, women went on strike as part of and in support of the IWW, were arrested in its free speech fights, stood with their fellow workers in speaking out against World War I, and were persecuted and prosecuted along with their male comrades all over the Pacific Northwest. At the same time, the IWW engaged in women's issues, such as birth control agitation, and advanced an economic argument regarding prostitution, seeing "fallen" women as part of the working class and victims of the capitalist system, rather than as morally deficient. Focusing on women changes how we see the IWW in a fundamental way. We see that its reach surpassed the lumber camps and hobo jungles, and that it was a valid avenue in which radical working-class women could organize, educate, and agitate for social justice.

While "official" Wobbly ideology, as espoused by IWW newspapers, IWW General Executive Board meetings, and the annual convention, did not offer much specific advice on the "woman question" other than noting the need to organize women, individuals within the union navigated the issues of sexuality, marriage, childcare, and domestic labor on a daily basis. The free-footed Wobbly with no wife or kids to hold him back was held up by some as the ideal member who could hop a train to join the fight at a moment's notice, but many Wobblies who were in relationships had to choose whether to get married, whether women would take part in the movement—and risk arrest—alongside their husbands, whether to use birth control, and in general how Wobbly ideals played out in daily life.

The title of this book signals my intent to take us beyond Elizabeth Gurley Flynn—often referred to as "the Rebel Girl"—as the focus for discussions of women and the IWW. Flynn spent considerable time in the Pacific Northwest and will still play a minor role here, but my goal is to not let her overshadow the other women who were valuable assets to the organization in a local capacity. The title also refers to women *and* the IWW, rather than women *in* the IWW; I purposefully did not limit myself to women who were dues-paying members of the organization. I also examine working-class women's support for the organization's activities, like birth control agitation, and legal defense, such as took place after the Everett free speech fight of 1916.

The IWW did more than offer women organization in an industrial union at their place of employment. The union also provided women the opportunity to participate in broader social and political issues. Unlike the feminist movement of the early twentieth century, the IWW provided a way for working-class women to move beyond the narrow issue of women's suffrage. Articles in IWW newspapers discussed issues affecting women such as marriage and free love, women's right to work, their role in the home, and birth control, as well as things not specific—but still important—to women, such as patriotism, war, the class struggle, and economics. Women were organized with and alongside the men of the IWW, not in separate female auxiliaries, as often happened in the American Federation of Labor (AFL); they fought for their own interests as women workers, not just as adjuncts to men. In this book I examine both the successes and limits of cross-sex organization in a union that advocated a radical reconstruction of society based on working-class solidarity, regardless of gender.

Relatively little scholarly work exists on women within the IWW, compared with the amount done on the organization as a whole. It is not difficult to see why. Little evidence of women appears in the national archives of the union, and the major source on Wobblies in the Northwest, the *Industrial Worker* newspaper published in Spokane, contains few examples of women's activities or interests. Official records and newspapers are often where historians studying the IWW have found the most material, so it is no wonder they haven't found reason to write about women's lives.

The standard history of the IWW, *We Shall Be All*, by Melvyn Dubofsky, published in 1969, made little of women's involvement outside of discussing Elizabeth Gurley Flynn. More attention was paid to women's involvement in works written in the 1970s and 1980s, but still with no large-scale treatment of or focus on the Pacific Northwest. More

Cover of the sheet music for Joe Hill's "The Rebel Girl," with image modeled after Elizabeth Gurley Flynn. Illustration by Arthur Machia. Walter P. Reuther Library, Archives of Labor and Urban Affairs, Wayne State University, 26677.

recent studies of the IWW have been mostly local or regional histories. Studies looking at the culture and gendered ideology of the organization have focused on maleness and masculinity.[3]

Clearly the IWW appealed to male workers and employed a gendered discourse of masculinity to promote revolutionary unionism. Despite the masculine ideology, however, women were still drawn to the organization. Many of them created a gendered imagery themselves, deriding the manhood of strikebreakers, urging workers to be "real men," and creating a new ideal of femininity, the Rebel Girl. This kind of female activism was used by male and female Wobblies to shame men who were not taking an active stance in the fight against the employing class. Regarding the three women arrested in the Spokane free speech fight, the *Industrial Worker* noted, "it ought to make some of you great, husky, imitations of men ashamed of yourselves when women suffer that you may have your right."[4]

If IWW culture appealed so strongly to male migrant workers, what about it appealed to women? These Wobbly women were drawn primarily to the ideology of the union, and then to its culture. The revolutionary syndicalism of the union focused on direct action in the workplace and on the streets that gave women a role to play outside the political realm, where many middle-class women focused on the fight for suffrage. Wobbly women wanted equality, freedom of speech, better workplace conditions, birth control, and the freedom to choose whether to get married, but they saw the answer to these problems in industrial organization and did not look to the state to "save" them in the way that middle-class activists did. In studies outside the IWW, historians have emphasized the importance of community and family ties to the labor movement in the West. Acknowledging how social relationships inspired or limited political action gives us a much fuller picture of working-class history than focusing solely on strikes and organizations.[5]

Were these Wobbly women feminists? The term "feminist" was coming into vogue during the early twentieth century, associated primarily with white, middle-class women whose main focus of activism was suffrage. Wobbly women felt more in common with their working-class brothers than with these women, and so distanced themselves from the term. Their critiques focused on the evils of capitalism, and although they advocated more freedoms for women, they often did not offer a critique of patriarchy to go along with it.

My work on the IWW suggests that women in the union sought solidarity with working-class men and denied that a common bond existed between women that transcended classes. As early as 1907, Lillian Forberg advocated women organizing with men. She wrote in the IWW newspaper, the *Industrial Union Bulletin*, "Wherever women are engaged in Industry let them organize, not by themselves, but together with the men with whom they work; let them take an active part in the control of the organization and the education of the unorganized; by doing so they will become a part of the embryo of the Industrial Commonwealth which is forming within the shell of capitalism."[6] Deriding upper-class women, and their well-fed dogs, was also a common theme in IWW papers. This is not to suggest that a few anecdotes mean that women never felt that their interests as workers and as women were in conflict, but only that women who advocated revolutionary industrial unionism often felt that ties of class were stronger than ties of sex. Historian Mari Jo Buhle notes that during this period many immigrant working-class women found middle-class suffragists wanted to "divert them from active class consciousness to a more abstract transclass loyalty, from the vision of the general strike to an endless electoral tug of war."[7]

Historians of the IWW, and some Wobblies, have often traced the radicalism of migratory workers, such as those in the lumber camps, to their lack of family ties. The popular association of the Wobbly as a single, male transient was utilized by the press, business owners, politicians, church leaders, and the American Federation of Labor to insinuate that Wobblies were not "respectable" citizens—that they did not possess the social respectability that came along with having a family. The notion of "respectability," often identified as having a family and owning a home, was utilized by the middle class and the "labor aristocracy" of the AFL. The politics of respectability were often used against the IWW, and family status was a key part of that. But the importance of family status was contested ground within the organization. The IWW in some instances played up that its members had wives and children or were mothers themselves, but it also rejected the argument that those with families should be treated differently than those without.

Examining female Wobblies interactions with the law, it becomes clear that legal institutions and individuals viewed the actions of Wobblies through a class-based and gendered lens of respectability. I define "respectability" in this case as the upholding of white Victorian ideals of a male-dominated household and monogamous marriage, complete with child-rearing, home-ownership, and modest dress and behavior. Members of the IWW faced accusations that they lacked respectability and therefore, in the view of some labor leaders, politicians, and vigilantes, forfeited claims to First Amendment rights and sometimes even legal protection.[8] It is important to remember that the majority of the women profiled in this study, even as they faced criticism or denial of their respectability, still maintained their privileges as white women, which allowed them to take actions that may have been more dangerous or risky for women of color.

Not all adversaries of the IWW defined respectability the same way. For conservative union members, virtually all male, respectability included knowledge of a skilled trade, union activism within a craft, stability in a community, and a family. The respectable union man's wife would not work outside the home, if at all possible, and was an active member of the union's women's auxiliary. For politicians, the Wobblies' defiance of laws they saw as unjust and the organization's disinterest in signing contracts with employers denied it respectability. Vigilantes obsessed with 100 percent Americanism viewed the IWW as unpatriotic and un-American. Respectability was tied to sexuality, race, ethnicity, and religion, with heterosexual, white, Anglo, Protestant workers as the standard-bearers.

Respectability can also be viewed in a relational sense, wherein those who have it define themselves in comparison with those who don't. Those "other people" are the rough, disreputable people who do not meet the norms set by the in-group. Wobblies were often seen as outsiders, the very definition of the "other." But they fought back against this definition of respectability with a definition of their own, based on solidarity, courage in the face of repression, and free choice in personal matters.[9]

The public roles that many female Wobblies played during strikes, speeches, and rallies took them out of the private sphere of the home and into the public arena. Middle-class women had increasingly gained social acceptance in their roles as public speakers for Progressive causes and suffrage campaigns, speaking to women and about women's issues. But female Wobblies used the language of working-class solidarity and spoke to a mixed-sex audience and with male speakers during free speech fights such as the one in Everett. They therefore bore a double threat to their respectability.

Sociologists have also demonstrated that, as recently as the 1980s and into the present, "nonlegal indicators of respectability will affect the sanctions that female defendants incur." Wobbly women were often arrested because of their connection with the union, and while on trial or being interrogated by the police, they were questioned about their personal lives on matters that had nothing to do with the case at hand. Prosecutors utilized relationship status to signify the defendant's lack of respectability and thereby increase the likelihood that a jury would find them to be disreputable in other ways. Respectability is still a factor today, both in legal cases and in public perception and media portrayals of radical and activist movements.[10]

The women in this study were not all wage earners themselves. Many were wives of IWW men and did not work outside the home. The question of whether housewives could be members of the IWW was explicitly posed to the *Industrial Union Bulletin* in 1908. The IWW constitution stated that none but wage earners could be members. Sophie Vasilio wrote in to ask if non-wage-earning working-class women had a right to belong to a mixed local of the union—that is, local branches that did not represent a specific industry, but represented all members regardless of occupation. The editor responded that "no reason is apparent women, married and wishing to aid in the propaganda work, should not be admitted to a mixed local; but no provision is made for such a person when the mixed local ends its activities and its members take their places in Industrial Unions." The editor also said that the issue would be addressed at the next convention, though it never was.[11] IWW housewives did not, however, wait for official confirmation of their role. In addition to their support of the union, housewives played key roles in free speech fights and on defense committees. Clearly women's roles in the IWW have been more profound and complicated than most historians have suggested.[12]

Thus in this book I follow those historians of gender and class who have begun to shift their focus from the workplace to the household and the community. This study takes an inclusive approach, and looks at women and the IWW in the workplace, community, and household, while attempting to understand how class and gender shaped their experiences in all those areas. Focusing on the Pacific Northwest allows me to examine small cities and resource towns, rather than lumber camps. The demographics are very different, as a result, and therefore expand our notion of what a Wobbly was and how the Wobbly community functioned outside the lumber camp and hobo jungle.[13]

My focus in this book is on the states of Oregon and Washington. A regional rather than a local study is important because women did not limit themselves to a single city. One woman who figures prominently in my study, Edith Frenette, traveled around the region, showing up in free speech fights and strikes in Port Alberni, British Columbia; Everett, Seattle, and Spokane, Washington; and Missoula, Montana. A regional perspective illuminates how the radical community of the Northwest functioned. Wobblies often held meetings in conjunction with Socialists, and hosted anarchist speakers such as Emma Goldman when she came through town. Major events such as free speech fights drew in Wobblies from all over the continent to participate. Restricting the study of the IWW to a city or industry restricts our understanding of it as a community and a movement.

As chapter 1 demonstrates, the Pacific Northwest also differed socially, ethnically, and economically from the rest of the United States and was particularly attractive to the IWW for many of these reasons. After a brief introduction to the region in chapter 1, the book follows a roughly chronological structure, with each chapter focusing on a major event or person. Chapter 2 analyzes the Spokane free speech fight, one of the early notable Wobbly-led fights in the Northwest and one of the first that brought women into the picture. Elizabeth Gurley Flynn, Edith Frenette, and Agnes Thecla Fair all spent time in the jails of Spokane during the fight, and their treatment caused a public outcry over the deplorable conditions that jailed women faced. Chapter 3 examines a small strike in Seattle in 1912. Although the strike itself was minor, the treatment of two of the strike leaders sheds light on how authorities tried to stigmatize and punish Wobblies for unorthodox beliefs about love and marriage.

Chapter 4 examines the 1913 Portland cannery strike. The IWW did organize female laundry workers, waitresses, and domestics in the region, but details of those labor struggles are difficult to come by. The Portland strike was the largest and most significant in the Northwest that involved primarily women. The cannery strike evolved into a free speech fight, with several women involved, and also introduced the Portland Wobblies to an eighteen-year-old girl named Lillian Larkin, arrested on suspicion of prostitution. This incident provides a welcome example for studying how the union related to prostitutes and saw prostitution as a by-product of industrial capitalism.

Chapter 5 focuses on the Everett Massacre and ensuing trial. The little-known role that women played in the events in Everett was the inspiration for this study to begin with. Women were jailed for speaking in Everett, and the audiences at most of the street speaking events comprised primarily women and children. The chapter examines women's pivotal role in the events leading up to the massacre, how women were used by both sides during the ensuing trial, and Wobbly beliefs on the institution of marriage.

In addition, chapters 2 through 5 examine the ways in which the notion of respectability was utilized by both the Wobblies and their detractors during legal proceedings and in public discourse. These two tactics—judging respectability on behalf of the law and defending respectability on behalf of the Wobblies—held strong until the beginning of World War I. As war hysteria mounted, constructs of respectability shifted and became more strongly tied to 100 percent Americanism, which meant patriotic support of the war. Although questions surrounding sexual morality did not stop completely, they were no longer the primary focus of interrogation. If officials felt that Wobbly beliefs threatened the traditional family before the war, they reasoned that Wobbly political beliefs threatened the entire nation during the war. The war also subsumed focus on women's issues such as birth control. Radical birth control activism peaked in 1916 and became a lesser focus as most radical activists turned their attention to the war.

Chapters 6 through 8 examine the toll that wartime repression took on the IWW and many of its members. Louise Olivereau and Marie Equi are two great examples of women connected with the organization who shifted their focus from women's issues to antiwar activism. Chapters 7 and 8 examine, respectively, the cases of these two women, who were arrested for speaking out against World War I. Their cases were widely known in the Northwest and are essential, as two infamous IWW supporters, to understanding the region during this period. The treatment that Equi and Olivereau received from federal officials and the support (or lack thereof) that they received from the IWW reflected the changing environment of a nation at war.

In addition to Equi and Olivereau, numerous uncelebrated women were affected by the crackdown on the IWW during the war. Women were arrested for work they did in support of the organization and many were threatened with jail time or deportation. Women also played a role in supporting the male Wobblies who were arrested around the Northwest. Through the examination of the tensions that split the organization, and how individuals suffered because of persecution and federal repression, we come to understand how the war years ultimately led to a decline in the family and female-friendly aspects of the organization and how the radical community of the Pacific Northwest ceased to function as it had in the years prior to the war.

Today, in a divided country where workers face an uncertain future and unionization is it at its lowest levels in a century, studying the IWW provides both instruction and inspiration. The union sought to organize all workers regardless of sex, race, or skill. It advocated organizing workers along industrial lines, rather than focusing on a single craft, plant, or city. It emphasized that workers in the United States shared common interests—and a common enemy—with workers in Mexico, China, and Russia. It advocated organizing the "unorganizable" and can be seen today representing fast food workers and championing the rights of prison laborers.

The Wobblies encountered tremendous persecution for their agitation. They faced daunting forces, both local (vigilantes) and national (federal restrictions on freedom of speech during wartime), with bravery and ingenuity. Repression did not kill the Wobblies, although it certainly caused suffering in the lives of many individual members and their families. Their fight reminds us of the importance of solidarity and of community. A movement made up only of those with nothing to lose cannot achieve lasting success. Risking arrest in defiance of laws restricting our rights, as the Wobblies did in Spokane and Everett, has its place, but so too do the actions of families coming together to picnic, play games, and sing songs just like the Wobblies in Aberdeen did a century ago.

1
Setting the Scene
Why the Pacific Northwest?

Those of us who live in the Pacific Northwest like to think that our region is unique, that the natural beauty and regional culture distinguish us from the rest of the United States. Cities like Seattle and Portland are beacons of white, liberal progressivism and environmentalism, drawing in newcomers from less "advanced" areas of the nation. These attitudes, like everything, have a history, and would not be too dissimilar to arguments made by northwesterners a century ago.

The story of the labor movement in the United States has often been told as a national story, with court cases, labor organizations, strikes, and laws that affected all workers. But that national narrative tends to focus on the industrialized cities of the East and Midwest as proxy for the nation as a whole. The IWW had success in these major cities, but it also had a different kind of success, and a different kind of membership, in the mills and fields and cities of the Pacific Northwest. In order to understand why so many major events in the union's history took place in this region, and why the organization appealed to so many people in the area, we need a better understanding of what makes this area unique. The industrialization that happened in the East over the long course of the nineteenth century happened in a few short decades in Oregon and Washington. The volatility of that transformation, as well as the independent nature of those who moved here from other areas of the northwest, made it a fertile ground for radicalism.

Just as the term "America" held images of streets paved with gold for immigrants from Europe and Asia, the Pacific Northwest also held an allure to those living in the Northeast and Midwest regions of the United States. As historian Carlos Schwantes has noted, a description of the Pacific Northwest based purely on statistics or geographical descriptions cannot quantify the importance of the image of the region to those who wished to settle here. The *idea* of the Northwest is what drew people here. Regional promoters and the Northern Pacific Railroad proclaimed the vast array of natural resources and the health benefits of the climate. They focused their appeals on white working-class men, noting that agriculture was so easy that a good work ethic was more necessary than funds to be successful in the region.[1]

The most familiar aspect of Pacific Northwest history is the image of pioneers in wagon trains crossing on the Oregon Trail. Those crossings peaked between 1840 and 1860, and our story begins decades later. Instead of covered wagons, steam locomotives are the mode of transportation essential to understanding the region. Connecting the Northwest to the rest of the country by rail spurred industrialization and massive migration in the late nineteenth century. Local lines were built as early as 1875, but it wasn't until 1887 that the Southern Pacific connected Oregon to California (and thus the rest of the United States). By 1891 Seattle was connected to Montreal via the Canadian Pacific Railway and, in 1893, to St. Paul via the Great Northern Railway. These railways provided a way to distribute Northwest products around the country, and the economy started booming. The railroads brought access to new markets, but they also came with the price of dependence on the line to distribute that product.

Railroad companies were the biggest boosters of the Northwest. They had agents around the country, and all over the world, handing out pamphlets and giving lectures about the availability of land and the absence of crop failure. By the 1880s, the local labor movement blamed boosters for creating false hope and enticing people to move to the Northwest, only to have them flood the job market and lower wages. One pamphlet distributed by the Union Pacific Railroad in 1889 falsely advertised that jobs were so plentiful in the Northwest that workers never resorted to the strike, and employers never locked out their employees.[2]

These kinds of advertisements portrayed the Northwest as a land of opportunity for white working men, and that is primarily who migrated there during this period. The racial makeup of the inhabitants of Oregon and Washington differed significantly from that in other parts of the country. From 1890 to 1920, both Oregon and Washington maintained a primarily white population, with larger populations of Asians and Native

Americans than of African Americans. An increase of African American migration to the region did not occur until World War II, when many came for jobs in the shipyards. Oregon was particularly notorious for its racist policies and practices. Although the state banned slavery in its 1859 constitution, it also banned free black people from living there. The results of these kinds of exclusionary policies are borne out when we examine how white the population was during this period.

In the late nineteenth and early twentieth centuries, the populations of Oregon and Washington grew dramatically. Oregon's population increased from 317,704 in 1890 to 783,389 in 1920. Washington's growth was even more substantial: from 357,252 people in 1890 to 1,356,621 in 1920. In 1890, 95 percent of Oregonians counted in the census were categorized as white, and by 1920 that number was up to 98 percent. Washington was similar, with 95 percent counted as white in 1890 and 97 percent in 1920.

The category of "white" tells us little about whether these people were native-born, or from which region of Europe they came. The Northwest was far from Ellis Island, the point of entry for many European immigrants, and most had settled for a while somewhere else in the country before migrating to the region. Of the European immigrants, Scandinavians were the most numerous. The majority of Scandinavian immigrants settled initially in the Midwest. As the center of the lumber industry shifted from the Midwest to the Northwest, immigration patterns followed.

The image of the Northwest populace tends to be that most members were native-born Americans. Census information shows, however, that Oregon and Washington maintained a higher percentage of foreign-born inhabitants than the average for the United States as a whole. Oregon's foreign-born population was 18.3 percent in 1890, and Washington's was 25.8 percent, dwarfing the US average of 14.8 percent. The largest numbers of foreign-born persons in the region came from our neighbor to the north, Canada. The borders were relatively fluid during this period, and we will see examples of Wobblies who moved back and forth between the two countries. England, Sweden, Finland, and Norway provided the majority of the rest.

Relative to the rest of the nation, Oregon and Washington also had large numbers of immigrants from China and Japan. Chinese immigrants arrived earlier than the Japanese, most to work on the railroads. Many that stayed in the region made their living as miners, though they were subject to tremendous violence and prejudice. The most infamous incident was the 1887 massacre at Hells Canyon in Oregon, where a gang of seven white men killed anywhere from ten to thirty-four Chinese miners, robbed them, and were not prosecuted. Much of the anti-Chinese violence was perpetrated by white workers and organized labor during this period. After the 1882 Chinese Exclusion Act, the number of Chinese immigrants declined; emigrants from Japan started arriving in larger numbers in the 1890s, until the 1907 Gentlemen's Agreement between Japan and the United States informally restricted emigration from that country. Laws targeting Japanese immigrants, such as the 1923 Oregon Alien Land Law, tried to restrict immigrants' ability to own homes. Japanese immigrants tended to work in agriculture.

Migration to the Northwest led to an imbalanced male-female ratio during this time period. In 1890, Washington had a female population of only 33 percent, while Oregon was at 42 percent. By 1920, the ratio had become slightly more balanced, with Oregon and Washington at 46 and 47 percent female, respectively. Although women did work for wages in the Northwest, their labor did not follow the industries, such as garment manufacturing, typical of women's work in the East and Midwest. The most common occupations for women in Oregon in 1910 were schoolteacher, dressmaker (non-factory), stenographer, saleswoman, bookkeeper or accountant, boarding or lodging housekeeper, farmer, housekeeper, milliner, waitress, store clerk, and midwife or nurse. And we cannot forget to include other forms of labor that often went unrecognized in the census, such as prostitution.[3]

Among Scandinavian immigrants, domestic service was one of the largest job categories, and 61.9 percent of all female Scandinavian immigrant women in the United States were listed as domestic servants in 1900. Domestic servants received room and board, so their wages were lower than those with factory occupations. They often worked longer hours and had less time to socialize with peers after work. Emmy Berg, who immigrated to the Northwest from Sweden in 1909 at the age of seventeen recalled several jobs she had in her first ten years in the Northwest, including domestic service, working at a bakery, waiting tables and running her own restaurant for a short time, and finally working at a laundry. Most of these jobs earned her about fifteen dollars per month, the equivalent purchasing power of about four hundred dollars per month today. It was estimated in Portland in 1913 that a young woman needed to make nine to ten dollars per week in order to provide for herself. Female occupations in the Northwest did not reflect the resource-based economy that the majority of male workers in the region participated in during this period.[4]

Businessmen and settlers from around the world were attracted to the Northwest for its bountiful natural resources, ripe for exploitation. The extractive industries were the economic backbone of the region. The accepted belief was that natural resources were there for the benefit of mankind. With a seemingly endless supply of trees and fish, no attention was initially paid to preservation. The main industries in the northwest were fishing, agriculture, and lumber.

Fishing (along with fur trading) was one of the earliest economic mainstays of the region. Salmon was the most well-known and profitable of the fish abundant in the Northwest. This led to the rise of canneries to pack the salmon for shipment, and by 1883 there were at least fifty on the Columbia River. The number of Columbia River canneries reached a peak in 1895, with the Puget Sound surpassing their number and peaking in 1913. After that point the majority of canned salmon came from Alaska. Most of the fishermen in the Northwest were Scandinavians or Finns; the workers involved in canning were primarily Chinese. Most were men, although women were involved in other types of canning, as we will see in chapter 4.[5]

Agriculture was the second-biggest industry in the Northwest. The Willamette Valley, the Walla Walla Valley, and the Palouse region were the centers of agricultural activity. Wheat, cattle, and apples dominated agriculture in the region, with sheep, pears, prunes, and cherries not far behind. Initially only the Willamette Valley (with its easy access to water) drew farmers in the 1850s. Areas in the more arid eastern parts of the region relied on irrigation. Irrigation initially began with individual efforts, but then larger companies got involved, and finally the federal government started large-scale "reclamation" projects.

Wheat and apples made up two-thirds of Washington's agricultural income by the 1920s. These crops called for a large supply of seasonal workers during the harvest, roughly thirty-five thousand a year in Washington. Most of these workers were year-round itinerant workers, spending time in the fields and in the lumber camps, and even shoveling snow in the winter. They spent the rest of their time either looking for work or spending their earnings (often in bars and brothels) in the bigger cities and towns. As Historian Greg Hall has pointed out, these workers, without permanent homes or ties to the community, were welcomed during the harvest but remained socially separated from the communities they served, and their presence was undesirable when the harvest was over.[6]

Lumber was the biggest industry in the Pacific Northwest, and the one with which the region is most closely identified. Because of the centrality of lumber organizing to the story of the IWW in Oregon and Washington, it is important to get a clear picture of how the industry functioned, who worked in the industry, and the working conditions they encountered.

While the earliest mills were operated by the Hudson's Bay Company in the 1820s, production didn't explode until the lumbermen of the Great Lakes region turned westward in the late 1880s. In 1849, the Midwest region of the country was cutting 54.8 percent of the lumber produced in the United States, while the Pacific states were at only 5.9 percent. By 1919, the Midwest was producing only 7.5 percent, while the Pacific states had jumped to 25.5 percent. The southern states were the only region that produced more, with 46.6 percent of the total. The dominance of the southern lumber industry (and their lack of unionization and lower wages) was constantly used by employers in the Northwest to justify low wages, long hours, and miserable conditions in lumber camps.[7]

Three major corporations dominated the lumber industry in the Pacific Northwest at the beginning of the century: the Southern Pacific Railroad, the Northern Pacific Railway, and the Weyerhaeuser Corporation. Weyerhaeuser, a vertically integrated organization founded in Minnesota, made its first large lumber purchase in the Northwest from the Northern Pacific Railway in 1900. This initial purchase of 900,000 acres would grow to 1,500,000 by 1905. In addition to these behemoth lumber corporations, there were a plethora of small timber owners.[8]

The timber industry was a volatile one. The completion of the Great Northern Railway in 1893 made it possible for Pacific Northwest lumber to be shipped all over the country. Around 1900 the industry really started booming, but instability brought fluctuations of prices and profits. The 1906 San Francisco earthquake provided a windfall for the lumber industry, but this was soon followed by a sharp fall in profits after the 1907 depression. Lumber prices could vary wildly. A report by the United States Bureau of Labor Statistics of wholesale prices per board foot of Douglas-fir (*Pseudotsuga menziesii*)—which was a majority of the timber in the Northwest—showed prices that jumped from $8.50 in December 1905 to $13.75 in January 1907. Prices increased again to hold steady at $14.25 from May through August of 1907. They rapidly dropped thereafter, not reaching that height again until May of 1917. Prices climbed again during the war years and shortly after, hovering around $18.50 through most of 1918 and jumping as high as $37.50 in early 1920 before dropping to $11.50 in January 1922. The report noted that chronic instability in the lumber industry was similar to that of agriculture, with competition between many small producers leading to overproduction and price-cutting.[9]

Fluctuations in lumber prices affected wages in the industry, which also fluctuated. Workers in the lumber camps made the modern equivalent of about a thousand dollars per month in this period, working eight- to ten-hour days for eighteen to twenty days a month. The unskilled sawmill workers were usually the lowest paid in the lumber industry, with slightly higher wages in the logging camps because of the harsh conditions found there, and the highest wages usually going to skilled shingle weavers. The industry was estimated to employ at least fifty thousand people in Oregon alone in 1907.[10]

The ethnic makeup of lumber workers matched the trends of the region as a whole. Although many of the workers were native-born Americans, Scandinavian immigrants made up the largest ethnic group, with Southern European and Asian immigrants as significantly smaller minorities. A 1924 government report noted that the only significant study of race and ethnicity in the Northwest logging industry was carried out by the Washington State Bureau of Labor in 1913. The report divided workers into only three categories. The first group, "Natives and North Europeans" made up 88 percent of the 20,538 workers in the mills and 93 percent of the 5,752 workers in the camps. The second group, "South Europeans" made up roughly 6 percent of those in the mills and 6 percent of those in the camps, while the third group, "Asiatics" also made up 6 percent of millworkers and less than 1 percent of workers in the logging camps. Although the southern European and

Asian workers made up 15.6 percent of the total, they "held only 2.3 per cent of the jobs which paid over $2.50 a day."[11]

The logging camps where most of these workers stayed were situated outside urban areas. Most workers were fairly young, since the work was physically demanding. While working in the camps the men lived in bunkhouses. Blankets were not provided, so the men had to pack their own from camp to camp, which gave rise to the nickname "bindle stiff," a term originating in the late 1890s in reference to the bundle of bedding and clothing that itinerant workers or hobos carried. The bunkhouses were notoriously overcrowded, sleeping thirty to forty men, often two to a bed. Lice were common. The men hung their wet clothes and socks to dry in the bunkhouse, adding to the stuffy, unpleasant atmosphere. As one would expect, the food served in the camps was also a constant source of complaint among the lumber workers. The variety and amount of food was acceptable, but the unsanitary conditions in which it was prepared and served was the issue.[12]

Along with the bunkhouse atmosphere, men in the logging camps had several other complaints. When a lumberjack received his paycheck, it was less several deductions. The first was a hospital fee, which would be understandable if the workers could expect to receive proper treatment for their numerous on-the-job injuries, but that was not the case. The workers were also charged for the mattress they slept on, which would be paid for over and over by each successive worker who slept there.

Conditions in the mills, although slightly better than in the logging camps, were also dangerous. The sawmills were increasingly mechanized and de-skilled in the early twentieth century. This, along with speed-ups, led to an increased number of mutilations and accidents in the mills, prompting an IWW pamphlet on the lumber industry to note, "Lumber is not the only product of the sawmills. There is also a bountiful harvest of cripples." An example of the injury rate at a major sawmill can be found in the records of the Port Blakely Mill in Washington, with roughly twelve hundred employees. There were 142 accidents and four fatalities in 1904. The majority of these accidents involved workers losing fingers after coming too close to a saw.[13]

Needless to say, with these kinds of working conditions, the lumber industry had a very high turnover rate, estimated to be an exorbitant 500 percent in 1915. While individual agency is certainly a factor in this migratory cycle, many workers did not leave the camps on their own volition, especially those who had been branded union agitators. A 1918 report found the main causes of high turnover in the industry were "long hours; low wages; unsanitary camps; lack of family life; absence of community life; unsatisfactory working relationships with foreman and superintendents."[14]

Regarding family and community life, one logging camp had reported that about 5 percent of the workers had wives living at camp, and 5 percent had wives in nearby towns. A government report noted that men were not as dissatisfied in the mills as in the camps, because "they are not so closely associated during their hours off duty, and there is less of latent dissatisfaction with what life offers, less of psychological foundation for revolt."[15] As in many other homosocial environments, male-male sexual relations occurred in the camps, usually between an older man and a youth.[16]

Prior to the founding of the IWW in 1905, other labor organizations were active in the Northwest. Some of this early labor activism stemmed from anti-Chinese hysteria. Large numbers of Chinese workers were recruited to work on the transcontinental railroad, and when it was completed they had to search for other work. Many white workers felt threatened by this, and believed that the Chinese workers would take their jobs since they were willing to work for less pay. White Americans viewed the Chinese laborers as unassimilable, their language and culture too different to be incorporated into American society. The Chinese Exclusion Act of 1882 restricted immigration by new Chinese workers (based on their nationality alone), but those who arrived prior to its enactment populated newly established Chinatowns in all of the larger Northwest cities. Chinese men vastly outnumbered women, and so the Chinese immigrants formed a primarily bachelor society. As Carlos Schwantes notes, "Sinophobia . . . blatantly combined job consciousness and class consciousness under the banner of white solidarity." Chinese workers were attacked in acts of mob violence around the Northwest, culminating in an attempt by a white mob to run Chinese immigrants out of the city of Seattle, prompting the governor to declare martial law in 1885. Even groups such as the Knights of Labor, which were open to organizing black and white workers in other parts of the country, were still virulently anti-Chinese in the Northwest. The anti-Chinese hysteria of the mid-1880s led to large increases in Knights of Labor membership in the Northwest. The Knights were the largest labor organization in the region during the 1880s and early 1890s before quickly fading out as the American Federation of Labor rose to prominence.[17]

The American Federation of Labor (AFL) was formed in 1886. The AFL's focus on organizing skilled workers and emphasis on "business unionism" did not garner them quick support in the Northwest. Although the organization gained influence in the East and Midwest, it did not start making inroads in the Pacific region until the early twentieth century. The labor activism of the 1880s dwindled during the depression of 1893–1897. But when prosperity returned, the AFL did make some headway in the late 1890s and early 1900s. Their focus on craft unionism left out large groups of migratory workers in the extractive industries of mining, agriculture, and lumber.

The American Federation of Labor paid minimal attention to the unskilled migratory workers in the lumber camps, as they were not the ideal candidates for membership in the AFL trade union system. The sawmills were not conducive either, since there would be only two or three men of each craft working in a mill. Cloice Howd surmised that since many of the skilled sawmill workers had risen up from unskilled work, they had a greater affinity with their former equals. The inconsistency of the AFL and their attempts to organize the lumber industry are exemplified in the many organizations formed, renamed, and combined during the first two decades of the twentieth century.

The first organization of Northwestern lumber workers came in 1890 among the more-skilled shingle weavers, who were affiliated with the AFL. In 1901 they successfully struck for higher wages. At the 1912 convention of the International Shingle Weavers' Union of America (ISWUA), a proposal was floated to switch affiliation from the AFL to the IWW. It was rejected. In 1905, a local of the AFL affiliated International Brotherhood of Woodsmen and Sawmill Workers was formed, but its membership peaked in 1906 with 1,250 workers. It was suspended in 1911 for not paying dues. In 1913, the Shingle Weavers' Union expanded to include workers in the sawmills and the logging camps and changed its name to the International Union of Shingle Weavers, Sawmill Workers, and Woodsmen. In 1914 the name changed again to the International Union of Timber Workers. Membership in this organization peaked in 1913–1914 and declined thereafter.

The AFL rescinded its jurisdiction over the sawmill and logging camp workers in 1915, and the organization was again called the ISWUA. The International Union of Timber Workers (minus the shingle weavers) affiliated with the AFL in 1917. This inconsistency reflected the difficulty the AFL had trying to organize the more-skilled workers—the shingle weavers—while unskilled workers dominated the industry. The IWW strategy of industrial unionism sought to organize all three branches of the lumber industry on equal footing in one union, though they did not achieve this on a large scale until the formation of the Lumber Workers Industrial Union No. 500 in March 1917.[18]

The coming-of-age of cities in the Northwest such as Seattle and Portland arose during a time of intense industrial conflict around the country. Populism gained some popularity in the 1890s as the depression of 1893 hindered economic growth in the region. In some ways, Oregon and Washington were politically solidly Progressive states in the early twentieth century, spearheading reforms such as the initiative, referendum, and recall, as well as the direct election of senators. Both states had passed measures giving women the right to vote by 1912. Many, however, believed that these actions did not go far enough. From the 1890s to the 1910s, the Pacific Northwest was home to anarchists, a popular socialist party, and a number of utopian communities.[19]

The Puget Sound region was home to several utopian communities between the 1880s and the 1920s. The most famous of these was the Home Colony. Founded in 1896 by three anarchists, the colony attracted numerous visitors such as anarchists Emma Goldman and Alexander Berkman, as well as IWW founder William "Big Bill" Haywood. Land was held individually, and no formal cooperative economic efforts were set out by the people who lived there. The colonists at Home Colony were left to themselves for the most part, although they faced some criticism stemming from their "free love" ideals and their practice of bathing naked in the sound. The community was robust until World War I, but the anarchist colony had ended by 1919.[20]

In addition to its popularity at the Home Colony, anarchist philosophy was advanced by Abe and Mary Isaak, editors of *The Firebrand*, an English-language anarchist newspaper in Portland from 1895 to 1897. Abe Isaak and fellow editors Henry Addis and Abner J. Pope were arrested in 1897 after publishing "A Woman Waits for Me" by Walt

Whitman, which was considered obscene by the authorities. Addis and Isaak were released on appeal, but Pope served a four-month sentence, after which Isaak had moved his family to San Francisco, while Pope and Addis headed to Home Colony.[21]

The Socialist Labor Party (SLP) held small sway in the region through the 1890s. Some members of the SLP met with members of the Social Democratic Party at a national convention in 1901 and formed the Socialist Party of America (SP). Socialist Party membership grew in Oregon and Washington, and each state boasted a number of Socialist newspapers in the early years of the century. By 1908, Oregon had seventy-four local chapters, and Washington had over one hundred, promising twenty-two thousand votes in the 1908 election. The AFL took a stronger stance in electoral politics in 1908, clashing with the SP over which organization should lead working-class voters toward voting their best interest.[22]

As with the SP nationally, the period of 1911 to 1912 was the high-water mark of socialism's popularity regionally. Whereas the Socialist Party candidate for president, Eugene Debs, received 6 percent of the vote nationally, he received 12.4 percent of the vote in Washington and 9.7 percent in Oregon. The Socialist Party itself was split into "Red" and "Yellow" factions, the former adopting a more revolutionary stance, and the latter willing to form alliances for political expediency. After a few years of increasing popularity, the war years brought difficulty for the SP. In 1917 the SP voted in a large majority for a resolution against the war, though some members subsequently left the party because of its antiwar stance. Socialist Party members faced repression for antiwar activities during World War I, just as the Wobblies did, but unlike the IWW, membership alone could not land a person in jail.[23]

After the Red Scare that followed World War I, membership in the Socialist Party declined in the Northwest, as it did nationally. Moderate Socialists moved toward the Democratic Party, while radicals moved toward the Communist Party. The Red Scare and overall conservative political climate of the 1920s claimed what was left of the membership.[24]

By the early twentieth century, this confluence of abundant natural resources, a largely unorganized workforce, and an interest in radical politics made the states of Oregon and Washington ripe for a new kind of unionism, one that would shake up the region and create front-page headlines on a regular basis. That union was the Industrial Workers of the World.

2
Spokane 1909
The Free Speech Fight

The migratory nature of work in extractive industries like lumber and mining, the mix of native-born Americans with immigrants from China, Japan, and the Scandinavian countries, and the popularity of socialist politics, labor activism, and utopian communities together made the Northwest an environment conducive to the inclusive unionism imagined by the Industrial Workers of the World. The region became the site of several IWW strikes and political actions, and the organization was known by workers and feared by employers by the early 1910s. It was in Spokane in 1909 that the IWW held one of their most successful free speech fights and cemented the reputation of the organization in the region.

Free speech fights were a tactic used by the IWW, primarily on the west coast, from 1909 into the war years.[1] In general, free speech fights occurred when IWW organizers were prohibited from speaking on the street about union or labor issues. This prohibition could be formal, by city ordinance, or informal, by vigilantes or police officers choosing to interrupt or arrest speakers. When a speaker or organizer was arrested, a call would then go out, usually in one of the IWW newspapers, for as many members as possible to flood the city and speak and be arrested until the jails were full or the city rescinded or stopped enforcing the speaking ban. Direct communication with workers in the streets was an important organizational tactic for the union, and so they fought to maintain their ability to reach workers in that way. Some free speech fights remained small and relatively nonviolent, as was the case in Missoula, Montana, in 1909, while others led to significant violence, as was the case in Everett, Washington, in 1916.

The Spokane free speech fight is significant to the history of the organization in that it popularized a form of protest the Wobblies would use throughout the West. It provided publicity for the organization in its early years and was seen as a success for the IWW. The fight was the real introduction of Elizabeth Gurley Flynn to the Northwest: the famous "Rebel Girl" of the IWW, the organization's most prominent female organizer, was nineteen and pregnant at the time of her arrival in Spokane and was one of the two Wobblies charged with conspiracy to break the law. Flynn was not the only female member of the organization who spoke on the streets and supported the many Wobblies in jail. Another woman, Edith Frenette, was jailed several times throughout the fight. Women involved with the IWW also publicized the conditions in the women's jail and ended up spurring reformers in the city to investigate and advocate the hiring of a matron for the jail. Although the Spokane free speech fight is a well-known chapter in IWW history, focusing on the women involved can provide us with a new perspective. But before we delve into the infamous events in Spokane, we need to understand the history of the union up to that point.

Faced with deplorable working conditions in many industries, labor advocates were increasingly frustrated by the limited utility of craft-based unionism popularized by the American Federation of Labor. In June 1905 activists who saw a need for a new type of union gathered in Chicago. The Industrial Workers of the World was formed out of this convention. There were 203 delegates present, including some who were already well-known nationally for their radicalism, such as Bill Haywood, Lucy Parsons, Mother Jones, Eugene Debs, and Daniel DeLeon.

Representatives attended from many unions, the largest of which were the Western Federation of Miners (WFM) and the American Labor Union (ALU). The Western Federation of Miners—later known as the International Union of Mine, Mill, and Smelter Workers—was founded in 1893 and had gained popularity for its militancy in mines of Colorado, Utah, Idaho, and Montana. IWW leader "Big Bill" Haywood came to the founding convention as a representative of the WFM. The ALU was a socialist labor organization popular in the same regions, though not focused specifically on mining.

The avowed purpose of the organization formed at this convention was to liberate the working class from their capitalist masters and put them in charge of the means of production. This would be accomplished through industrial unionism, inclusive of all workers, regardless of sex, race, or skill. From its inception, the IWW explicitly rejected the methods of the AFL, which separated workers and often ignored or overtly discriminated against unskilled workers, women, and minorities. At the founding convention of the IWW, twelve of the 203 delegates were women. Only one, Mother Jones, signed the founding document of the IWW, the "Industrial Union Manifesto," and none were on the executive committee.

Mary Harris Jones, more popularly known as Mother Jones, was an Irish American former schoolteacher and widow, nationally recognized for her work on behalf of the United Mine Workers. The second most notable female attendant was Lucy Parsons, a well-known speaker active in anarchist and socialist circles from the 1880s until the end of her life in 1942. Parsons was born to an enslaved woman in the pre–Civil War South and rumored to be the child of her white master, but she portrayed herself as the descendent of Mexican and Native American parents.[2] She was the widow of Haymarket martyr Albert Parsons, who served as a confederate soldier prior to moving to Chicago and becoming an outspoken anarchist. Parsons did not go to the convention as a delegate of a particular union, but represented herself. She described

Mrs. L. E. Parsons, 1886,
photographer A. Brauneck, Library
of Congress, LC-DIG-ds-10459.

her reason for coming to the convention, speaking for herself and other individual delegates: "Because we had eyes to see misery, we had ears to hear the cry of the downcast and miserable of the earth, we had a heart that was sympathetic, and we believed that we could come here and raise our voice and mingle it with yours in the interest of humanity." Other women present at the convention included Luela Twinings of Denver, Mrs. E. C. Cogswell of Kansas, and Mary Breckon of Chicago. Lillian and Isora Forberg, Mrs. Bohlman, and Miss Libby Levinson all represented the Industrial Workers Club of Chicago.[3]

On the third day of the convention, Lucy Parsons addressed the crowd:

> We, the women of this country, have no ballot, even if we
> wished to use it, and the only way that we can be repre-
> sented is to take a man to represent us. You men have made
> such a mess of it in representing us that we have not much
> confidence in asking you. . . . We are the slaves of slaves. We
> are exploited more ruthlessly than men. Wherever wages
> are to be reduced, the capitalist class uses women to reduce
> them, and if there is anything that you men should do in the
> future, it is to organize the women.[4]

Parsons made clear the necessity of women's organization and participation in the union from its very beginning. When the question of dues arose, she spoke of female textile workers who made only $3.60 a week, and the delegates had this in mind as they adopted a policy of low dues and initiation fees. The second convention lowered dues even further for women.[5]

IWW members were often referred to as "outsiders" by the press and by business owners in the communities where they were active. But in order to be successful, Wobbly organizers had to learn how those communities functioned, be able to work within preformed formal and informal alliances, and understand what the community was looking to achieve. Although there were a few paid organizers in the IWW, every member was encouraged to spread the word about the union and its philosophy in their workplace and promote membership.

The IWW philosophy did not take root immediately around the nation, but initially took hold in places where the WFM was already strong. In 1906, miners associated with the WFM and IWW went on strike in Goldfield, Nevada, though they were unsuccessful. Also in 1906, WFM leaders Big Bill Haywood, Charles Moyer, and George Pettibone were arrested and accused of murder in the death of former Idaho governor Frank Steunenberg. Their trial received international publicity, and they were all acquitted in 1907. In 1907 the IWW was also involved in a lumber strike in Portland, Oregon, where about three thousand workers struck for better wages and conditions. Lumber operators did not meet all of the union's demands, but the strike did spark an interest in the IWW regionally.

The year prior to the Spokane free speech fight—1908—was a transformational year for the IWW. The question of political action had inspired rancorous debate among Wobbly leadership. Daniel DeLeon, labor intellectual and head of the Socialist Labor Party, and his supporters made a grab for control of the union. At the 1908 convention, held in Chicago, DeLeon and his supporters were the delegates from New York. In Portland, Oregon, IWW organizer John H. Walsh gathered a group of men and formed what came to be known as the infamous Overalls Brigade. Nineteen men in overalls boarded the "red special" and hopped trains all around the Northwest on their way to Chicago, singing and propagandizing all the way. Mrs. Dollie Walsh joined them, though she rode in the passenger car. Mrs. Walsh helped set up meetings as the group traveled; when the men left the jungles to head into Centralia, she was there waiting for them with "the whole bunch of congregants." After that they stopped in Tacoma, Seattle, and Spokane before heading farther east. DeLeon derogatorily referred to them as "the bummery," implying that his group owned the mantle of respectable radicals. The two factions debated the role politics should play in the organization. Did political action need to happen to make industrial action possible? Or would voting distract workers from necessary action in the workplace? Would the IWW be a union affiliate of the Socialist Party, or something else entirely? "The bummery" made a convincing argument, and the convention decided to remove any reference to political action from the preamble of the constitution.[6]

This was an important transitional moment for the IWW, and although most have viewed this as the triumph of the "hobo element," the organizers themselves, Mr. and Mrs. Walsh, were not hobos. Historian Todd Depastino argues that the Overalls Brigade rang in a new era of hobo imagery in the West. He notes that Walsh "and his floating fraternity celebrated their identities as 'sons of rest' who preferred 'the simple life in the jungles' to the workaday world of the homeguard."[7] The homeguard referred to workers who had homes and families and did not travel for work. While this "sons of rest" lifestyle was certainly the reality for many members of the organization in the Northwest, Walsh himself was obviously "tied down" to his wife, since she accompanied and helped them on their journey. While this imagery of the hobo jungle and distrust of the "homeguard" is prevalent in IWW literature, when examining many of the major IWW events in the Northwest, it is clear that women were involved and that many men involved were married. This "triumph" of the bummery at the 1908 convention was less about the power of the male migratory workers and hobo imagery, and more about focusing on the workplace and community rather than on political action. A focus on political action would have given females who did not yet have the right to vote no role to play, and left untapped the real strength of the organization finding imaginative and daring ways to improve work and community life in the region.

Although the IWW leadership chose not to link their organization officially to the Socialist Party, some of its members were socialists. But another vocal portion of the Wobbly rank and file derided what they termed "slowcialism" and focused more on industrial unionism than electoral politics. In a 1912 issue of the *Industrial Worker* the Marshfield, Oregon, IWW local reported, "We have a Socialist local here, one of the mild and ladylike ones—that would not hurt the capitalists in a thousand years."[8] The infamous Mr. Block from Wobbly cartoons is often mocked for his belief in electoral socialism. Joe Hill's 1913 song about the character "Mr. Block," explains what happens when Block votes for the Socialist ticket:

> Election day he shouted, "Socialist for Mayor!"
> The "comrade" got elected, he happy was for fair,
> But after the election he got an awful shock,
> A great big socialistic Bull did rap him on the block.
> And Comrade Block did sob,
> "I helped him to his job."[9]

Historian Jeffrey Johnson articulates this conflicted relationship between the IWW and the Socialist locals in Oregon and Washington: the Socialist locals "recognized the interconnectedness of IWW-Socialist Party activity but did not always welcome IWW members, particularly given false public perceptions that the two organizations were mutually and constantly cooperative." The Socialist Party locals of the Northwest tended to be more radical than their national counterparts, voting down referendums to modify the party's constitution to allow them to dismiss any member who "opposes political action or advocates crime." This would include Wobblies who were against political action as well as those who advocated sabotage. As with the time period following the Russian Revolution in 1917, when anyone with any kind of leftist ideas was labeled a Bolshevik, during this period the public often conflated members of the two groups. And while many people did belong to both, the relationship between the two organizations remained unstable.[10]

Despite the antipathy felt by some Wobblies toward the Socialist Party and toward organized political action, when it suited them the two groups worked together, holding joint meetings or benefits or cosponsoring visiting speakers. For example on November 2, 1910, the Seattle local of the IWW organized a remembrance celebration for Francisco Ferrer, the Spanish anarchist and founder of the Modern School Movement. It hosted the event along with the Workingmen's Circle, Russian Workingmen's Association, Radical Library Association, and the Socialist Party. The *International Socialist Review*, published by Charles H. Kerr in Chicago, often printed stories about Wobbly activities and included articles by prominent members like Elizabeth Gurley Flynn.[11]

But the IWW and the Socialist Party had no formal connection, and after the decision was made in 1908 to omit political action from the organization's constitution, the fledgling IWW struggled. In March 1909, a lack of funds caused the General Executive Board to suspend publication of the IWW newspaper, the *Industrial Union Bulletin*. Though *Solidarity* took its place later that year, the future of the union was still uncertain, especially in the East. But events in 1909 would lead to one of the Wobblies' most memorable fights, and one of their biggest victories.

In the early twentieth century, Spokane was Washington State's second largest city, boasting a population of 104,402, with 39 percent women. By 1909 it had become one of the largest IWW strongholds in the West.

Workers engaged in the lumber industry or in agriculture came to Spokane to find jobs or a place to stay during the break between forest work and harvest season. Spokane was also the home of the *Industrial Worker*, the official western organ of the IWW, from 1909 to 1913. By April of 1909, the IWW hall in Spokane boasted a library with a reading room—no talking or smoking allowed—a cigar and newsstand, and an assembly hall that held hundreds. The hall showed motion pictures at five cents admission, though the *Industrial Worker* lamented the fact that a lack of revolutionary films meant that comedies were the only movies shown. Workers could buy hospital insurance at the hall for fifty cents a month, which guaranteed them ten dollars a week protection. The *Industrial Worker* estimated twelve hundred to fifteen hundred members in good standing locally, with three thousand or so in total on the books.[12]

The Spokane IWW hall was more than a community center: it was a place where people could gather for entertainment as well as for information, films and lectures, help finding employment, and a place to sleep and store their belongings. The Spokane hall welcomed families of members, as well as those who were active members themselves. By June of 1909 the Spokane local had its own band to entertain the workers with songs of class struggle. The *Industrial Worker* boasted that the band included four female members: Mrs. Zella Biebel and her daughter Bessie Biebel, Jenne Corbin, and Anna Arquett. This was in addition to the traveling brass band organized by J. H. Walsh, which included his wife Dollie Reid Walsh, as well as Edith Frenette and her husband Charles. While advertising for new band members, Walsh stipulated that they "must be able to play in the band, sing, lecture, sell literature, etc., and even before this, they must be IWWs from head to foot."[13]

Many of the women involved in the Spokane free speech fight, such as Anna Arquett, could often be found at the Spokane Wobbly hall. Others, such as national organizer Elizabeth Gurley Flynn, traveled to Spokane for the event. Although Flynn had already been working for the IWW for two years, she gained national notoriety for her role with the organization during the Spokane free speech fight. Flynn grew up in New York, the child of parents who were involved in both the Socialist and Irish nationalist movements. At the age of sixteen, Flynn gave her first speech, "What Socialism Will Do for Women." She joined the IWW in 1906 and was organizing for the union by 1907. In 1909 she was

Elizabeth Gurley Flynn at the Paterson, New Jersey, silk strike, 1913. Walter P. Reuther Library, Archives of Labor and Urban Affairs, Wayne State University, 26675.

nineteen years old and pregnant, married to IWW organizer Jack Jones (the relationship wouldn't last long). While her family took over much of the care for her son, she continued to agitate nationally. She was involved in many of the major strikes of the 1910s, including the Bread and Roses strike in Lawrence, Massachusetts, in 1912, the silk-weavers strike in Paterson in 1913, and the Mesabi Iron Range strike in 1916. While Flynn had a falling out with the IWW during the war years, she continued her activism throughout her life, joining the Communist Party in the 1930s and continuing her membership until her death in 1964.[14]

Edith Frenette, also arrested in Spokane, is one of the many female members of the IWW whose stories have not been recorded in the history of the organization. In her autobiography, Flynn described Frenette as a camp cook. Frenette took an active role in the free speech fights in Missoula, Spokane, and Everett. She and her husband Charles traveled and worked in both Washington and British Columbia in the early 1910s and counted Spokane as their home in 1909. We can find a few details about the Frenettes, as they were living in Tacoma, Washington, during the 1910 US census, and Port Alberni, British Columbia, during the 1911 Canadian census. Charles was born in 1878 in Minnesota, to

parents who were born in Canada and were classified as French by ethnicity. Edith was born in 1881 in Maine, to parents who were both born
in Canada and listed as "Scotch." Interestingly for a Wobbly—they
were usually secular in belief—in the Canadian census Edith listed her
religion as Methodist, while Charles listed none.[15]

During the Spokane free speech fight, the Wobblies gained another female recruit who would be with the organization for the rest of
her short life, then ten-year-old Katie Phar, the "songbird of the IWW."
Introduced to the union by her parents, Phar began singing for the
organization during the fight, and the local repaid her with a locket
that Christmas. She took out her first red card—as membership cards
for the union were known—in 1916 during the Everett trial, paid for by
defendant Tom Tracy. Phar continued to be a member of the organization until her death in 1943, and the IWW honored her with a memorial
edition of the *Little Red Songbook* in 1945. She was remembered far and
wide by Wobblies as a tremendous singer. When famous Wobbly singer

Katie Phar holding IWW
flag, ca. 1910s. IWW
Photograph Collection,
University of Washington
Special Collections, UW3505.

and martyr Joe Hill was in prison in 1915 awaiting execution, Phar wrote to him, and he replied to her with a copy of his song "The Rebel Girl." He expressed his hope she would sing it when Gurley Flynn came to speak in Spokane, "because Gurley Flynn is certainly some Rebel Girl and when you and her get together there will be 'two of a kind.'" [16]

Together with Elizabeth Gurley Flynn and Katie Phar, Agnes Thecla Fair was another female Wobbly cited as inspiration for Hill's "The Rebel Girl." Fair, a well-known female hobo, had lived for a time in Alaska and published a book of poems and songs titled *Sour Dough's Bible* in Seattle in 1910. There is little evidence of Fair's activism in Wobbly sources after her arrest in Spokane until her tragic suicide in January 1917. "Weary with illness," Fair threw herself in front of a train in Portland. Her fellow Wobblies rumored that she never recovered from Joe Hill's 1915 execution, and that caused her to end her life. Many Wobblies were present at her funeral, including Dr. Marie Equi. Harry Lloyd, an IWW organizer who was arrested with Fair during the free speech fight, gave the oration. Her mourners spread red carnations on her casket and then sang Wobbly songs in her memory. The *Oregonian* noted that the body was to be cremated, and the ashes were to be taken by Fair's ex-husband, W. P. Dougherty of Coalinga, California.[17]

While Fair, Flynn, and Frenette made headline news in Spokane, this was not the first free speech arrest for the last two. A previous IWW free speech fight had taken place a few weeks before in Missoula, Montana. Flynn and her husband Jack Jones had been organizing in Missoula, a town near the centers of lumber and mining in western Montana, as well as a university town, when street speaking was banned. The police arrested several Wobblies, who were sentenced to fifteen days in jail before they put in the call for more to come to the city. Both Flynn and Edith Frenette were arrested during the fight. The *Industrial Worker* reported that "when Mrs. Frenette was arrested there was an enormous crowd followed her to the jail, and while not riotus, were certainly indignant." An anonymous "Free Speech Fight Diary" published in the *International Socialist Review* in November 1909, noted that Frenette was a member of the Spokane local and a member of the advisory board. The diarist also noted that when she was arrested the crowd was a little more than indignant, and "threw stones at the police, severely injuring Officer Hoel" while they were taking Frenette to jail. In her autobiography, Flynn recalled that college professors joined in the fight for free speech once the two women had been arrested. The women were "treated with kid gloves by the Sheriff and his wife," though Flynn noted that this same sheriff had badly beaten up Flynn's husband a few days before. This points to one of the most important contributions IWW women made to free speech fights: they were usually released earlier and often treated more leniently than male Wobblies. While most Wobbly women objected to the preferential treatment, it allowed them to be out on the street within a few days, publicizing their experiences and continuing the fight.[18]

In Missoula the free speech fight continued, with new tactics, such as what Flynn described as "an amusing tussle" over who would be feeding all of the Wobblies in town. "We held our meeting early so the men would go to jail before supper. The police began to turn them out the next morning before breakfast, forcing us to provide rations for the day." The authorities finally caved, and the charges against the men arrested were dropped. The Missoula fight was declared over by the October 20 issue of the *Industrial Worker*; October 25 marked the beginning of the fight in Spokane. [19]

In towns where migratory laborers gathered, like Spokane, employment agents, or "job sharks" as they were known by the Wobblies, gathered as well. For a dollar or two, an agent would give the worker information about a job at a farm or lumber camp, often far enough away to be impossible for the worker to verify. When the worker arrived at the indicated location, he might find the job did not exist or had already been filled. If he was hired, he was often fired soon after. The Wobblies complained of the "perpetual motion" system employed by the job sharks, in which the agent would have one man on his way to the job, one at the job, and one who was fired and heading back to town to look for work.

The IWW fought long and hard against the job sharks, and one of the best ways of doing this was street speaking. It was the only way to reach the workers who hung around in the skid row areas of town where the agencies were located. IWW agitators often shared street space with the Salvation Army or other religious speakers. Wobblies stood directly in front of employment agencies, urging workers not to "buy jobs." The employment agencies organized against the IWW, forming the Associated Agencies of Spokane to urge the city council to adopt a resolution against street speaking: to combat the IWW presence, in

1908 the City of Spokane passed an ordinance prohibiting all types of street speaking. A group of Wobblies, led by John Walsh, were arrested. They agreed among themselves to make Walsh's arrest a test case for the constitutionality of the street speaking statute and for his charges to move forward in return for the release of the rest of the men. At the insistence of religious groups such as the Salvation Army, the original ordinance was replaced by a new one in August 1909, which allowed for religious speakers with the consent of the mayor.[20] The IWW saw this as a threat to their right of free speech. While the free speech fight that ensued eventually led the Wobblies to defy the ban outright, they initially sought to work with the city government. At the IWW Spokane Executive Council meeting on September 19, 1909, a motion was carried to appoint a committee "to see the Mayor and try and get a permit to speak on the streets."[21] A week later, at the September 26 executive council meeting, a motion was carried to have lawyer Fred Moore see the city council "and present our case in regard to street speaking."[22] It is unclear what happened at those meetings, but in later testimony Douglass, the acting secretary of the IWW Spokane locals, reported that "the city officials promised the IWW committee that they would frame an ordinance satisfactory to us if we would stay off the street until Mr. Walsh had his trial in the Supreme Court." He then noted that while they were waiting for that to happen, the Salvation Army spoke on the street, which is what prompted the Wobblies to take to the street to challenge the law, believing that both religious and labor organizations should have equal rights to speak.[23] The lower court found Walsh guilty, but then the case was dropped, so it never made its way to the Supreme Court.

The free speech fight is commonly viewed as direct action in response to an unjust law, but the Wobblies clearly did not move immediately toward outright defiance. They wanted to present the case that street speaking was necessary for the organization to reach its potential membership. Their first response was not to test the law by disobeying it, but to get permission from the Spokane city council.

The members were unsuccessful in their efforts to work within the law, and on October 25, Spokane authorities arrested IWW organizer James Thompson for speaking on the street. The *Industrial Worker* then sent out a call for all available Wobblies to flood the area, marked November 2 (the day of Thompson's court date) as "Free Speech Day," and asked "all lovers of free speech . . . to be in readiness to be in Spokane on that date."[24] The Wobblies would hold a public meeting, whether or not Thompson was acquitted. Judge Mann declared the second ordinance unconstitutional, but left the first ordinance in place, and the Wobblies took to the streets. Several were arrested and charged with disorderly conduct.[25]

Although the court declared the ordinance allowing for religious street speakers unconstitutional, the first ordinance banning all street speaking was left to stand. During the court case following the arrests, Elizabeth Gurley Flynn testified to the organization's belief in free speech, and how she defined what was constitutional. Prosecutor Pugh, in language that illustrated his opinion on the intellectual abilities of the IWW, asked Flynn in court,

> Were you teaching them to look to the courts as the interpreters of the constitution of the United States, or were you teaching them that they themselves—rabble though they might be—had the right, if they could read English, to read the constitution and say what it meant, and then go out and assert their interpretation—and go out and back it up by force of numbers?[26]

Flynn initially replied that she advised members to look at their own interpretation as well as that of the courts, but when further questioned, admitted that she believed the members of the IWW "should respect the courts' decision in so far as it expressed the rights of the working-class." Mr. Pugh then asked again if Flynn believed that the working class "whether it could read and write, and whether it was washed or unwashed," had the right to interpret the law how it saw fit. Flynn reiterated her belief that "when the courts will not regard their rights as the people . . . then in the last analysis they are to be the judges." Thus, to Flynn, the IWW had the right to interpret the Constitution within the best interests of the working class, not as defined by the capitalist court system. The prosecution implied the "unwashed" and uneducated masses might not be respectable enough to be afforded that right.[27]

The free speech fight continued, and on November 3 the organization's headquarters were raided and four men were arrested, including the editor of the *Industrial Worker*, James Wilson. In the November 10 issue of the *Industrial Worker*, Flynn recounted the situation in Spokane. So far over a hundred men were in jail, some sentenced to thirty days, some to thirty days plus fines of one hundred dollars. James Wilson, James P. Thompson, E. J. Foote, C. L. Filigno, and A. E. Cousins were all charged with criminal conspiracy, which carried a potential sentence of five years, though only Filigno, along with Flynn, would be tried.[28]

By November 10 there were three IWW women in the Spokane county jail for street speaking: Edith Frenette, Agnes Thecla Fair, and a Mrs. McDaniels. The *Industrial Worker*, which often exhorted its readers to "be a man" and fight with the union, noted "it ought to make some of you great, husky, imitations of men ashamed of your-selves when women suffer that you may have your right." Historians are not exempt from using this kind of gendered rhetoric, and Melvyn Dubofsky continued this line of thought in *We Shall Be All*, referring to Elizabeth Gurley Flynn: "If repression could not break the spirit of a pregnant, slightly built, teenage girl, how could it crush the Wobblies' free-speech fighters flooding into Spokane in an unending stream?" Frenette had been released and arrested two more times by November 24. In cases like this, where sustained action on the street or on a picket line was needed, it was an asset to the organization to have women who were willing to go back on the street after being released from police custody. [29]

It was not only speaking on the street that led to arrest. Edith Frenette was also arrested and tried for disorderly conduct after singing "The Red Flag" in front of the Franklin school where many of the ar-rested men were held. "The Red Flag," written in 1889 by Irish Socialist Jim Connell, was a popular anthem for radicals in the early twentieth century. It contains these stirring lyrics:

> The People's flag is deepest red.
> It shrouded oft, our martyred dead;
> And ere their limbs grew stiff and cold
> Their life-blood dyed its every fold.
> *Chorus*
> Then raise the scarlet standard high
> Beneath its folds, we'll live and die.

Though cowards flinch and traitors sneer,
We'll keep the red flag flying here.[30]

The very first version of the Wobbly *Little Red Songbook* appeared two months prior to the Spokane free speech fight. Edited by an informal committee in Spokane, they chose "The Red Flag" as the first song included. It obviously held deep meaning for Frenette and the other Wobblies in Spokane.[31]

During Frenette's trial, as reported by Elizabeth Gurley Flynn, the chief of police, as well as six other officers, testified that she "acted as if she were drunk, that she had carried on in a disorderly manner on the streets since this trouble started, and one said she acted like 'a lewd woman.'" Frenette recited "The Red Flag" by request of the court, and did so "with such dramatic force that the Judge was horrified at its treasonable and unpatriotic sentiment." Frenette was then sentenced to thirty days and a one-hundred-dollar fine. She was held for the next two days in the city jail. Her actions of speaking out in the street, and her association with the disreputable Wobblies, were cause for the officers to impugn her respectability by moving her actions outside the context of social protest and into the category of "lewd woman," a category that also included the drunks and prostitutes they picked up on a regular basis.[32]

The arrests of Wobblies in Spokane were not limited to adults speaking on the street. Gurley Flynn also reported that, on December 1, Spokane authorities raided the IWW hall again and arrested eight newsboys, ranging in age from eight to sixteen. The police interrogated the children, who then spent the night in jail. As Elizabeth Gurley Flynn noted, though a simple case on the surface, "it is a subtle attempt to undermine the right of a parent to teach a child ideas different from the established order."[33] A poster with a picture of the boys, which referred to them as "young Americans of the rebel type," asked "How about you men? Are boys to go to jail for you?" The poster was found in the evidence file for the IWW trials and was most likely hung in the Wobbly hall and confiscated during a raid. Most of the parents of the IWW newsboys promised to keep their children away from the IWW hall or claimed ignorance of their activities. But one prominent Wobbly family fought for their son's rights.[34]

Outraged mother Florence Thompson rushed to court to defend her family and their belief system. She spoke out against Spokane judge

Boys arrested during Spokane Free Speech Fight, 1909. Spokane City Clerk Files, Washington State Archives-Eastern Region Branch.

John D. Hinkle's opinion that the IWW hall was a disgraceful place, and that by entering willingly a woman lost any claim to respectability. Joseph Thompson was the only one among the newsboys who refused to boycott the hall. His mother accompanied him to the hall and "was in full accord with the IWW." Judge Hinkle concluded that "the IWW hall is no fit place for a woman, and no good woman frequents it." The judge also noted that Joseph looked "dirty and uncared for." He then accused Mrs. Thompson of being an unfit guardian for the boy.

The next day Thompson's father James was tried for his role in the fight. Mrs. Thompson and Joseph watched from the courtroom, but the probation officer saw them in attendance and ordered Joseph to go home. The following day, during the continuation of Joseph's trial, the courtroom was filled with women who visited the IWW hall regularly, whom Flynn described as "not in a pleasant frame of mind." Faced with these women he had offended, the judge "blustered around" and "tried to make amends" for his comment about Mrs. Thompson being an unfit mother. He then dismissed the juvenile cases. The women in his courtroom saw themselves as part of the IWW community and stood together to show that their association with the union did not hinder their ability to care for their children or to be respectable and responsible mothers. Respectability was a double-edged sword. It was used against women associated with the IWW by policemen, judges, and officials who felt that association with the organization was a sign of moral shortcoming. The women themselves defiantly sought to disprove this mischaracterization and the middle-class morals that defined the realm of respectability.[35]

Flynn was also the target for assumptions about respectability, but she refused to discuss her personal life in courtroom appearances. Women had taken an interest in all aspects of the free speech fight, and Flynn's trial was no different. The *Spokesman-Review* noted that the majority of people in the packed courtroom during Flynn's testimony were women. The newspaper described Flynn as the "little woman in red" and noted her defiant tone and the lack of fear present in her testimony. Flynn responded to questions about her personal life by ignoring them; as the attorney asked Flynn questions about her husband and their relationship, "with a hint that the realm of personal affairs was being invaded [Flynn] began to take an interest in the surroundings of the courtroom" and the prosecutor moved on to another subject."[36]

At the end of the courtroom battle, C. L. Filigno was found guilty of conspiracy, while Flynn was found innocent. As one of the jurors noted, "of course sympathy for the little woman figured somewhat in the verdict," but what had moved the jury the most was a telegram sent by Filigno to Flynn asking her to come to Spokane, therefore making him the greater offender and ringleader in the conspiracy. The telegram provided proof that he asked her to come, but the sight of nineteen-year-old, pregnant Flynn likely swayed the jurors just as much as the evidence. Although Wobbly women did not advocate preferential treatment in the court system, they were often given lesser sentences than their male comrades. Wobbly women attempted to fight side by side with men in the streets, but a court and jail system that saw women as the weaker sex treated them more gently than it did their male fellow workers.[37]

Thus the treatment that Flynn, Frenette, and Fair received in jail, although inappropriate, was nothing compared with the inhumane treatment of the male prisoners. The majority of men arrested received a thirty-day sentence, and some also received a hundred-dollar fine. According to Flynn's report in the *International Socialist Review*, twenty-eight to thirty men at a time were crowded into a six-foot-by-eight-foot cell, with steam heat turning the cell into a "sweatbox."

They were then removed and placed in a freezing cold cell with the windows open. Some of the men were ordered to work on the rock pile, which they refused to do, and as punishment were fed a diet of bread and water. The men who received a full meal joined them on a hunger strike in solidarity. So many Wobblies were arrested that they filled the jail and were sent to two overflow facilities, the old Franklin schoolhouse and Fort Wright. Those at the school were taken to the city jail once a week to bathe. After enduring the ice-cold water, they then had to march outside in freezing temperatures back to their unheated cells.[38]

Although not as overtly brutal as what the men faced, the treatment that Wobbly women received in jail was also subject to scrutiny. Reports on the conditions in the women's jail earned the Wobbly women support from the citizens of Spokane, as well as reminding male Wobblies that the police were harming "our women." The *Industrial Worker* reported that "the women members of the organization have been insulted, clubbed, and all other manner of brutalities heaped upon them."[39] Edith Frenette was reportedly struck by a policeman on the way to jail.[40] Agnes Thecla Fair wrote a letter to the *Workingman's Paper* outlining what happened to her in jail. She reported that during the interrogation, when she refused to answer any questions, one officer said "We'll make her talk," and she quoted another as threatening, "F—k her and she'll talk." Fair wrote, "Just then one started to unbutton my waist, I went into spasms from which I never recovered until evening." Later that evening, a "man disguised as a woman" was brought into the cell with her. As she tried to sleep she "felt a large hand creeping over me. It's too horrible to put on paper. I jumped into an enclosure, screaming frantically and frothing at the mouth." After her release, to publicly present her fragile physical state, she had the Fellow Workers carry her on a stretcher to her room, "as it cost money to hire cabs and it would only keep from the public the brutality of the bulls."[41]

The Spokane *Spokesman-Review* was interested in these arrested women, more for entertainment or prurient interest than because of their radical ideas. The paper described Agnes Fair as a "slim girl in a black waist with a flaming red scarf"—symbolic of her support of the IWW—who advocated eight dollars a day for four hours of work. Anna Arquett was also arrested at the IWW hall. The paper described her as "a tall, masculine woman who had been haranguing the crowd at the hall with much vehemence, and a younger girl who was much excited." Under the subheading "Pretty Woman Arrested" the *Spokesman-Review* detailed the case of Edith Frenette, described as "plump and pretty" and "by far the most attractive of the day's batch of guests at the station." During her trial, after a few days in jail, Frenette "seemed as neatly groomed and pink-cheeked as though she had spent the time at home." Although Arquett's "masculine" look may have suggested deviant sexual behavior or a reason she would be attracted to the IWW's radical ideology, the description of Frenette denotes surprise that a normal, "pretty," respectable-looking woman would get involved with such a disreputable organization.[42]

A month later, Elizabeth Gurley Flynn reported on her treatment during her arrest and imprisonment. Flynn described her fellow cellmates and how they treated her:

> I was placed in a cell with two other women, poor miserable specimens of the victims of society. . . . Never before had I come in contact with women of that type, and they were interesting. . . . These miserable outcasts of society did everything in their power to make me comfortable.[43]

This included giving her blankets, fruit, soap, and clean towels. They also accommodated Flynn, as she noted, by trying to "moderate their language, apologize for their profanity, and pathetically try to conform to some of the standards of decency when they see that you are 'different.' They have been so accustomed to being ill-used and browbeaten they rather expect it, yet become indignant when it is done to another." Flynn saw herself as a step above these "fallen" women: "Content to sleep and eat, they seem to be as happy inside jail as out. They are unconscious of their degradation and solicit no sympathy. Perhaps they shouldn't be conscious, for society is to blame and not they." Flynn also noted that the women were on terms of "disgusting familiarity" with the jailers, who took one of the women out of her cell several times during the night to visit a "sweetheart" in another cell. It seemed to Flynn that the woman was "practicing her profession inside of jail as well as out."[44]

During this ordeal Flynn was very careful to maintain her own image of respectability. Although she thought it silly that an old Wobbly felt it was improper of her to be speaking in public while she was pregnant, she still took pains to separate herself from the immoral women she was jailed with:

> It is certainly a shame and disgrace to this city that a woman
> can be arrested because of union difficulties, bonds placed
> so high that immediate release is impossible, thrown into a
> county jail, where sights and sounds, horrible, immoral, and
> absolutely different from her ordinary, decent mode of life
> can be forced upon her.[45]

When Flynn publicized her jail experiences, Mayor Pratt of Spokane wrote an open letter denying Flynn's "wild and hysterical inferences," which was published in the *Spokesman-Review*. The IWW then asked the mayor to apologize or face a libel charge. The mayor refused, and so the IWW sued him and two other officials for $10,000 each. Flynn charged that her "reputation and efficacy" as a writer and speaker had been damaged by the charge that she was wild and hysterical, which could therefore make her potential audiences view her as unreliable or untrustworthy.[46] "Hysterical" is a word not often used to describe men, and when the mayor used that phrase to describe Flynn's account of events, he was not only calling her a liar, but insinuating that she was emotional and irrational. Flynn noted that though the IWW didn't intend to collect the $30,000 as "spending money . . . we certainly intend to force these officials, who so commonly brand one as hysterical and libelous, to prove their assertions." The result of the case is unknown.[47]

After Flynn and Fair published their experiences, the women of the City Club of Spokane demanded that the city place a matron in the women's jail. This led to an investigation of the conditions in the city jail. The results were published in a report titled "In the Matter of the Investigation of the Police Department of the City of Spokane by A Committee Consisting of Dr. Thomas L. Catterson, and Others," commonly known as "The Sullivan Report" because it was directed to police chief John Sullivan. In addition to Dr. Catterson, the committee included Mrs. F. F. Emery, Inez de Lashmutt, E. O'Shea, Carl E. Gundlach, and W. J. McElvoy. The committee members were well-known in the city of Spokane. Dr. Catterson had been practicing medicine in the city since the 1880s; Inez de Lashmutt, a Wellesley alumni and member of the Daughters of the American Revolution, hosted teas discussing hot topics in her studio; and Mrs. F. F. Emery was a member of the Pacific Coast Red Cross Society. In their two-hundred-plus-page report, the committee interviewed guards at the jail, policemen, and female nurses who saw the prisoners, as well as asking women who had been jailed about their experiences. The existence of the report is testimony to the effect that Wobbly claims about the conditions in the jails had on the city of Spokane, for it is unlikely that the investigation would have taken place without them.[48]

The Sullivan Report revealed the ideals of appropriate and inappropriate female behavior that Spokane authorities projected on the prisoners and how they decided which women were worthy of protection. The *Industrial Worker* reported that the mayor and the sheriff both agreed that a matron was a good idea, but the chief of police protested, saying that the women in jail were of a "low type" and did not need a matron. In their report, the committee did not find evidence of abuse by the jailers. The committee found it important to interview women who had experienced the jail as prisoners, but these women's perspectives were often undercut by the authority figures in the jail. What the officials interviewed did not directly state, but insinuated in several of the testimonies, is that they could not rely on the jailed women's statements because those women were by nature unreliable. They described them as low women addicted to drugs and drink, and therefore not respectable and not to be trusted. What is not mentioned in the report is that the women may have feared reprisal if they spoke out against their treatment in jail and ended up back there again. Although Fair's claims of abuse were never substantiated, the outcry in response to both Fair and Flynn's reports of conditions in the jail was enough to warrant investigation and, ultimately, to gain support for the hiring of a full-time matron for the jail. Mary Caroline Davidson Seymour was appointed and served as the matron from 1910 to 1932.[49]

The Sullivan Report also revealed possible tensions among the female Wobblies over tactics and publicity. The committee questioned several officials regarding Agnes Thecla Fair's claims that she was abused by the police, but the officials revealed that they did not believe Fair because fellow Wobbly Edith Frenette did not take her seriously. Dr. John O'Shea, a surgeon at the Spokane emergency hospital who frequently visited the jail, believed Fair's claims of ill-treatment to be "absolutely false." O'Shea said that he saw Fair three or four times while she was in jail, but did not give any details about her condition. When pressed as to how he knew her claims were false, he said he depended on the word of one of Fair's fellow prisoners. He admitted, "you can't depend entirely on that," but still took her words at face value. O'Shea then named Edith Frenette as the woman who said Fair was lying.[50]

The committee also interviewed Captain Bertha Smith, the matron of the Salvation Army Rescue Home. Smith reported that she had never heard a complaint from the women in the jail until Agnes Fair. She had searched Fair at the request of the police captain, who claimed to believe Fair had letters from Moscow on her person. Smith said that Fair asked her to be gentle, and said that she had been feeling well until she was arrested, and since then "so unwell and miserable that now she was nearly fainting." Smith said she was kind to Fair, dressed her, made her bed, and gave her something to drink. She also reported that Edith Frenette was in the room and was laughing at the whole scene. Smith said that Frenette was a "strong woman" and a "strong character" and everyone there thought that Fair "made a little put-on." She described Fair as a woman "of not great physical strength and a hysterical woman." She saw Fair on Saturday when she was arrested, and then not again until Monday. During the Monday visit, Fair told her she would die if she had to stay in jail much longer. Smith helped Fair into the courtroom, and reported that Fair made such a scene that Frenette was laughing at her, as were the men in the courtroom. Fair was told in the courtroom that she would be released if she promised to stay off the street, but she would not make such a promise. According to Smith, she was then taken to the emergency hospital, at which point the IWW brought her a stretcher and, in a bit of attention-grabbing street theater, "made a parade with her through the streets."[51]

Smith also reported that Fair said that one of the arresting officers had treated her very cruelly. Though neither O'Shea nor Smith detail what kind of cruel treatment Fair complained about, Smith's further testimony revealed that it was difficult to get the IWW women to work with her since she was from the Salvation Army, a group that the IWW frequently lampooned in songs and competed with for workers' attention on the street. One jailer, Robert Wilson, described an interaction with Fair over prison food. She complained about the food and refused to eat it. Wilson said that, if he were not in such a hurry to get home, he would have "jammed it down her throat." After she threw the food at him, he told her, "You will be glad to lick where they lay someday."[52]

This aggressive behavior could be emblematic of the treatment the women received from the other jailers, or it could be an isolated case. It was the only incident of negative behavior toward Fair in the committee's report. None of the testimonies corroborated the story that Fair told in her letter to the *Industrial Worker*. This is not surprising, since those who testified worked in the jail and had an interest in its reputation.

A fourth prison representative, Detective Thomas Lister, also reported that Frenette spoke to him privately, said that Fair was lying, and proclaimed "that woman is crazy" and that "as an organization we don't recognize her." Lister then asked why the crowd followed her down the street in the stretcher, and Frenette repeated that the organization did not recognize her. Evidence of this nature is difficult to interpret. It was in the best interest of those connected with the jail to discredit both Frenette and Fair. But the number of officials who believed that Frenette was, at the very least, amused by Fair's "performance," suggests some truth to the matter. It is possible that Frenette believed that Fair's dramatic behavior was detrimental to the cause and made the IWW, and the women associated with it, look hysterical and irrational, not like serious rebels testing their constitutional rights. Fair may have felt that by promoting her femininity, fragility, or need for special treatment, she garnered publicity that would be advantageous to the Wobbly cause. Regardless of whether or not Frenette privately felt that Fair was an embarrassment to the cause, the organization made no public statements other than those in support of Fair. It is not surprising that women within the IWW did not fully agree on which tactic was most appropriate.[53]

Many women during the Progressive Era felt this tension between asserting equality for women and using notions of female difference when advocating reforms such as restrictions on working hours. Middle-class Progressive reformers often argued that men and women were fundamentally different in order to enact protective legislation. The City Club women of Spokane advocated for a matron at the city jail, and the Wobblies were supported financially during their fight by the efforts of middle-class and upper-class women. Flynn, along with other members of the IWW, had mixed feelings about this. The January

1910 issue of *Solidarity* reported that two of the leading suffragists in Spokane refused to help put up bail for Elizabeth Gurley Flynn when she was jailed there. Flynn herself brought up the issue years later in an article titled "The IWW Call to Women" in *Solidarity*. She wrote,

> I have seen prosperous, polite, daintily-gowned ladies
> become indignant over police brutality in the Spokane free
> speech fight of 1909, and lose all interest—even refuse to
> put up bail for pregnant women—when they realized that
> the IWW intended to organize the lumber, mining and
> farming industries, whence the golden stream flowed to pay
> for their comfort and leisure.[54]

IWW women defined themselves primarily by class. Although upper-class women could be allies on some issues, such as free speech or improving factory conditions, they would never support the full IWW program. In that same article, Flynn wrote that the "sisterhood of women, like the brotherhood of man, is a hollow sham to labor. Behind all its smug hypocrisy and sickly sentimentality loom the sinister outlines of the class war."[55]

The Wobbly women who believed that gender did not transcend class barriers were proven correct in the issue of appointing a matron to the city jail. The City Club women who supported the idea also publicly stated that they did not agree with the goals of the IWW. The Spokane *Press* printed a letter from Mrs. Philip Stalford to Mayor Pratt. Stalford was one of the leaders of the investigation into conditions in the prison, and Pratt had publicly stated that, if Stalford was "a good citizen," then she should come forward with her proof of misconduct at the jail. She responded that the committee had affidavits from women in the jail, none of them connected with the IWW, and her work with the City Club proved her good citizenship. She also responded to allegations by Chief Sullivan that she was an IWW sympathizer: "No woman who attended the council meeting on the night of February 23 was an IWW, and to most of them no worse epithet could be hurled than IWW sympathizer." The actions of the female Wobblies inspired the City Club women to demand an investigation into the conditions in the jails, but for these women, being labeled as an IWW sympathizer was an insult. This is the kind of response Flynn referred to in the aforementioned

Industrial Worker article: even if upper-class women agreed with a tactic or supported the Wobblies in a strike or free speech battle, they did not, and would not, support the fundamental goals of the organization.[56]

Victory in labor agitation can be defined in many different ways. The free speech fight was a public relations victory, spreading information about the IWW throughout the country and, especially, within the Pacific Northwest. The free speech fight as a tactic continued to be used by Wobblies in the West over the next several years. Although it did not have the desired effect of drastically reshaping the power structure in Spokane, the fight was a victory in several concrete ways: stopping the enforcement of the ban on street speaking, enacting harsher regulations on employment agencies, and instigating the appointment of a matron in the city jail. As would happen again in Portland in 1913, Wobbly women who were jailed for street actions publicized their jail experiences and called attention to the issues of corruption, sanitation, and exploitation that the women in jail faced, and therefore played an important role in the appointment of a matron.

The Spokane free speech fight was a real test for the IWW. Historians have noted that the fight was a defining moment for the IWW as a movement that fought for workers, the right to organize, and civil rights, but it may also be read as an example of the role women played in the organization and how they were treated by authorities when questioning the law. Women wanted to stand with their brothers in the organization to fight for their right to free speech, yet they decried any treatment by the authorities that put them on the level of other working women, who just happened to sell their bodies for a living. From this early point, Wobbly women demanded that they be seen as respectable, both as mothers and activists, even though they were will willing to speak in public and be jailed—behaviors often categorized as male—in their fight for free speech.

3
Seattle 1912
Becky Beck and the Seattle Tailors' Strike

By 1912, the IWW had grown in popularity in the Pacific Northwest as well as around the nation. That year saw strikes in Lawrence, Massachusetts, and Grays Harbor, Washington. In May there was also a much smaller and less widely known series of strikes among tailors in Seattle. The strikes barely received mention in IWW newspapers, much less in the national press. The report of the Seventh Annual IWW Convention, in October of 1912, described the events: "Ten small strikes lasting from a few hours up to two months. All of the strikes successful—except one." When examining this group of strikes (for simplicity conflated in this chapter to a singular "strike") in terms of IWW ideology or national success, it is easy to dismiss it as insignificant. But when examining the strike and ensuing legal battle with an eye on gender and respectability, it is remarkable because of the presence of women and the ensuing legal repression that targeted radicals because of alleged immoral behavior.[1]

Seattle was a quickly growing city in the early twentieth century, with a population of 237,194 in 1910, and 42 percent women. Though there were not many large IWW-led strikes in Seattle, the organization was active and hosted speakers, socials, and other events in the city. The 1912 tailors' strike was a small affair, involving perhaps a few dozen workers and lasting less than a month. Though small, it was complicated, as both the Industrial Workers of the World and the American Federation of Labor–affiliated Journeymen Tailors Union organized tailors in Seattle during this period. Coordination and competition between the two organizations varied by shop and oftentimes by individual tailor.[2]

The Journeymen Tailors Union (JTU) was at the forefront of organizing tailors in the Seattle area early in 1912. The *Seattle Union Record*, the city's labor newspaper, reported eighty new tailors signed up for the JTU since January 1 of that year, and a total of eighteen shops running with the eight-hour day as of April 27. Things began to go awry the following month, when three employers fired and intimidated union employees. The *Union Record* reported that the Budd & Nelson shop fired two workers for being members of the JTU, McGrath Bros. discharged three for union involvement, and a strike had begun at the P.O. Wold shop because it refused to pay workers the union rate. At the same time, relations between the IWW and JTU were strained as the two organizations pursued different tactics and strategies. The *Union Record* reported that there was a "stumbling block" in the organization of tailors because of "an organization which attempted to call a strike on shops signed up without giving the employers an opportunity to be heard." That stumbling block was the IWW, which, unlike the conservative American Federation of Labor (AFL) union, was not inclined to seek compromise and collaboration with employers. The employers sought the advice of organizer Biggs of the Journeymen Tailors Union on how to handle the IWW. Biggs's advice led to a "complete rout of the other organization and better and more friendly relations being established" between the journeymen tailors and the employers.[3]

The differences in ideology and tactics between the AFL and the IWW were exemplified in the tailors' strike that occurred in April and May of 1912. While the JTU wanted to establish friendly relations with the employers, the IWW believed that the workers and employers had a fundamentally oppositional relationship. In April, IWW organizer F. H. Allison reported that there had been successful strikes for the eight-hour day in four different shops, but that they had trouble with the AFL-organized workers: "They tried to put the local out of biz this morning but the IWW picketed the bunch and told the scabby bunch that they could take out cards in the IWW by paying $1.50 and they would then be considered union men and could work only 8 hours a day." He noted that all but one joined, and the shop now runs eight hours a day with "a full crew of reds."[4]

Although the JTU may have wanted and felt it had established "better and more friendly relations" with employers, some workers were still unsatisfied, and the IWW did not feel that the JTU fully represented workers in the industry. In May, the IWW continued to strike at select shops, and ended up making front-page headlines for altercations on the picket line. According to the B & R Company, the strike was the result of the discharge of a woman named Mrs. Shaw, who was fired for using "very insulting language to the managers" after being reprimanded for doing unsatisfactory work. At that point the other workers quit, although local newspapers reported that they had signified willingness to come back to work if they were reinstated.[5]

The legal aftermath of the strike brought two Seattle-area Wobblies, Jack Solomon and Rebecca Beck, to the forefront, and it is through their legal struggles that we learn how morality laws were used to target radicals, especially those who were recent immigrants to the United States. Solomon, age thirty-five at the time of the strike, was born in Kovna, Russia, where he lived until around the age of fourteen, at which time he moved to London. He remained in London until roughly 1905; while there he married a woman named Deborah Levine with whom he had four children, who were between the ages of six and fourteen in 1912. From London he moved to Toronto for about six months, Cleveland for nine, and Chicago for two or three years before moving to Seattle. Solomon claimed to have supported his family until he moved from Seattle to Alaska and conveniently "lost track" of them, which had been about a year prior to the strike.[6]

Rebecca "Becky" Beck was twenty-nine years old in 1912. She was born in 1883 in Vitebsk, Russia, to a poor Jewish family, and moved to London at a young age. Beck then moved with her family to Chicago around 1904. Chicago was a hub of radicalism, and Beck was right in the middle of it. She visited Hull House, a settlement house for recent immigrants, and there met well-known Progressive reformer Jane Addams. Since Beck could speak both Yiddish and English, Addams sent her out to talk to immigrant workers about trade unions. Beck saw anarchists Emma Goldman and Voltairine de Cleyre speak in Chicago, and in a 1974 interview, Beck claimed this was when she became an anarchist herself. She moved to Seattle in 1910 with her brothers Abe and Morris, and got a job as a tailor. She worked with Louise Olivereau at the Labor Temple and became involved in the local labor movement.[7]

Becky Beck started working at the B & R Company in January of 1912. She quit on her own accord, because of illness, around the beginning of May. At that time she convalesced at Home Colony, the anarchist colony in Washington, and returned to Seattle on May 12. Recollecting the event later in her life, Beck said that the women had decided to go on strike because they worked a forty-hour week, but the men in the shop had to stay two hours longer per day, which they felt was unfair.

She said that she attempted to get the "regular" union to help, but when they refused she appealed to the IWW.[8]

The strikers asked Beck to go to the shop and talk to some of the women who were crossing the picket line. Beck and fellow Wobbly Friede Clyde, along with thirty male members of the organization, then had a confrontation with women crossing the picket line at the B & R Company, where the two women allegedly scratched and slapped other women who attempted to enter the shop to work. Beck's involvement drew attention from the local newspapers and brought a gendered lens to the discussion of the strike. The front-page headline of the *Seattle Daily Times*, "IWW Amazons Beat Tailorshop Employees for Trying to Work," portrayed the Wobbly women as unfeminine, asexual warriors. The *Times* also claimed that although many of the women who worked at the shop were members of the IWW, most joined only because of coercion or because they thought they were joining a different union altogether, which insinuates both that the female workers were unintelligent and that the IWW exploited that weakness. Beck was arrested later that day, on a complaint brought by fifty-eight-year-old Thea Steen that Beck had slapped her in the face. Beck in turn claimed that an unnamed female strikebreaker hit her in the head with her purse, leaving her in need of stitches.[9]

The next morning, Friede Clyde and several male members of the IWW continued to picket. Jack Solomon, the chairman of the strike committee, issued these demands:

> All employees now working in the shop, with the exception of one girl, to be discharged; all strikers to be taken back to former positions and paid the former wages; no employee to be discharged without two weeks' notice; the B & R Company to pay the IWW $30 which the union had expended in attorney fees, and all the wages of the reinstated strikers to start on May 13.[10]

Solomon and six other male members of the IWW were arrested later that day. Over a hundred members of the organization were arrested for violating an injunction against picketing during the strike.[11]

The strike ended a few days after the altercation on the picket line, but Jack Solomon and Becky Beck were arrested again on May 24, this time on charges of violating the 1903 Immigration Act. They were both released on bond, but Solomon was held at the detention house in Seattle after defaulting on his. Under the 1903 Immigration Act, also known as the Anarchist Exclusion Act, the United States Congress prohibited the following groups from admission to the country:

> All idiots, insane persons, epileptics, and persons who have been insane within five years previous; persons who have had two or more attacks of insanity at any time previously; paupers; persons likely to become a public charge; professional beggars; persons afflicted with a loathsome or with a dangerous contagious disease—persons who have been convicted of a felony or other crime or misdemeanor involving moral turpitude; polygamists, anarchists, or persons who believe in or advocate the overthrow by force or violence of the Government of the United States or of all government or of all forms of law, or the assassination of public officials; prostitutes, and persons who procure or attempt to bring in prostitutes or women for the purpose of prostitution.[12]

According to historian Matthew Frye Jacobson, while the Anarchist Exclusion Act worked well as a threat to those entering the country, it had relatively little effect on the actual safety of American society by deporting such "dangerous" persons. Between 1903 and 1921, the US government refused only thirty-eight intended immigrants because of their anarchist beliefs, and only fourteen alien anarchists were deported during the period from 1911 until the Red Scare and mass deportations in 1919. These laws instead served to define the ideal "American" behavior, characterizing what kind of people should or should not be welcomed in American society. Jacobson notes that, "together with the state's expanded powers of deportation, these antiradical immigration and naturalization laws amount to a decision at the federal level, not only to disavow homegrown radicalism with a language of Americanism and anti-Americanism, but to export discontent through a machinery of repressive speech codes, unforgiving alien laws, and ever-vigilant government bureaucracies." These laws designated radicalism as anti-American behavior, and though many Wobblies were US citizens, those that were not could find themselves targets of exclusion laws.[13]

The Anarchist Exclusion Act applied to persons trying to enter the country, as well as to those who had made it through the initial screening but were found to belong to one of the listed categories within three years of their arrival. The initial accusation by the Seattle Jewish aid society inaccurately accused Beck and Solomon of entering the country together in 1911, which would have put them within that three-year time frame. Although local business owners had reason to want the two agitators deported, it was the local aid society that initially gave the authorities a reason to arrest them. A Jewish aid society in England had contacted the Council of Jewish Women in New York in March of 1912 asking for help in tracking down Solomon, because his wife and four children had been left destitute in England. They forwarded the request to Jewish societies around the country, and after Solomon's arrest for the altercation during the tailor strike, the aid society in Seattle alerted the Department of Commerce and Labor Immigration Services Division. This initial report also accused Solomon not only of abandoning his family in England, but also of bringing Beck into the country for immoral purposes. The local authorities then requested warrants for their arrest and proceeded to prosecute them for anarchist beliefs and immoral activities.[14]

In order to maintain their innocence, Beck and Solomon had to prove three things: that Beck was not a prostitute, that they had not been involved in any immoral activity, and that they were not anarchists. As the charges were both moral and political, they were questioned along both of those lines. Solomon and Beck both denied being anarchists, but admitted membership in the IWW. When asked if he believed in the government of this country, Solomon replied, "Not if I could get a better one." And in answer to the question, "Do you believe in the overthrow of these governments?" he replied, "Sure, I believe in the overthrow by votes." He denied that he believed in the use of violence to overthrow the government.[15]

Beck similarly denied a belief in overthrow by violence. After she admitted that she studied philosophical anarchy, she was questioned about what exactly her beliefs were. She said that rather than overthrow by force, she believed in "intelligence and betterment of humanity through the mind." When asked if this meant she wanted to use argument and persuasion to convince people to overthrow the government, she replied, "No, a person has to know their own mind. If a person own mind one knows [sic] he can do good for every living thing. I think it may be possible to do without laws gradually, the things should be eliminated gradually, but through intelligence." When asked if she thought it was possible that people could become so intelligent that government would no longer be necessary, she replied, "It is a dream of mine, I don't know whether it will ever come true, but it is a dream."[16]

It was established early on in the hearings that Beck had entered the country prior to Solomon, and therefore he was not guilty of bringing her into the country for the purposes of prostitution. He could, however, still be guilty of violating the Mann Act, which was punishable by a fine not to exceed five thousand dollars and/or five years imprisonment.[17]

The Mann Act was passed in 1910 to curb what was termed "white slavery," young girls forced into prostitution against their will. The act, also known as the White Slave Traffic Act, aimed to convict those who took women across state lines against their will to practice prostitution. But the legal wording of the act gave it much broader scope, and it was rare to find cases that actually involved coercion. Section 2 of the act prohibited interstate transport of women for the purposes of "prostitution or debauchery, or for any other immoral purpose." "Immoral" is not a legally defined term, and left much power in the hands of local officials to decide which acts could be considered immoral. Consummation was not required for those charged to be convicted; prosecutors had only to prove the transport was made with immoral intentions.[18]

What officials typically deemed immoral was any kind of implied sexual activity outside of the bounds of marriage. Mann Act prosecutions often involved the transport of willing adults; whether or not sex actually took place was not usually the issue. In the case of Solomon and Beck, who were consenting adults, their immoral activity constituted living together as man and wife, when they were not legally defined as such.

The case against Solomon and Beck centered on a move the pair had made to Ketchikan, Alaska, in 1911. Solomon denied that the two had ever lived together as man and wife. He reported that he had lived in the same house as Beck and her brother, but that was all. In order to violate the Mann Act, Solomon would have had to pay for her transport to Alaska. The evidence supplied to prove this was a money order made out to Becky Solomon, in the amount of ten dollars, signed by Jack Solomon in Alaska in May of 1911. Solomon and Beck argued that the check was actually repayment of a loan made to Solomon by Beck.[19]

While questioning Solomon during the investigation, the immigration agents asserted that Beck had admitted that she and Solomon had lived as man and wife in her earlier interview. Solomon maintained that she had given the wrong answer and that it was never true. In Beck's second examination she denied she lived with Solomon as his wife in Seattle, but said that they "were known as man and wife as it was necessary to do that in Alaska." They asked her about another man named Andrew Saunders, who she had previously lived with. She claimed they had intended to marry, but the relationship ended because of an undisclosed disagreement. The officers also showed evidence of a letter received by Beck from a man at Home Colony named Pease, which implied that the two had intimate relations. Beck denied this and said they spent a "pleasant hour" together, but that nothing more had happened. As we will see in cases involving Wobbly women, whether or not immorality was the actual charge, they were often interrogated about their personal relationships with men.[20]

Officials accused Beck of believing in free love, a term they used in a derogatory manner but that was embraced by many radicals of the era. The early-twentieth-century version of free love was less about encouraging people to have multiple partners and more about critiquing the institution of marriage. In her 1911 essay "Marriage and Love," Emma Goldman argued that "marriage and love have nothing in common; they are as far apart as the poles; are, in fact, antagonistic to each other." She argued that marriage was an economic arrangement akin to prostitution, in which a woman trades sex for economic security.[21]

But Goldman herself experienced the difficulty of putting free association, in which partners coupled and decoupled as their feelings dictated, into practice. She struggled with jealousy and possessiveness in her relationship with Ben Reitman, even knowing full well that this conflicted with her beliefs. When interviewed later in life, Becky Beck described her dislike of Reitman, recounting, "He once took me home from a lecture and immediately asked me to sleep with him. I said no, and he said 'Don't you believe in free love?' 'Yes,' I answered, 'I believe in choosing my lovers.'"[22]

In the Pacific Northwest, Beck and Solomon were not alone in their unconventional arrangements, or in suffering under the moral ambiguity that resulted when spouses and families (such as Solomon's in England) were deserted. Louise Bryant, a feminist and journalist, left her husband for Portland native John Reed, the journalist who brought the stories of the Mexican civil war and the Russian Revolution to the American people. Another well-known Portland couple, the Socialist poet Sara Bard Field and radical author and attorney C. E. S. Wood, carried on an affair that ruined both of their marriages. Free love did not come without consequences, but the attraction of living life freed from the bonds of traditional marriage drew in many active in the radical community.[23]

During this period the discussion of sex and sexuality was becoming more open in radical circles. Becky Beck was no prude, and had nude photos taken of herself around the time she came to the United States. These were produced as evidence of her immoral behavior. Beck denied that she gave the photographs to anyone, or that they were made for distribution for profit. When asked why she took them, she explained that she wanted to remember how she looked when she was older.[24]

In the findings of her examination by immigration officials on June 14, Beck was described as "of good physique" and "above the average intelligence." But the agents still found her to be morally deficient as evidenced by "her relations with men, her false statements during the examination, and the fact of her having had nude photographs taken of herself." This, along with her admitted relationship with Saunders and the alleged relationship with Pease, was enough evidence to convince the agent that she be placed "in a class of immoral women generally and commonly known as prostitutes." Even though she had several character witnesses testify on her behalf, they "impressed [the agent] very unfavorably as they are all persons imbued with the same beliefs, ignorant and uneducated except along socialistic and anarchistic lines." Radical political and social beliefs were enough to discount witness testimony, which again signifies how difficult it was for radicals to find justice in a system that deemed them deficient because of their beliefs.[25]

In a letter dated July 5, 1912, the commissioner of immigration in Seattle, Ellis DeBruler, wrote to the commissioner-general of immigration in Washington, DC, to discuss the cases of Solomon and Beck. The commissioner admitted that both had been in the country for more than three years, so deporting them because of anarchist views was not lawful. However, DeBruler believed that the two were "morally deficient, being believers and followers of the Free Love cult." In his view, "their presence in the country is a menace to law and order and a disgrace to the community and the nation and I believe that they should be removed from the country, if the law can possibly be construed to warrant such action." DeBruler also noted that the case had been forwarded to the US attorney for his district, but he advised that a White Slave Act violation was not warranted. Clearly Beck and Solomon were seen as guilty and dangerous regardless of whether or not there was any legal basis to designate them as such.[26]

DeBruler admitted in his letter that the charges with which he had hoped to deport the pair were unfounded, but still hoped that there might be a way to "construe" the law to deport them anyway. A letter to the secretary of commerce and labor from the counsel for Beck and Solomon, Channing Coleman, demolished any chance of that happening. Coleman argued their case point by point and showed the immigration commission had no evidence of prostitution or anarchism. He argued that the case was instead directly related to their activity in the tailors' strike and that they were targeted because of their labor activities.

As evidence of the political nature of the case, Coleman noted that the inspector refused to give the name of his "local source" that had reported the pair as involved in anarchism and prostitution. Coleman believed the shop owners who had been struck were the anonymous informants. Since they knew that Beck and Solomon had recently entered the United States, they reported them to remove them from the center of agitation and strike activity. Furthermore, Beck had testified that the inspector initially asked her about the strike, which proved to Coleman that he had previously had communication with the business owners the tailors were on strike against.[27]

Coleman was not alone in his belief that the immigration service was being used to punish strike leaders. Shortly after their arrest, a petition was filed on Beck and Solomon's behalf that tied the arrest to their participation in the strike:

> The undersigned citizens and residents of Seattle, being convinced that a great wrong is being done to Jack Soloman [sic] and Becky Beck by arresting and detaining them for

deportation, and being convinced that the Immigration Officers are deceived by false information given by interested parties for the purpose of breaking the strike against the B & R Tailors, which strike they are leading, respectfully petition the Honorable Secretary, to order the immediate release of said Jack Soloman and Becky Beck from custody.

The petition carried over seven hundred signatures.[28]

The petition and Coleman's letter worked, and on July 11, 1912, acting Secretary of Commerce and Labor Benjamin S. Cable informed DeBruler that, after careful review, Cable found that the facts did not justify deportation, though he "regrets that such is the case." At that point Solomon was released and Beck's bond was returned. After the accusation by Coleman that the warrant was actually based on involvement in the strike, Cable wrote to Samuel Gompers, president of the AFL, to assure him that the arrest was not related to the strike, and that not enough evidence had been provided to warrant deportation.[29]

For many of the women involved in trials such as these, their subsequent actions are difficult to track down. Luckily, Beck lived a long life and continued to be an activist into the 1970s, during which time she was interviewed twice. In a 1973 interview, Beck referred to Solomon as her first husband, and mentioned that she had a child with him in 1912 that died shortly after it was born. When the interviewer asked Beck when she married Solomon, she replied that they had a common-law marriage recognized by the state of Washington. So it is likely from Beck's later admission that both Beck and Solomon lied about their relationship in order to avoid deportation based on issues of morality.[30]

Beck and Solomon's relationship proved to be short-lived, and Beck married Benjamin August in Seattle around 1916–1917. They left Seattle about a year later to go to New York, but returned to Seattle and helped organize the 1919 general strike. She then lived in the Bay Area and subsequently Los Angeles, left her husband in 1931, and moved to the Home Colony in Washington. In a 1974 interview she noted that she still belonged to the International League for Peace and Freedom, founded by Jane Addams. She ended the interview by proclaiming that her motto was "Down with hatred! Love to all mankind!" Beck, at that time known as Rebecca August, passed away in 1978.[31]

The cases of Becky Beck and Jack Solomon provide an example of the way that issues of morality were used to persecute radicals. Beck and Solomon were known for their labor activities and their membership in the Industrial Workers of the World. But since those actions were not in themselves illegal, morality laws such as the Mann Act or immigration exclusions were used against those labor activists who questioned traditional middle-class beliefs regarding gender, sex, and marriage. The frequent references to Solomon and Beck as members of the "free love cult" insinuate that not only did they want to transform industrial life and the relationship between the working class and the employing class, they also wanted to transform familial relationships. The vague wording of such morality laws provided a way for prosecutors to attempt to stifle radical, but not illegal, activity in the workplace, by attacking the private lives of those involved.

The Seattle tailors' strike had limited effect on the IWW as a labor organization in that it did not lead to lasting or widespread unionization of the industry within the IWW. But the trials of Becky Beck and Jack Solomon make it clear that the legal troubles that followed their organizing efforts were based on the judgment of officials who believed that by virtue of their radical beliefs they did not belong in the United States. This exemplifies the legal risks that male and female Wobblies faced in their organizing efforts. Radicals were questioned on a moral, rather than legal, basis and had to account for any relationship outside of marriage that could be deemed immoral. Women's behavior in this regard was more closely scrutinized than men's. The courts put women's personal lives on trial for actions they took to protect their bodies and their rights in the workplace. Any hint of behavior outside the bounds of traditional marriage and sexuality put them at risk. The legal system that was set up to persecute political radicalism also persecuted those who questioned middle-class moral values.

4

Portland 1913

The Oregon Packing Company Strike and the Case of Lilian Larkin

As during the tailors' strike in Seattle, women's sexual behaviors again became a focal point during a strike of cannery workers in Portland in 1913. Examining the strike and its aftermath reveals how women within the IWW rejected or renegotiated popular views on the causes of prostitution. During the strike, the women held signs declaring that "40¢ a day is what makes prostitutes," blaming low wages, rather than loose morals, for pushing women into selling their bodies for a living. The Industrial Workers of the World shared this view. Its support of the female strikers led to a showdown between radical and progressive forces in the city, each battling to define what was respectable and acceptable behavior for young females. As the strike ended, the battle took on a new turn, pitting the IWW against one of the nation's first policewomen, Lola Baldwin, in the case of Lilian Larkin, an eighteen-year-old with "immoral tendencies" who had been accused of vagrancy.

The 1913 cannery strike also typifies the tensions during this period between Progressive reform and radicalism. The justice system, as we have seen in chapters 2 and 3, was a tool for enforcing "respectable" behaviors, as it judged women on their personal and political beliefs, regardless of the legality of those beliefs. The strike is also an example of the paternalistic nature of progressivism, as reformers effectively took the strike out of the strikers' hands and settled it in the way they thought most beneficial to the workers. While Progressives enforced what they thought was best for young women, the IWW supported what the young women thought would be best for themselves. Progressives believed they were acting in the best interests of young women, protecting them from immorality or vice. The Wobblies and the young women they represented fought to have control over their labor and their bodies, and argued against morality being forced on them.[1]

The 1913 strike at the Oregon Packing Company (OPC) lasted less than two months and affected only a few hundred workers, but it led to a dramatic showdown between radicals and Progressives in the city of Portland, the largest city in Oregon, with a population of 207,214 in 1910. Recent studies of the strike have examined how Progressive Era reformers commandeered the negotiations between the workers and the employers and settled the strike according to their standards of justice and fairness. The strike and the ensuing Larkin controversy reflect the discordant views on prostitution and female sexuality espoused by middle-class reformers and working-class women, especially those associated with the Industrial Workers of the World.[2]

While the 1913 cannery strike could be catalogued as one of many conflicts between labor and business during the Progressive Era, the class struggle was complicated by the atmosphere of anti-vice panic in Portland and throughout the nation. Progressive reformers were highly concerned about women's working conditions and female sexuality, and feared that low wages made young women vulnerable to moral decay. To protect young women's moral virtue, numerous efforts were made to understand and alleviate the problems of low wages and vice in Progressive Era Portland.

First gaining popularity in the 1890s, regulations on hours and conditions of female work outside of the home had been a contentious issue. While most radical groups like the IWW did not advocate different workplace standards for men and women, throughout the Progressive Era many reformers focused on women's unique qualities, especially their role as mothers, to advocate shorter working hours and better conditions. When different states started to mandate a limit on the hours one could work during the day, in the case of *Lochner v. New York* (1905), the United States Supreme Court invalidated these laws on the grounds of the doctrine of "freedom of contract," which had long been used against unions and reform groups. According to "freedom of contract," a worker had the "freedom" to make any agreement she wanted with her employer regarding hours, wages, or conditions, and the government had no right to interfere with that employer/employee relationship. One can imagine how little freedom a mother desperate to feed her children felt in this relationship.

More and more often, reformers pointed out the injustice inherent in "freedom of contract": desperation led people to agree to low pay, long hours, and deplorable conditions. It was a fundamentally imbalanced relationship, where, as the Wobblies often pointed out, the interests of workers and employers were at odds. Just three years after the *Lochner* case, *Muller v. Oregon* (1908) justified treating men and women differently under the law when it came to maximum hours. In 1903, Oregon had set a maximum of ten hours a day that women could work outside the home. Curt Muller, who owned a Portland laundry, had been convicted and fined ten dollars for keeping his workers longer than the maximum hours. He took his case to the United States Supreme Court. In this landmark decision, the court justified women's shorter working hours because of their biological differences. Women were protected by the state because of their ability to reproduce and the importance of healthy motherhood. This had less to do with the rights of workers and more to do with the state's responsibility of keeping women healthy enough to reproduce. The IWW generally rejected laws that treated men and women differently and advocated for shorter hours for the entire working-class. The union argued that laws enforcing maximum hours for women would hurt women in the long run because employers would just fire them and hire men, who could work longer hours.[3]

Along with laws regulating maximum working hours, Progressives also investigated the issue of low wages. In 1912 the Consumer's League of Oregon undertook a study, headed by reformer Caroline Gleason, that would provide information in support of a minimum wage law for women that the group wanted to introduce to the state legislature the following year. Gleason's study, the *Report of the Social Survey Committee of the Consumers' League of Oregon on the Wages, Hours, and Conditions of Work and Cost and Standard Living of Women Wage Earners in Oregon with Special Reference to Portland*, was published in 1913 and used much of the same language prioritizing women's roles as mothers that was used by future Supreme Court judge Louis Brandeis, a lawyer for Oregon in the *Muller v. Oregon* case. The minimum wage bill was passed in February 1913, and also included a provision to create the Industrial Welfare Commission. The commission was made up of representatives of workers, employers, and the public and was established to oversee and regulate hours and conditions of labor. Catholic priest Edwin O'Hara was appointed to represent the public, pottery manufacturer Amedee Smith to represent the employers, and Bertha

Moore, listed as a retired teacher, to represent workers. Gleason was named executive secretary. The Oregon Industrial Welfare Commission (OIWC) was established June 3, less than a month before the OPC strike began. The role the commission played in the strike was the first effort of this new regulating body, and the members approached it with zeal, no doubt eager to prove their worth. While O'Hara and Gleason had reputations as Progressive reformers, it should be noted that Smith was a member of the Portland Non-Partisan League, an organization formed during the strike that passed a resolution endorsing police action against the strikers. Smith signed the resolution, demonstrating that he was not impartial on the issue of the strike. The Wobblies and Socialists opposed the OIWC and its mandate, and Father O'Hara was a subject of particular scorn. The Strike Press Committee referred to him as "His Oilyness," and accused him of telling the striking women in his parish that they would go to hell if they did not go back to work.[4]

The Oregon Packing Company strike also coincided with a nationwide scare over the issue of prostitution, often termed "white slavery." Reaching its peak in the United States in years prior to World War I, beliefs about white slavery combined the moralistic attitudes of Progressive reformers with the Victorian fear of sexual impropriety. The fear was that young, white girls were being kidnapped and forced into a life of prostitution and drug addiction. The term itself elevated concerns over the well-being of white women above women of color. Panic over prostitution during the Progressive Era had three distinct but related elements. The first was public panic that young girls were being kidnapped and sold into slavery. The second stemmed from the increased freedom of young girls working in factories and moving to cities, where their families no longer could keep close watch on them. The third focused on vice in major cities and what local governments could do to stop it. The threat of kidnapping was largely imagined, and although young women breaking free from parental control threatened Victorian moral standards and traditional family life, little could be done to stem the tide of immigrant and American-born young women flocking to the cities for work. Vice in cities, however, drew the attention of Progressive reformers because it was a demonstrable problem and steps could be taken to fix it. These issues are worth exploring more carefully in order to fully understand the context of the actions of both strikers and Progressive reformers in Portland in 1913.

The panic over white slavery was reaching fever pitch by the time of the 1913 OPC strike. The term itself was coined only a few years earlier by George Kibbe Turner, in a 1907 article in *McClure's* on vice in Chicago. Several sensationalized reports in newspapers and by politicians claimed that a widespread prostitution ring existed in the United States. This ring allegedly preyed on native-born American girls and was said to be run by foreigners: Russian Jews in the East, and Chinese in the West. Novels and movies such as *A Traffic in Souls* (1913) and *The Inside of the White Slave Traffic* (1913) were popular and played into the hysteria. Although it is difficult to tell with much accuracy how much forced prostitution actually existed, several studies have shown it to be roughly 5 to 10 percent of all cases of prostitution. The other causes of prostitution, often economic, were ignored as reformers focused on their own sense of threatened morality and fear of behavior they could not control.[5]

The propaganda over the fear of kidnapping and drug addiction led to federal laws aimed at preventing traffic in women. The first attempt at federal legislation making it illegal to import alien prostitutes was ruled unconstitutional in 1909, when the United States Supreme Court decided "the provisions against importers and employers were an unconstitutional assumption of police powers reserved for the state." A more successful (and still in effect) federal law was passed in 1910, known as the Mann Act. Unlike the laws that had been declared unconstitutional, the Mann Act focused on the act of taking women across state lines for prostitution or other "immoral behavior." This could include premarital or extramarital sex and was used against people, including radicals, who had unconventional relationships, as we saw in the previous chapter.[6]

The public obsession with white slavery reflected the fear of changes brought on by mass immigration, industrialization, and urbanization. Young women had more freedom than ever before and were able to interact with men in the workplace and in new social spaces such as movie theaters and amusement parks. As Joanne Meyerowitz points out, these "women adrift" moved to cities for economic opportunities, to escape abuse, or to have more freedom. Regardless of their reasons for joining the workforce, young women now spent more time in the outside world than in the private sphere of the home, as previous generations had, which was cause for consternation. But employers, to justify low wages, used the prevailing notion that young female workers were only working for "pin money" and had other means of support.[7]

In response to these social changes, Progressive reformers focused on restricting young women's sexuality and punishing female delinquency. Historian Mary Odem points out that "reformers assumed the authority to define an appropriate code of morality for female youth, one that was based on middle-class ideals of female sexual restraint and modesty." Although often purporting to "protect" young women, most of these new regulations focused on limiting their freedoms and subjecting them to detention if they did not conform.[8]

The fear of young women "adrift" in cities led to the creation of new institutions responsible for policing and reforming their behavior. The Oregon State Industrial School for Girls was a product of these newfound fears of female delinquency. It opened in July 1913, during the cannery strike. The school was to hold delinquent young women between the ages of twelve and twenty-five, "the purpose being to protect them, to protect society, and if possible to so train and educate them that they will become good and useful women." There were six offenses for which one could be admitted: immorality, larceny, vagrancy, incorrigibility, evil associates, or delinquency.[9] A teacher visiting the school found that the students learned tasks such as cleaning, laundry, and cooking, which were "a very important part of every girl's education." Each young woman spent the morning in some kind of manual labor and the afternoon in school. As well as being graded on these activities, they were marked in the following categories: "effort, tidiness, truthfulness, obedience, promptness, honesty, good influence, and clean talk." Most of those categories were subjective, so the occupants were at the mercy of those supervising and judging them. The young women also worked on the farm located on the grounds, and attended Bible study and church services on weekends. A three-year term was the standard for all females committed, though they could be paroled for good behavior. While on parole, they had to write a letter to the superintendent once a month to check in, and send in one-fourth of their earnings. Once the women were fully released, those earnings would be returned to them. The reform institution attempted to enforce respectable behavior by imposing strict rules and regulations, and often left young women sentenced to the school with little choice but to obey.[10]

The treatment of "immoral" young women by state authorities often conflated moral judgment with assessment of mental abilities. As Ruth Rosen points out in her pioneering study of prostitution, *The Lost Sisterhood*, prostitutes were often accused of being feebleminded. According to the Massachusetts white slave commission, some common characteristics of feeblemindedness were "general moral insensibility, the boldness, egotism and vanity, the love of notoriety, the lack of shame or remorse, the absence of even a pretense of affection or sympathy for their children or for their parents, the desire for immediate pleasure without regard for consequences, the lack of forethought or anxiety about the future." Rosen notes that "rather than indicating mental deficiency, the label feeble-minded instead referred to the prostitutes' refusal or failure to conform to middle-class values and behavior patterns." "Refusal or failure to conform to middle-class values and behavior patterns" could also be used to describe the stance of the majority of IWW membership.[11]

While historians have concluded that the focus on white slavery and female sexuality during the 1910s was largely an overreaction to changing social circumstances, it did coincide with the very real existence of prostitution in the nation's cities. Vice districts known for drinking, gambling, and prostitution were found in all major cities and were targets of Progressive reformers in their quest to control and reshape working-class behaviors. These would often also be the areas where migrant workers came to spend their paychecks, and therefore where an IWW office could usually be found.

Portland too was swept up in this reform movement. In 1912, the Portland Vice Commission presented a report to the mayor "on immorality in places of public resort and accommodation, namely, hotels, apartment houses, rooming and lodging houses which by advertisement solicit the patronage of the public." The commission investigated 547 establishments. Of these, only ninety-eight were found to be moral, while eighteen more were listed as "doubtful" in terms of morality. The other 431 were listed as immoral, and separated into three degrees of immorality: 113 were "wholly given up to prostitution or assignation," 124 were listed as "immoral tenants desired or preferred," and the final 194 were listed as "immorality countenanced or ignored." The commission report also pointed out that many of these establishments were in buildings owned by prominent businessmen in the city, suggesting that city leaders were profiting off these immoral activities. One of the solutions they recommended, which was adopted in 1913, was the so-called tin-plate law. It required "owners of hotel, rooming and lodging houses and saloons to maintain a conspicuous plate or sign with the owner's name and address," with a penalty of fines of up to one hundred dollars a day for those who did not obey. This was meant to shame the well-known businessmen who owned these buildings into making sure their tenants were moral.[12]

The local and national obsession with prostitution and changing freedoms for young women cannot be separated from the strike. The strikers were clearly aware of the panic over prostitution and teenage sexuality when they explicitly blamed low wages in the workplace for turning young women to prostitution. The reformers feared that the young female strikers mingling with the "dangerous" male Wobblies were being taken advantage of and would be turned into prostitutes. Reformers believed that state and local government should intervene in the workplace to promote their standards of fairness, morality, and respectability. This strike gave them a chance to apply their belief in the positive nature of governmental intrusion to a real world situation.

Attention to vice and morality was also reflected in the local news-papers accounts of the strike. The *Oregonian*, the Portland *Telegram,* and the Oregon *Daily Journal* all came down on the side of the employ-ers and Progressive reformers. The Portland *News* (previously known as the *Daily News*), an avowedly working-class paper, supported the strikers and gave much more attention to the strike, often as front-page news. The mainstream newspapers shed light on how the "dangers" of young women's association with the Wobblies were relayed to the pub-lic. The working-class paper, while providing a more dramatic reading of the strike, paid more attention to what the strikers had to say about the events, and castigated police and local officials for their behavior toward the strikers.

Now that we understand the context of the strike, the actions of all parties involved can be seen in light of local and national issues. In June of 1913, the cherry crop was ready to be canned at the Or-egon Packing Company, located on Eighth and Belmont in southeast Portland. The women had previously been canning strawberries and making about a dollar a day, but the cherries took longer and were of lower quality, so some women ended up making as little as forty cents a day. Twenty-year-old Pauline Haller, one of the leaders of the strike, later testified that the workers had been complaining about conditions and wages and, on June 27, decided they would ask for more money. If they were rebuffed, they would go out on strike. They approached the supervisor, Mr. McPherson, and as Haller recounted,

> He spoke to us first and then he kicked us out. He didn't give us our wraps or anything. He said "if you don't like it here get out." I told him we wanted more wages and I don't think $1.50 is any too much for any girl to live on. Nobody agitated—we all walked out together and the majority of the old women ran back and got to work.[13]

The women who joined the strike later testified that they were told they would be making two dollars a day, but ended up only making twenty-nine to fifty cents. They also complained of hand injuries and getting sick from the rotten fruit.[14]

The local branches of the IWW and the Socialist Party immediately supported the women who walked out on strike. A few days into the strike the women formed a strike committee to negotiate with the OPC, which initially refused to meet with the strikers. The committee requested a wage increase to $1.50 per day, which was the strikers' initial demand, but they did not stop there. They wanted double time for overtime and Sunday work and an increase in pay for the forewoman to twenty-five cents an hour. The strikers had concerns beyond wages, and demanded that the company provide a lunchroom, sick room, lockers, a dressing room, three aprons per week, and sufficient towels. Low wages inspired the strike, but hygiene was clearly important to the strikers.[15]

Along with organizing the strikers' demands, the strike committee also tried to keep order. Fearing that trouble from businessmen and onlookers would cause the police to break up street meetings, the Wobblies physically encouraged people such as local businessman M. C. Banfield to move along and not clog the sidewalk. Banfield later testified that Wobbly "self-appointed police" put their hands on his shoulders and forcefully kept him moving so the congestion would not cause a street meeting to be broken up.[16] Along with security, the committee was also charged with feeding the strikers. On July 4 the strikers had

THE STRIKE COMMITTEE

Two Strikers with Banners
Are a 14-Year-Old Girl and
a Full-Blooded Indian Girl.

Images of the Strike. *International Socialist Review,* September 1913.

an "all day picnic. Sympathizers sent over an abundance of ice-cream for the women, and a brass band is in attendance in front of strike headquarters."[17] There was "speaking, singing, music, and dining" in front of the plant from 6 a.m. to 6 p.m. daily, and after that time the strikers would head downtown for large rallies.[18]

The IWW and the local Socialist Party assisted the strikers by providing financial aid during this strike. There were newspaper reports that they were paying full room and board for the strikers, though that amount of funding was unlikely. OPC superintendent McPherson was dismissive of the workers' complaints and believed that the agitators were "conducting the strike merely for the pleasure of causing trouble. The girls find this an easy way of making a living."[19] The strikers, however, saw it differently. During a hearing with Oregon governor Oswald West, striker Mrs. Miller noted that "if it were not for the assistance given by the despised agitators I couldn't eat. They paid my rent, kept my table going, and cared for my sick boy." Whereas McPherson and the *Oregonian* thought that aid to the strikers meant paying troublemakers to not work, those who were assisting the strikers knew that it was a necessity if they were going to stay out long enough for the strike to be successful.[20]

Local radicals weren't the only ones interested in representing the strikers. The newly formed Oregon Industrial Welfare Commission organized a committee to investigate conditions in the factory. Strikers were suspicious of the OIWC's efforts. Tom Burns, notorious Portland radical and chairman of the strike committee, claimed the OIWC "butted into this affair" and was "composed primarily of parlor reformers." He continued, "It seems to me that their principle function is to break a strike, and not assist in ameliorating the conditions of the helpless workers."[21] An unnamed strike supporter told the committee that the OIWC asked the girls to leave the picket line and promised they would settle the strike for them in thirty to ninety days. When they discussed wages with the commission, the strikers said they needed a minimum of $1.50 a day, but the supporter reported that Father O'Hara "thought that was too much but said he would see what he could do." The strikers refused to leave the picket line. Later they found out at the commission brokered a settlement without their input or approval.[22]

The strikers' suspicions of the OIWC proved correct: the commission ignored many of the workers' requests regarding safety and sanitation and instead came to an agreement with the OPC that improved wages but still fell below the amount requested by the strikers. The Portland *News* reported on the deal with the headline, "They Weren't Told About It." The agreement, dated July 1, listed the following conditions:

1. That a minimum flat time rate shall be a dollar a day on a basis of a 10-hour day.
2. Piece rate shall be determined on the basis of work of the average worker who shall be able to earn the above minimum at piece rate, in 10 hours.
3. Old or crippled workers shall be given permits by the Industrial Welfare Commission for time rate.
4. No worker who works under permit from Industrial Welfare Commission, or from the Child Labor Commission, shall be considered in the computing of piece rate for the average worker.[23]

The Portland *News* reported that those still working at the plant knew nothing of the new agreement, and that the wage minimum had not yet been implemented. The dollar a day minimum wage fell far short of the nine to ten dollars a week that even the mayor of Portland agreed was necessary for the women to support themselves, let alone any family members that relied on them.[24]

The OIWC declared the strike over after the agreement, but the majority of the women on strike refused to go back to work and continued to picket the OPC. They had played no part in the negotiations, and the OIWC agreement did not meet the strikers' list of demands. On July 8, eleven women who had continued to work in the factory were sent in cars to complain to Mayor Albee about the treatment they received from the strikers. They were followed by a march of one hundred strikers who wanted to tell their side of the story. At this point the strike turned into a free speech fight. On July 9, Mayor Albee issued an order to the chief of police to "permit no person, striker or other, to use abusive obscene, vulgar or threatening language. Permit no person to block the street or sidewalk. Permit no rowdyism, threats or violence of any kind. Arrest forthwith all violators of the penal ordinances of the City of Portland or violators of these orders."[25] The Portland *News* claimed that Albee only prohibited street speaking after an appeal by the Employers Association, which suggests that the prohibition was about the strike and protest, rather than about the language used.[26]

On the morning of July 9 the first arrests for street speaking were made. Mrs. Schoen and Rudolph and Mary Schwab were arrested. Rudolph was the son of Michael Schwab, who was a defendant in the 1886 Haymarket trial, during which eight anarchists were convicted of conspiracy after a bomb was thrown during a street meeting in Chicago supporting the movement for an eight-hour workday. While the case and ensuing trial were full of evidence of bias against the radicals on the part of the judge, jury, and police, four of the men were ultimately executed for their political beliefs. Schwab's sentence was commuted to life in prison, and he was pardoned by Illinois governor John Altgeld in 1893. Rudolph Schwab and Mary Charsky met in San Francisco and were married in 1912. They were members of the Socialist Labor Party (SLP) and went up to Portland to support the strike once they heard about it. Years later in an interview, Mary reported that since the strike wasn't officially sponsored by the SLP, they were kicked out of the party for it.[27]

On July 10, Mary Schwab was arrested again, along with Mrs. Rice, Mrs. Agness O'Connor, and Mrs. Belle Goldish. All these women

SCENE IN COUNCIL CHAMBER DURING HEARING GIVEN STRIKING CANNERS YESTERDAY BY GOVERNOR WEST

City council hearing for the striking cannery workers. *Oregon Daily Journal*, July 13, 1913.

were listed in the local papers as in their late twenties and early thirties. On July 11, Governor Oswald West addressed the crowd picketing the OPC, promising to help resolve the strike. On July 12, the strikers, as well as supporters, crowded city hall to testify about the conditions they faced at the plant to an audience of the governor and the members of the OIWC. Mayor Albee did not attend. At the meeting twelve of the women spoke of low wages, unsanitary conditions, and the poor quality of fruit that they were forced to work with.[28] Tom Burns and Mary Schwab, representing the strikers, tore into the officials present, goading OIWC member Father O'Hara into admitting that he was the one who announced to the press that the strike was over before the strikers had been consulted. At one point during the meeting Governor West was so incensed that he stood on a mahogany table shouting at Burns, "Don't think because you wear a red flag I am afraid of you."[29] West's anger was a result of what he believed were insults to OIWC member Bertha Moore, a retired teacher and the state-appointed representative for the workers on the OIWC, who had taught West when he was a boy.[30]

Later that day the strike took a more violent turn when mounted police charged the female picketers, in an incident the press committee hyperbolically called "the most atrociously brutal act in the history of Oregon." Approximately seventy-five women linked arms on the picket line, and they reformed time and time again after the police charged and broke the line. Three women were injured: Mrs. C. H. Hart, Mrs. Mitchell, and Mrs. Kennedy. Strike supporters Edith and Andy Kohler were arrested at the scene. Also arrested on Saturday was George Stevens, the night watchmen at the OPC, for kicking striker Eva Bale. The strikers vowed to continue to picket, and the injured women secured a lawyer and made plans to sue the policemen who gave the order to charge.[31]

Tension escalated over the next few days. On July 15, the police arrested Tom Burns while he was speaking to raise donations for the strikers and beat him so badly that he required an operation. In one of the biggest street meetings, on July 16, the police arrested ten more. At this point Dr. Marie Equi became a focal point of the strike. Equi, whom we will read more about in chapter 8, had been a supporter of Progressive causes and was radicalized by the OPC strike. The *Oregonian* seemed equally fascinated and repulsed by Equi, making her out to be insane and violent and reporting that she punched the deputy and the night watchman at the jail. "She apparently courted arrest, applying picturesque epithets to the deputies and to the police." They then quoted Sheriff Word as warning "certain women that they went too far last night and that they cannot expect to be treated as women if they act like hooligans."[32]

It soon became clear that the women arrested were going to bear the consequences for stepping outside of the bounds of appropriate female behavior. On July 17, women went out again in defiance of the orders against street speaking. Approximately three thousand people were present at the meeting, and violence escalated into hand-to-hand combat between Wobblies and police. In all, ten women and six men were arrested. The women arrested were between the ages of sixteen and fifty-seven, suggesting the significance of this issue to younger and older workers. Again, Equi was at the forefront, purportedly leading a group of seventeen girls, screaming "that she would kill anyone who tried to make her stop talking."[33] Equi, Mary Schwab, Pauline Haller, Jean Bennett, and Belle Goldish were all charged with assembling

> with intent and with means and preparation to do an
> unlawful act, to wit to resist the Chief of Police of the City
> of Portland and the Sheriff of Multnomah County in their
> efforts to preserve the peace and prevent the said officers
> from maintaining law and order, the said defendants being

armed with weapons consisting of pieces of gas pipe and
other weapons and were by speech and otherwise endeavor-
ing to incite others to resist lawful authority at said time
and place.[34]

Since Equi was a doctor, the papers hyperbolically stoked fear of her
medical knowledge. The *Oregonian* reported that she claimed to have
infected a hairpin with a deadly virus, and she would stab anyone who
tried to come near her.[35]

The following day the labor-friendly Portland *News* led with the
headline "Crazed Cops Let Run Amok." Their coverage of events filled
the front page and featured stories recounted by the numerous citizens
who had nothing to do with the strike yet were clubbed and beaten
by police. The *News* also reported that it had received threats of an
organized group coming to ransack the plant and destroy the paper. To
this the newspaper replied "Now, listen, you anarchists, you starvers of
women, you protectors of white slavers, you pardoners of degenerates,
you grafters in high office, you haters of labor. . . you come right up to
325 Fifth Street and try it on."[36]

One example of onlooker involvement during the violent episode
that the *News* reported was the case of Mr. and Mrs. Arthur Kite. Mr.
Kite had grabbed a police club while protecting his wife from the officers. He was then beaten badly enough to require stitches, and when
his wife interfered in his defense, she was also arrested. The Kites, unlike the majority of the strikers who lived in Portland's working-class
east side, lived in the upscale Portland Heights neighborhood and were
in the downtown area to see a show. Mr. Kite, a department store employee, said that they were wedged in the crowd and had nothing to do
with the strike itself. The disorderly conduct charge against Mrs. Kite
was dropped, though Mr. Kite was found guilty.[37]

In efforts to clamp down on the street speaking and avoid any further violent confrontation, Mayor Albee proposed a "flag ordinance,"
which would prohibit any speech or language that created "disturbance
or disrespect for the governments of or in the United States," which
included the city government. Albee's detractors attacked this as a
way of prohibiting any attempt to criticize his policies or to accuse the
government of graft. City Commissioner Brewster, a lawyer, blocked
the passage of the law, saying that it was inadvisable considering the

current temperament of the people. He likely believed it would only add fuel to the free speech fight and provoke more violence. His arguments must have been persuasive, because by July 29 it was noted that the flag ordinance would not be up for debate at the city council's next meeting.[38]

By late July, attention had turned away from the strike and was focused on the free speech battle. As late as July 22, the strikers had issued another appeal for funds, but little attention was paid to the fate of the strikers in the local papers after that point. A free speech league was formed and held its first big meeting on July 27, with an audience of five thousand. The speakers included a lawyer and a Spanish-American War veteran. No mention of the strike or strikers that had instigated the free speech battle was made in any of the reports of the event, signifying that the focus had transitioned from the strike to the issue of free speech. By August 1, thirty free speech prisoners in the county jail had been released, and Mayor Albee had extended the "free speech zone" downtown. The free speech league and the indignant citizens, who had been beaten by police for merely walking by the street speakers, felt their fight had been won. But the fight was not yet completely over, for on August 13, ten people were arrested for speaking on the street, including Lucy Parsons, widow of Haymarket martyr Albert Parsons. That was, however, the last mention of any free speech arrests. The strike wound down, and media attention dwindled.[39]

The Oregon Packing Company strike happened at a time when the city of Portland, and the nation as a whole, had been paying very close attention to the issue of female sexuality—whether by force or by choice, for money or for marriage—and the language used when describing the strike reflected this preoccupation. Although the Wobblies offered an economic explanation for why women became prostitutes, they also defended women's right to have control over their own sexuality and fought back against the power of Progressive reformers to make choices for the "good" of young women, just as the OIWC had done during the strike.

Wobbly Jean Bennett and the working-class women on strike at the OPC, like the Progressive reformers, were concerned with prostitution. But unlike the reformers, they did not blame mysterious "white slavers" or the moral failings of troubled young women. Instead they focused on the economic imperative. The signs they carried on the picket line, stating "40¢ is What Makes Prostitutes," linked economic and physical exploitation. Thus the strikers not only stepped beyond the bounds of proper female behavior by standing up for themselves and publicly going on strike, they also flirted with vulgarity, and connected selling one's labor for wages to selling one's body for wages. Both were economic transactions, and one could lead to the other if workers were not properly paid. During the strike, a letter printed in the Portland *News* by "One Lonely Woman Worker" explained the dilemma that working women faced. After describing herself as a widow with children, making thirty-five dollars per month, she asked,

> Will some wise newspaper, man or woman, tell me the best
> way to spend said thirty-five to the best advantage—pay
> rent, buy clothing, feed, shoes, fuel, pay for lights and
> water, carfare and dentists' bills? As hard as I manage, I
> simply cannot do it. I'll not mention how I make ends meet
> for fear of creating a "moral wave," for while I assure there
> is not always a market for labor there is always a traffic in
> souls and bodies.[40]

The IWW also viewed prostitution as a decidedly economic, rather than moral, concern. Low wages turned women into prostitutes, and low-wage seasonal labor made it difficult for men to support a family, so they therefore turned to prostitutes for companionship. IWW newspapers were full of stories about prostitutes. Wobblies did follow the Progressives in connecting prostitution to official corruption. Stories appeared in IWW newspapers about small towns that needed new sidewalks built. To raise funds, the police would make a sweep of the local red light district and the women's fines would fill the city's coffers.[41]

Wobbly newspapers linked women selling their bodies for a living to men who sold their labor for a living. This line of reasoning made the most sense in areas like the Northwest, where migrant labor was common. Men living in the lumber camps did not often interact with women other than prostitutes. It was difficult to maintain a stable family life for those moving from camp to camp. Historian Melvyn Dubofsky infamously characterized the western Wobbly solidarity, noting that timber workers were perfect recruits for the IWW: "Mostly native Americans or northern Europeans, they spoke English, lived together,

drank together, slept together, whored together, and fought together."
Philip Foner even noted a case of solidarity among male Wobblies and
prostitutes in Louisiana. During a lumber strike the women refused to
offer their services to strikebreakers, and in return, when the women
of the brothel went on strike themselves, the Wobblies stood in solidarity. This solidarity is hinted at in a cartoon appearing in the *Industrial
Worker* comparing the conditions of lumber workers and prostitutes.
It showed a picture of a hobo and a prostitute, with the caption "He
can't afford to have a home. She never had a chance. That's why they
are both selling themselves to the highest bidder." The IWW's economic
argument against white slavery hinged on the belief that low wages led
to prostitution, as was explicitly stated in the strikers' signs.[42]

Contemporary beliefs regarding prostitution often blamed high
levels of sexual desire or wanting to get rich as reasons why women
entered prostitution. While a few women undoubtedly hoped to get
rich by living the life, many more simply hoped to get by. This logic
is exemplified in famous Wobbly songwriter Joe Hill's 1913 song "The
White Slave." Hill had been a member of the Portland IWW local and
was familiar with labor conditions in the Northwest.

> One little girl, fair as a pearl,
> Worked every day in a laundry;
> All that she made for food she paid,
> So she slept on a park bench so soundly;

TWO VICTIMS OF SOCIETY

He can't afford to have a home. She never had a chance. That's why they are both selling themselves to
the highest bidder.

Cartoon from the
Industrial Worker,
January 26, 1911.

An old procuress spied her there,
And whispered softly in her ear:

Chorus
Come with me now, my girly,
Don't sleep out in the cold;
Your face and tresses curly
Will bring you fame and gold,
Automobiles to ride in, diamonds and silks to wear,
You'll be a star bright, down in the red light,
You'll make your fortune there.

Same little girl, no more a pearl,
Walks all alone 'long the river,
Five years have flown, her health is gone,
She would look at the water and shiver,
Whene'er she'd stop to rest and sleep,
She'd hear a voice call from the deep:

Girls in this way, fall every day,
And have been falling for ages,
Who is to blame? You know his name,
It's the boss that pays starvation wages.
A homeless girl can always hear
Temptations calling everywhere.[43]

The Wobblies can be credited for sympathizing with the plight
of women who turned to prostitution for economic reasons, but their
economic determinism ignored the specificity of sexual exploitation, its
emotional aspects, and how it differed from economic exploitation. The
Wobblies saw prostitution as a result of the capitalist system, and as a
form of labor, but they did not extensively discuss the issue in Wobbly
newspapers or songs. As with the subjects of marriage and free love,
the Wobblies were against any system that forced women to behave
in a certain way, and generally left the details vague. In the Wobbly
worldview, once capitalist exploitation was history and the One Big
Union had arrived, it was assumed that problems of sexual exploitation
would also disappear.

The discourse surrounding prostitution was present in the way that strikers, reformers, and city officials discussed the strike and the female strikers. The issue of vulgar language, often referring to pimps and prostitutes, by strikers, strike supporters, employers, and police was discussed nearly as much as the working conditions at the Oregon Packing Company. Both sides in the strike emphasized the importance of decent and respectable language, and accusations of impropriety flew fast and furious. Elmer Buse, secretary of the Socialist Party of Portland, wrote a letter to Congressman A. W. Lafferty complaining of police brutality and improper language during the free speech fight. "Old women and girls, peaceful, law abiding, and defenseless, have been trampled on by mounted police of this city. Many were hurt, three being severely injured in an unnecessary, damnable, and atrociously brutal charge of the mounted police." Buse directed his vitriol toward Sheriff Word, calling him "one of the most brutally ignorant and putridly foul mouthed characters in Portland." He accused Word and his deputies of "using the most atrociously filthy, obscene, profane, and indecent language, to men, women and children" during the strike.[44]

Buse's complaint apparently caught the attention of the congressman, for a month later, Mayor Albee wrote a letter to United States district attorney Clarence Reames and agreed to investigate the charges. Albee gave his side of the story and declared that there was nothing truthful in Buse's letter. Albee claimed that interference by the IWW, whose members he referred to as "outsiders" and "notorious trouble-breeders," "made of a trivial matter a more or less serious one." Albee claimed that he had offered to help the women and would back their claims for higher wages, but because of "hired agitators" and a newspaper "of the muck-raking variety," the strikers "refused to be guided by sane counsel." He complained that just as he was about to settle things with the strikers, Governor West came in and interfered, speaking to the strikers in the street and holding meetings in the city council chamber without Albee present. On the subject of the free speech fight, he claimed "profane, abusive and very vulgar language finally became so bad that I deemed it my solemn duty to suppress all public speaking, temporarily." Albee claimed to be a firm believer in free speech, though he would not "suffer the flag to be insulted" or "tolerate profane, obscene, or abusive language."[45]

City officials and businessmen once again insinuated that the Wobblies were outsiders and not respectable citizens. Albee's comments also ignored the agency of the striking women, and instead implied that they would have been complacent and happy to work with the city council if it were not for the outside agitators and newspapers riling up emotions. During testimony to the city council, one local businessman, A. E. Holton, said that he heard the strikers yelling things "not fit to repeat" at the strikebreakers. When prodded by the mayor, Holton said "damn scab," "dirty scab," and "pimp" were words used frequently. When Mr. McPherson testified, he said that he heard a man on a soapbox call the manager of the company a "syphilitic degenerate" as well as a pimp. Belle Goldish and Mrs. Rice had been arrested during the strike simply for using the world "scab." This language not only signified the "roughness" of the Wobblies and the strikers, but also mirrored the discussion of low wages leading to prostitution by referring to the company manager as a pimp.[46]

Along with the focus on "profane" language, much attention was paid during the strike to the danger of close contact between male Wobblies and younger female strikers. The *Oregonian* believed it a sinister scheme. They reported "indications" that white slavers—claiming to be Wobblies—had established a "recruiting station" in a home across the street from the OPC. "IWW agitators, many of them rough men from the North End sections, mingle freely with these girls, talk with them . . . and in general affect some intimacy."[47] There were also reports of a "flashily dressed woman" mingling among the strikers. Anna Spaniol, the woman whose home was in question, sued the *Oregonian* for twenty thousand dollars for the libelous accusation that she was running a prostitution ring. It was later noted by strikers that the "flashily dressed woman" was a striker wearing a black velvet dress that she had owned for several years and had taken good care of.[48]

Prostitution and female sexuality were central to the discourse surrounding the strike. The strikers feared being forced into prostitution because of low wages. They referred to employers as pimps. The newspapers feared the strike was cover for a white slavery operation. A woman could be accused of running a prostitution ring just for wearing a fancy dress. Rough male Wobblies working with young female strikers made Progressives uncomfortable. And an eighteen-year-old young woman could be sentenced to three years in the Industrial School for suspicion of prostitution.

When the female strikers were arrested for speaking on the street during the strike, they continued spreading their beliefs in the county jail, as Wobblies were wont to do. It was in the county jail that striker and Wobbly Jean Bennett, eighteen years old, met Lilian Larkin, also eighteen. Though the strike was effectively over, the Larkin case would continue the IWW battle against Progressive forces in the city.

Lilian Larkin's case history was outlined in a letter from Lola Baldwin, superintendent of the Municipal Bureau for the Protection of Women in Portland, to Mayor Albee in November of 1913. Lilian was first brought to the attention of the Boys and Girls Aid Society in May 1911, at the age of fifteen. Her mother was "a fast woman," and her father was reported dead. Lilian was described as out of control, "bold, with immoral tendencies, showed an inclination to be dishonest." The Girls Aid Society placed her with a family in Portland at that time.[49]

In July of 1913, Lilian turned eighteen, and started "consorting" with soldiers at the Vancouver Barracks, across the state line in Washington. She was involved in a Mann Act case with one of the soldiers there, in which he was accused of taking Larkin across state lines for immoral purposes. Between April and October, she served time in the Vancouver jail. After she was discharged, the police chief sent her to Portland. A few weeks later she spent the night in a hotel with another soldier from the Vancouver Barracks, Claude Laughlin, after which Mrs. Franzin, whose house Larkin was staying in, brought her to Baldwin. Baldwin sent Larkin to a doctor, because she believed Larkin to have a venereal disease, which was then treated. Baldwin suspected Larkin could not be relied on to tell the truth and filed a vagrancy charge against her. Larkin was accused of being a "common prostitute" and a vagrant on October 25, 1913.[50]

What prompted Baldwin's letter to Albee recounting Larkin's troubled history was the commotion caused by the female Wobblies:

Since the IWW women have been in our jails it has been
simply awful to try to do anything with the women with
whom they have come in contact. They have promulgated
their doctrines and put ideas into the heads of the other
women which they had never thought of before. These ideas

have made our girls unwilling to take our advice and counsel and have turned them against authority of every kind.[51]

Baldwin wrote that Wobbly striker Jean Bennett had visited her office
repeatedly and interviewed people there and asked Albee for advice
on how to deal with Bennett. Bennett and the IWW also hired a lawyer, Mr. Isaac Swett. Why was Bennett so interested in the case? She
believed Larkin had been "railroaded" and had not done enough to
warrant three years in the industrial school.[52]

Jean Bennett also spearheaded an unsuccessful effort to remove
policewoman Lola Baldwin, whom she blamed for incarcerating Larkin.
Bennett circulated a petition with the following claims:

1. [Baldwin] is utterly heartless and coldblooded and not a fit
    person to judge of human flesh and blood.
2. She makes no attempt whatever to secure work for these
    unfortunate girls but railroads them to some institution as the
    easiest way out of it.
3. She has never been known to make one kind remark, but
    instead every word she utters makes these girls despise her.
4. We feel that a motherly person would have a tendency to make
    the girls better instead of worse.[53]

If Baldwin epitomized the spirit of Progressive Era Portland, with
her focus on moral uplift, suffrage, and decent wages and conditions,
she also epitomized the conflict between radicals and Progressives, especially on the subject of female sexuality. Bennett's judgment of Baldwin mirrored the Wobblies' judgment of the Oregon Industrial Welfare
Commission. Both were progressive in nature, claiming to protect the
interests of young women. But instead of protecting them, they silenced
these young women's voices and instilled the solution that they deemed
the most appropriate, without consulting those affected the most.

The Wobblies petitioned for Larkin's release but were refused.
They wrote a letter to Larkin, urging her to "cheer up," but it was
not delivered to her. On November 7 Larkin was moved to the State
Industrial School for Girls. On November 21, three Wobblies—Bennett,
F. E. Hals, and I. D. Ransley—went to Salem and requested an interview
with Larkin. The committee then visited Governor Oswald West and,

according to the *Oregonian*, "intimated that unless the Board of Control liberated the girl, she would be liberated anyway." The governor "gathered from their conversation that a large number of the order might be brought to the Capital City for the purpose of freeing Miss Larkin."[54]

Bennett also requested that Larkin's mother be able to visit, which was approved. On November 22, Mrs. Emma Thompson visited her daughter for the first time in four years. Bennett requested to accompany her but the authorities refused, and Mrs. Thompson entered with Baldwin. On November 24, the IWW filed an appeal to Larkin's case, claiming that she was unaware she was on trial, didn't have a fair trial, and that when she sought help from Baldwin, instead of receiving aid she was charged with vagrancy. The Portland *News* reported that Larkin would be giving a public speech telling her story while she was in town for the appeal.[55]

Since Lilian Larkin's appeal was denied, it is unclear what happened to her after entering the Industrial School. The *First Biennial Report of the State Industrial School for Girls* listed thirty-six girls admitted between July 1913 and September 1914. Of that number, sixteen were paroled, two transferred to other institutions, one escaped, and one was returned from parole.[56] We will never know for certain whether Larkin was a prostitute or a rebellious teenager having fun. Her former employer described her as "romantically inclined" and "fond of stories of army life." He warned her not to read any more of the "sensational books she purchased" but she continued to do so in spite of this.[57] It is possible that Larkin was engaged in a practice called "treating." Treating was fairly common among single young women in the 1910s. Historians Kathy Peiss and Joanne Meyerowitz have described treating as a practice in which working-class men and women exchanged sexual favors for dinner, drinks, movies, clothing, and the like. Elizabeth Alice Clement points out that this practice was part of a continuum of sexuality between courting with the intention of marriage and exchanging sex for money. Premarital sex among working-class women was increasing in the first three decades of the twentieth century, reaching 26 percent for women who reached courting age between 1910 and 1920. Larkin's mother was reported to be a "fast" woman, but whether she was a prostitute or someone who became pregnant out of wedlock is difficult to ascertain. That the board of the Industrial School allowed her to visit Larkin for the first time in four years, in 1913, meant that she had improved her ways at least enough to be seen as not a danger to the girl's future, unlike the Wobblies, who were too dangerous to be admitted. I would also suggest that if Lilian Larkin were engaged in direct cash-for-services prostitution, she would have left the home she was staying in, where she was listed as a domestic, and entered a brothel, where she would have had steadier access to clients and likely the protection of a madam.[58]

Why would the IWW choose to support Lilian Larkin? To put it bluntly, why did the local Wobblies care? She was not involved in the strike and, as far as we can tell, did not know any of the Wobblies before her arrest. That Jean Bennett, herself an eighteen-year-old Wobbly, was able to rally the support of the local is itself remarkable. She may have bonded with Larkin, who was the same age, over a shared jail experience. Bennett understood that Larkin's arrest, trial, and sentence were unfair, likely already distrusted Policewoman Baldwin, and saw this as a perfect excuse to mount a campaign against Baldwin. Bennett was able to convince the local that Larkin was worth fighting for. The Wobblies felt that the cause was worthy of support and stood behind Larkin and Bennett in their campaign.

The IWW's involvement in the strike and in Larkin's case served two purposes for the organization. It helped make membership more attractive to women, something IWW newspapers and annual meetings continuously stressed the need for. The publicity of helping with a strike involving mostly women and standing up for a female victim of the criminal justice system signaled to young working-class women that the organization had their interests in mind. It also served as another battleground for the continuous Wobbly war with Progressive values of morality and respectability. The organization advocated an autonomous working-class culture that saw prostitution as the result of the capitalist system, and sexuality between consenting persons as a matter of personal choice.

The young female strikers' affiliation with the IWW gave them agency, unlike affiliation with the Progressive reformers, who wanted to act for them. Poor working conditions, long hours, and low pay were causes popular with reformers in Portland and around the country, and the OPC strike was a perfect avenue for reform groups like the OIWC to flex their muscle. Beyond the question of who could represent young female workers in wage disputes, the strike is also an example of female sexuality as contested territory during the Progressive Era. All of the blame placed on the IWW by city officials and local business leaders sought to discredit the women who chose to go on strike by themselves and insinuated that, without the IWW, the workers would have been happy to take whatever was offered them and go back to work. The strikers tied fears over prostitution to their claims that they deserved better working conditions. At the same time, the Larkin case shows that an organization normally thought of as unwelcoming to women would stick up for an eighteen-year-old girl who had gotten herself in trouble and had nowhere else to turn. The IWW support of the strike and of Larkin stemmed from the organization's belief in direct democracy and individual freedom. In both cases the IWW rejected Progressive reformers' attempts to impose solutions predicated on what the reformers perceived to be respectable behaviors for young women. In the case of the strike, their solution involved a minor pay increase but ignored many of the workers' demands regarding sanitary issues and more control over the workplace. In the Larkin case, their solution was detention in the State Industrial School for Girls, which ignored both Larkin's plea of innocence and her freedom to engage in sexual activity if she chose to do so. Rather than telling the women what should happen to them, the IWW supported these women's voices and their ability to make their own decisions about what was in their best interest.

5

Everett 1916

The Everett Massacre and the Tracy Trial

> Many of those who had gone on the witness stand for
> the defense afterwards took out membership cards in
> the IWW. The women of Everett—considerably more
> inclined toward revolutionary ideas than the men
> there, by the way—were among the first to ask for a
> "red card."
> —Walker Smith, *The Everett Massacre*[1]

On November 5, 1916, 250 Wobblies boarded the ferry *Verona* in Seattle
and headed to nearby Everett, Washington, to join a free speech fight
that had been building over the preceding few months. Everett sheriff
Don McRae, along with several newly deputized inhabitants of the city,
gathered along the dock in an attempt to stop the boat from landing. In
an event that has come to be known as the Everett Massacre, a shoot-out
occurred between the Wobblies and the deputies, ending with at least
five Wobblies and two deputies dead, and many more wounded. Hundreds of Wobblies were arrested after the shoot-out, and the ensuing
trial of Thomas Tracy, the first of seventy-six to be tried, roused support
for the Wobblies throughout the nation.

The Everett Massacre is one of the most infamous events in the
history of the IWW, but little investigation has been made into the role
women played in the events leading up to the massacre and during the
trial. Examples of their participation are evident in Wobbly Walker
Smith's history of the event, as well as newspaper accounts of the time.
The funeral procession in Seattle for three of the martyred Wobblies
included eighteen female pallbearers. Edith Frenette, who was also
involved in the Spokane and Missoula free speech fights, was active
in Everett in the months leading up to the massacre. Historians of the

IWW have made little mention of women's role in the Everett Massacre; this dismissal is in sharp contrast to accounts by activists and writers at the time, who found it important to note the involvement of Frenette and the women of Everett, and serves once again to focus attention only on the male hobo element of the IWW. All the passengers on the *Verona* and the majority of those arrested after the shooting were men, which makes it easy to view the Everett Massacre as part of the story of rough-and-tumble young radical men in the West. But focusing on women and gender provides a new perspective. The many examples of women's involvement all point to the radical community that the IWW was part of in the Northwest.

It is important to investigate the role that women played in Everett, but a gendered analysis also sheds light on how notions of appropriate male and female behavior permeated the trial that followed the massacre, in which female Wobbles were interrogated about their personal lives in order to question their status as respectable women. The respectability of the organization and its members was on trial, at times taking more precedence than the issue of the guilt or innocence of Thomas Tracy. Respectability itself was gendered—tied to stability, home ownership, and family status. Examining the events in Everett through this lens gives us a more complete picture of how the Wobblies functioned within communities like Everett, and the important role that women played in connecting the townspeople to the organization.

The Everett free speech fight occurred during a shingle-weavers strike that began in May 1916. Everett, about thirty miles north of Seattle, was a town of thirty-five thousand people, with lumber, shingles, and shipping dominating industry. Nearly everyone in town had a stake in the strike in some way. The shingle weavers of Everett belonged to the International Shingle Weavers' Union, affiliated with the American Federation of Labor. The generic term "shingle weaver" applied to "sawyers, filers, and packers who worked as a crew in the mills that produced these shingles."[2] Shingle weavers were considered more skilled than workers in lumber mills and therefore commanded higher wages. As new machinery increased production in shingle mills, it also increased the chance for injury. Shingle weavers were notorious for missing fingers and sometimes even limbs. A good shingle weaver could trim thirty thousand shingles in a ten-hour shift. That meant thirty thousand chances that a slip of the hand meant injury.[3]

The shingle weavers in Everett were organized in 1901. Walker Smith recalled that in 1911 the shingle-weavers union had about two thousand members, many in sympathy with the IWW, but a vote to affiliate with the union was lost. Smith hints that this was because of shady dealings by conservative union officials. Many of the radicals left the Shingle Weavers' Union, and the depression of 1914–1915 also decreased membership. In the spring of 1915, with shingle prices dropping, the mill owners announced a wage reduction. The workers went on strike to protest, but lost the strike. Part of their return to work was thanks to a "gentlemen's agreement" that wages would be raised when prices rose. By the spring of 1916, prices had risen significantly and workers demanded a return to the old wage scale beginning on May 1. On that day, union stewards made their demands, the mill owners refused, and the men walked out. The mill owners imported strikebreakers from out of town and hired men to protect the mills. On May 19 the picketers were checked for weapons by the police and marched away from the mills, where a group of strikebreakers, led by the owner of one of the mills, attacked them while the police looked on. That night the picketers returned with 150 Everett citizens and union members, to get revenge, and attacked the strikebreakers. Ten days later another Everett mill owner marched his strikebreakers through town to the Everett Theater, "in appreciation of their efficiency." A "near-riot" broke out between the strikebreakers and strikers when they left the theater.[4] Everett was clearly a community divided. A Pacific Coast–wide AFL longshoremen's strike going on at the same time had also increased tensions in the city. The shingle-weavers' strike wore on, and picketing dwindled to between ten and eighteen men by August. All of this had taken place without IWW involvement. It was easy for observers at the time to blame the "outsiders" of the IWW for the troubles that followed, but they were entering a town where nerves were frayed and the threat of violence was ever-present.[5]

It is unclear when the IWW first established a local in Everett, but it was announced in the February 22, 1912, issue of the *Industrial Worker* that the local was closing down temporarily. In the summer of 1916, the northwest branches of the IWW were planning an organizing drive of the lumber workers in the area and sent James Rowan to Everett to find out what support the IWW had. According to Walker Smith, Rowan had no idea the shingle-weavers' strike was in progress. On July 31, Rowan was arrested for speaking on the corner of Wetmore and Hewitt Avenues, which would become the center of street speaking during the free speech fight. Given the choice of thirty days in jail or leaving town, he left, and on August 4, Levi Remick was sent in as an organizer. He opened up a Wobbly hall at 1219½ Hewitt Avenue on August 9 and started selling Wobbly literature. Remick arranged for James P. Thompson (who had sparked the free speech fight in Spokane) to come to town to speak on August 22. No hall in town would rent to the IWW, so they decided he would speak on the street. Sheriff Don McRae announced he would not allow it and threatened to throw out of town any Wobbly he could find. Thompson and twenty or so Wobblies traveled to Everett from Seattle, and Thompson commenced speaking on the street, primarily summarizing a recent report by the United States Commission on Industrial Relations, which contained sections outlining the difficult conditions for lumber workers in the Pacific Northwest. That lasted about twenty minutes before the police came to break up the meeting. After Thompson and his wife Florence were arrested, James Rowan, Edith Frenette, Lorna Mahler, and several others all attempted to speak but were arrested.[6]

In one of the most publicized moments of this initial free speech fight, Everett citizen Letelsia Fye—in her mid-thirties and mother of two—stepped up to the soapbox and began to recite the Declaration of Independence. According to her testimony during the subsequent trial, all of the Wobblies present had been arrested and the crowd was yelling for someone else to speak. Someone suggested Fye, and so she started to recite the Declaration, adding commentary on the current situation in Everett. Then "the officer started toward me, and I jumped off the box and ducked into the crowd, for I'm a mother of two children, and I didn't want to spend the night in jail." As she stepped off the platform she asked, "Is there a red-blooded man in the audience who will take the stand?" Jake Michel, secretary of the Building Trades Council, answered her call and was arrested after commenting on free speech.[7]

The next morning James and Florence Thompson, Herbert and Lorna Mahler, and Edith Frenette were all deported back to Seattle. Frenette, Lorna Mahler, and James Thompson spoke at a meeting in Seattle that night, raising fifty dollars for the cause. By September 7, the Wobblies were back at it in Everett; Edith Frenette, H. Shebeck, Bob Adams, J. Johnson, J. Fred, and Dan Emmett were all arrested for street speaking. The Everett *Tribune* noted that Sheriff Luke "encountered considerable trouble in placing Mrs. Frenette under arrest when she displayed indignant resistance." The men were all sentenced to thirty days, though Frenette was released the next morning. That night two more Wobblies were arrested, and a "crowd of Everett citizens, in company with the few IWW members present" marched to the jail to demand the release of the prisoners. The Everett *Tribune* described the crowd as consisting of "an element of youths and general loiterers, curious pedestrians and a large representation of women."[8] While they were there the crowd knocked over a fence, which led to Frenette being arrested and charged with inciting to riot. She was later released on a one-thousand-dollar bail, a significant amount for a labor activist in this period.[9] The *Tribune* warned its readers that these street meetings were no place for children, and that women and girls "who lately have been in the thick of the excitement" should also stay away.[10]

Everett officials started checking incoming trains for Wobblies, so on September 9 a few Wobblies—including Edith Frenette—took the train to the nearby town of Mukilteo and boarded the *Wanderer*, a boat that Frenette had arranged to take them to Everett. They were met on their way to Everett by another boat carrying Sheriff McRae and sixty deputies. The sheriff and his men fired six shots at the *Wanderer*, and then McRae boarded the boat and arrested everyone on board, including the captain. McRae and the other deputies beat the men repeatedly while they were in jail. On September 11, Rowan returned to Everett and was arrested as soon as he stepped off the train. That night McRae took Rowan from the jail and dropped him off outside of town on the road leading back to Seattle. After walking a little way down the road, Rowan was met by a group of a dozen or so men with guns. They threw a cloth over his head and beat him with guns and clubs before they tore his clothes off, leaned him over a stump, and whipped him fifty or more times. Bloody and bruised, Rowan returned to Seattle after the beating and had photographs taken of his wounds. These photos were circulated around Seattle, encouraging, rather than deterring, more people to join the free speech fight.[11]

Frenette approached police chief Kelley and told him that vigilantes were beating Wobblies in the town. She told Kelley,

> It seems that there is an ordinance here against street speaking and we feel that it is unjust. We feel that we have a right

to speak here. We are not blocking traffic, and we propose
to make a test of the ordinance. Will you have one of your
men arrest me or any other speaker who chooses to take the
box, personally, and take me to jail and put a charge against
me, and protect me from the vigilantes who are beating the
men on the street?[12]

Using tactics similar to those used in the Spokane free speech fight, the
IWW attempted to employ the protection of law enforcement while at
the same time breaking a law they felt unjust. Kelley's response was
noncommittal; he would do what he could, but he claimed Sheriff
McRae was really in control of the situation.[13]

The IWW did not seek to break the law simply to cause chaos and
waste the city's money, but to prove a point about their constitutional
right to free speech. In Spokane the organization initially attempted to
get permits to speak in the street, and as Elizabeth Gurley Flynn demonstrated in her court testimony, the organization felt it had the Constitution—as interpreted in the best interest of the working class—on its side.
In Everett, the IWW tested the constitutionality of the street-speaking
ban and felt they had the right to do so without risking vigilante repression. But in a town like Everett that had already seen tensions between
the working class and the business interests, the threat of violence was
near. The commercial interests had a stake in stopping the Wobblies
from speaking, and the police and sheriff's deputies did not feel that
they needed to protect the rights to free speech of these "outsiders."

Events calmed down in Everett for most of October, but there was
one last gory episode before the infamous events of November 5. On
October 30, forty-one Wobblies traveled to Everett by boat to attempt
to speak on the street. Deputies met the boat at the dock. According
to Smith, the deputies outnumbered the Wobblies five to one, putting
their number at around two hundred. The Wobblies were loaded into
cars and taken to Beverly Park, on the road to Seattle. When they arrived at Beverly Park, the deputies formed two lines, and the Wobblies
were forced to run the gantlet as they were beaten with clubs, guns, and
axe handles. Ruby and Roy Ketchum, who lived near the park, heard
the sounds of the men screaming. Roy and his brother Lew ventured out
to see what was going on, and reported the following:

The deputies were formed in two lines ending in six men, three on each side of the cattle guard. A man would be taken out of the car and two deputies would join his arms up behind him meanwhile hammering his unprotected face from both sides as hard as they could with their fists. Then the man was started down the line, one deputy following to club him on the back to make him hurry, and the other deputies striking with clubs and other weapons and kicking the prisoner as he progressed. Just before reaching the cattle guard he was made to run, and, in crossing the blades the three men on the east side of the track would swing their clubs upon his back while the men on the west clubbed him across the face and stomach.

This was not the first time Wobblies had been the victims of this kind of vigilante justice, but Everett had a very organized—and deputized—group of antiradical citizens.[14]

Who were the men doing the beating? Many were members of the Commercial Club, which was made up of business owners, including officials from the local lumber mills. The Commercial Club was founded in 1912 when the Businessmen's Association and the Chamber of Commerce merged. Initially the club was formed as a broad coalition of industrialists, union representatives, clergy, physicians, school officials, and others important to the Everett community who sought to promote growth and cooperative industrial relations, but by the time of the strike and the events of 1916, it was firmly anti-union and anti-IWW. By September 1916, Sheriff McRae had deputized several hundred members, and it was those men who took part in the Beverly Park beating. Not all members approved of the vigilante violence, and when the volunteer deputies started practicing nightly drills at the Commercial Club, many ministers, attorneys, and businessmen resigned from the club in protest. While the vigilantes intended to run the Wobblies out of town, their tactics had the opposite effect. The Beverly Park beating stoked the fire of Wobbly resistance, and they planned a huge street meeting for November 5.[15]

The citizens of Everett woke on the morning of November 5 to a town divided. The front page of the Everett *Tribune* screamed the headline "IWW ENTITLED TO NO SYMPATHY." The article continued to heap contempt on the organization and its supporters:

> Sympathy? Sympathy for what? Sympathy for a bunch of men who loathe toil, who despise law and who only are happy when they can turn a town into a bear [sic] garden and then swoop down on another for the same purpose? The kind of men who are wining [sic] about getting walloped in Everett are the kind who deserved all they got and they're not entitled to any pity. Everett doesn't want a man who comes here to sow discontent. Everett wants law and order with peace and a contented community. There can be no honest sympathy for such a man no matter how roughly he is handled, there can be no regrets for punching a man who regards it a privilege to be sent to jail.[16]

This hostile atmosphere advocated by the Everett newspaper again exemplifies how the Wobblies were portrayed as "outsiders." This outsider status, tied to the lack of home and family, meant they were not entitled to the basic protections of the law. Citizens of Everett who chose to support these outsiders forfeited their respectability as well. After excoriating the IWW, the *Tribune* then turned on the Everett citizens who supported the Wobblies, writing that they "have no pride in their home town and no care for the quality of its citizenship."[17]

The events of November 5 have been seared into the consciousness of Wobblies and other radicals in the Pacific Northwest. It is one of the most brutal examples of repression that the union faced, and is the single deadliest event in the union's history. What follows is a brief account of Smith's version of the events of "Bloody Sunday." From Seattle the band of free speech fighters boarded the *Verona*. When the maximum capacity of 250 was reached, including a few non-Wobblies aboard whose fares were paid by the group, the rest (approximately thirty-eight) boarded the *Calista*. Smith reported that all aboard were jovial, singing union songs on the way to Everett. He also noted that a spy was among the group, who informed the Commercial Club that the Wobblies were on their way—though this should have come as no surprise since the event was well publicized. Thousands of Everett citizens were also awaiting the Wobblies, many to attend the mass meeting,

Funeral of Felix Baran, Seattle, 1916. IWW Photograph Collection, University of Washington Special Collections, UW11504.

but surely many out of curiosity. As the boat came close to the dock, McRae shouted, "Who is your leader?" to which the men responded, "We are all leaders!" McRae then replied "You can't land here!" and the Wobblies yelled "The hell we can't!" After this exchange a shot was fired, leading to a shoot-out in which two deputies, including Jefferson Beard, and several Wobblies were killed.[18]

The *Verona* turned around amid the shooting and headed back to Seattle, where the police were waiting for them. Four of the deceased Wobblies—Hugo Gerlot, Gustav Johnson, John Looney, and Abraham Rabinowitz—were sent to the morgue, and the thirty-one wounded to the hospital. Wobbly sympathizer Dr. Marie Equi later examined the body of Felix Baran, who died in the hospital, and pronounced that "with surgical attention there would have been more than an even chance of recovery." In the final tally, six men were unaccounted for; it was assumed that they had been shot and drowned, as witnesses recounted seeing deputies shooting at men in the water trying to swim to safety.[19]

Wobbly sympathizers portrayed Everett citizens as having gendered reactions to the massacre:

> So wanton was the slaughter of the helpless men and boys
> that strong men who witnessed the scene turned away

vomiting. From the hillside the women—those whom the deputies were pretending to protect from the "incoming hoarde" [sic]—casting aside all womanly fears, raced to the dock in a vain endeavor to stop the commission of further crime, crying out in their frenzy, "The curs! The curs! The dirty curs! They're nothing but murderers!" They, as well as the men who tried to launch boats to rescue the men in the water, were halted by the same citizen deputies whose names head the list of Red Cross donors.[20]

The injustice of it all shamed and sickened the men, while it angered and emboldened the women, almost reversing the "natural" gender order. It turned "respectable" nonviolent citizens into angry mobs castigating the vigilantes. The leaders of Everett, those influential citizens who would often support charity efforts, saw the Wobblies as such a threat that they would not allow the injured to be rescued. The female citizens of Everett, those who were assumed to need protection, ran to the scene to attempt to stem the violence. A second description similarly describes how shooting upended the social norms:

Your correspondent was on the street at the time of the battle and at the dock ten minutes afterward. He mingled with the street crowds for hours afterward. The temper of the people is dangerous. Nothing but curses and execrations for the Commercial Club was heard. Men and women who are ordinarily law abiding, who in normal times mind their own business pretty well, pay their taxes, send their children to church and school, in every way comport themselves as normal citizens, were heard using the most vitriolic language concerning the Commercial Club, loudly sympathizing with the IWWs. And therein lies the great harm that was done, more menacing to the city than the presence of any number of IWWs, viz., the transformation of decent, honest, citizens into beings mad for vengeance and praying for something dire to happen. I heard gray-haired women, mothers and wives, gentle, kindly, I know, in their home circles, openly hoping that the IWWs would come back and "clean up."[21]

The conclusion in both of these articles is that the injustice done to the Wobblies during the massacre was enough to reverse gender norms, the wrongs committed so intense that mild-mannered women and respectable male citizens were turned into angry radicals clamoring for justice.[22]

In Seattle, during the commotion immediately after the shooting, all the Wobblies from the *Verona* were arrested. They were put through a screening process to determine which ones would be charged with the deaths of two deputies. The person peering at the Wobblies from a darkened room, pointing fingers at those responsible, was George Reese, a member of the IWW. Charles Smith, employed by the notorious strikebreaking Pinkerton agency, who had also been on the *Verona*, joined Reese to identify several of the Wobblies. Seventy-four men in total were charged with the death of Jefferson Beard. Of the seventy-four, only fifteen were born outside the United States. The ages of the accused ranged from seventeen to fifty-six, with most of the men in their late twenties. Only two were from Washington, and none from Oregon. Demographically, this would be representative of Wobbly membership in lumber camps of the Pacific Northwest. The other 128 men who had been arrested were released on November 13.

A few days after the arrests, the Wobblies held a funeral for those killed during the massacre. The funeral for three of the Wobblies killed—Felix Baran, Hugo Gerlot, and John Looney—took place in Seattle on November 18. Over fifteen hundred men and women marched behind the hearses to Mount Pleasant Cemetery, where the coffins were borne by eighteen female pallbearers. I have not been able to find the names of these women, or their relationships to the deceased, but their presence in such a visible role does bear testament to the important role that women played in this struggle. A memorial at the cemetery took place on May 1, 1917. A photograph of the event shows several rows of women and children present.[23]

During the entirety of the free speech fight and the ensuing Tracy trial, jailed Wobblies received a tremendous amount of financial and material support from the local community and from sympathetic people around the country. Women played an important role in the support of these prisoners by bringing them meals and making them gifts. For Thanksgiving of 1916, only weeks after the massacre, some of the citizens of Everett, helped out by the Cooks' and Waiters' Union, prepared a meal for those in jail. They had received permission from jail officials,

Memorial for Victims of Everett Massacre, Seattle, May 1, 1917. Walter P. Reuther Library, Archives of Labor and Urban Affairs, Wayne State University, 393.

but when they arrived Sheriff McRae denied them entrance and would not let the meal be served. A few months later a committee of women from Everett brought the men another meal in jail, though they had to serve it through the bars. On April 22, 1917, women in Seattle successfully held a banquet for the men in the county jail. It lasted two and a half hours, during which time Elizabeth Gurley Flynn updated them on news from the outside while they had their dessert of ice cream and cake. The meal was finished with a cigar and "boutonniere of fragrant flowers furnished by a gray-haired old lady" for each prisoner. Women also provided moral support, and Smith's *Everett Massacre* includes a photograph of a large group of men and women singing to the prisoners from outside of the King County Jail.[24]

After the arrests, the Wobblies assembled a team of lawyers, including Fred Moore as chief counsel, George Vanderveer, E. C. Dailey, Caroline Lowe, Harry Sigmond, and J. L. Finch. Vanderveer, Moore, and Lowe would all go on to defend the Wobblies in Chicago during World War I. The Everett trial did not begin until March 5, 1917. It took place in Seattle after a change of venue request was granted because of prejudice in Everett. Since women were granted the right to vote in Washington State in 1910, there were several women on the jury. The jurors were listed by occupation or, in the case of the women, their husbands' occupation. The jurors were questioned about their familiarity with the IWW, their union affiliation, and their political beliefs. The male jurors agreed on by the defense and prosecution consisted of a rancher, a bricklayer, a farmer, an awning maker, a contractor, and a machinist's helper. The women on the jury were identified as the wives of a steamfitter, a master mariner, a harness-maker, a druggist, a lineman, and one woman listed as "widow, working-class family." That the jury was evenly split between men and women is important to note when looking at the arguments made by the defense and prosecution. [25]

The primary argument of the prosecution was a familiar one for IWW cases: the men on trial were outside agitators. The prosecution called a few members of the Commercial Club to the stand to testify to shooting coming from the *Verona*. The prosecution then read a series of IWW articles and pamphlets, including *Sabotage* by Walker Smith. The prosecution also tried—unsuccessfully—to tie the IWW to a number of fires around Everett in 1916. One police officer testified that several IWW men left a street meeting with sections of gas pipe, to be used as weapons, in their hands. It was later proven that the men were holding legs to the podium they had set up for the meeting. They were unable to prove anything more than that the Wobblies were not from Everett.[26]

Legal strategies on both sides built on conceptions of gender. The prosecution witnesses were primarily men: business owners, law officials, and members of the Commercial Club. The defense relied on the testimony of women to prove both that respectable citizens had suffered at the hands of McRae and the vigilantes and that their association and support of the IWW made the organization more respectable. The defense used witnesses to testify that meetings were conducted in an orderly fashion and obeyed rules regarding keeping the streets clear of people. The defense called several female Everett citizens to testify that they had been at meetings and seen violence perpetrated by the deputies, not the IWW. Ina Salter, Elizabeth Maloney, Letelsia Fye, Dollie Gustaffson, Avis Mathison, Mrs. Peter Aiken, Annie Pomeroy, Rebecca Wade, and Hannah Crosby all testified on April 4 and 5, 1917. Walker Smith believed that "the fact that these citizens, and a number of other women who were mentioned in the testimony, attended the IWW meetings quite regularly, impressed the jury favorably. Some of these women witnesses had been roughly handled by the deputies." Most of the women were wives of Everett workingmen, but a few—Fye, Wade, and Crosby—were widows, which shows that the IWW had an appeal to women beyond just those whose husbands worked in the sawmills.[27]

Edith Frenette was also called to testify. Though Frenette had played a large role in the events leading up to the massacre, she was not on the *Verona* on November 5 and therefore was not one the Wobblies on trial for the murder of Jefferson Beard. Frenette had spent the night of November 4 in Everett. This was proven during the trial after one of the witnesses for the prosecution claimed to have seen her in Seattle the morning of November 5 discussing bringing red pepper to Everett to use against the vigilantes. The defense disproved this by submitting as evidence the ledger from the hotel in Everett where Frenette stayed the night before the massacre. Immediately after the shoot-out in Everett, Frenette, along with Lorna Mahler and Joyce Peters, had returned to Seattle, where they were arrested. All three were in their thirties at the time, and were described as housewives. It was initially reported that all three were arrested for attempting to throw cayenne pepper in the face of Sheriff McRae as he was being transported to the hospital. Edith Frenette was eventually charged with first-degree assault after witnesses declared she had pointed a gun at McRae after the shooting. She was jailed for three weeks and released on $2,500 bail. The charges were later dropped.[28]

During the trial, Frenette was portrayed as one of the main organizers of the Everett free speech fights. When Everett mayor Dennis Merrill testified regarding confrontation between Wobblies and city officials preceding the massacre, he claimed that the Wobblies, specifically Frenette, had tried to intimidate him. In his report for the *Seattle Union Record* of the days' proceedings in the Tracy trial, Albert Brilliant referred to Frenette as "the terror of the prosecution, . . . who during the entire trial has been pointed to by the state as the center of a conspiracy which had for its object the invasion of the city of Everett, the assassination of city authorities, and the destruction of the city by fire." Although she was not one of the defendants in the trial, she was still viewed by authorities as the mastermind behind the Wobblies' presence in Everett.[29]

As we have seen with other radical women, Frenette's morality was on trial. When Frenette was brought up to testify for the defense, after

*Figures Prominent in Legal Proceedings
Resulting From I. W. W. Riot at Everett*

70 MORE I.W.W. ARE JAILED ON SAME CHARGE

Held for Unlawful Assembly in Connection With Invasion of Everett November 5

From left to right, Joyce Peters, Edith Frenette, and Lorna Mahler. Seattle *Post-Intelligencer*, November 15, 1916.

asking her in detail about the massacre, defense attorney Vanderveer—probably in anticipation of what the prosecution would ask during the cross-examination—asked her if she had lived in the same room as Earl Osborne, another IWW member, while she lived in a rooming house in Seattle during the time of the massacre. The cross-examination did indeed press the point, asking Frenette questions about her personal life, trying to get information about her relationship with her husband and where exactly she called her home. The prosecution asked where Mr. Frenette's home was, to which she answered Vancouver Island. They asked her when she last lived there, to which she answered, a year ago. They asked if she had been "home" since. She said "not to that home. Any place one stops is a home. A hotel is a home."[30] They continued to press her on whether or not she had ever lived in the same place as Osborne, and she replied that she had never made it her home. By debating the meaning of home, she managed to evade questions that implied that by leaving her husband she was less than respectable. Where she had lived and with whom had nothing to do with her actions in Everett, yet as was the case with many Wobbly women, these questions were asked to demonstrate her character and to insinuate that the Wobblies believed in changing not only economic relations, but social relations as well. A woman who left her husband and lived with another could be seen as morally suspect, easier for a jury to view as an outsider and thus not trust her testimony nor believe she was entitled to the same protections as respectable Everett citizens.[31]

When Joyce Peters took the stand for the defense, she also was subjected to questions regarding her marital status. Although she had been referred to as Mrs. Peters in the IWW and mainstream press since the events in Everett began, and throughout the trial, the prosecution interrogated her regarding her marital status. Attorney Cooley asked Peters if she had a husband at the time of the events in Everett. She replied that she considered Mr. Peters her husband. Cooley then pointed out that the two had been married only the day before, right before her testimony. Peters admitted to this, and at that time the counsel for the defense objected, and the judge sustained. It is unclear why they decided to marry directly before the trial. While the Peters could have just decided to marry on a whim, it is more likely that they decided, or were urged by the counsel for the defense, to legalize their union because it would make them more legitimate and respectable as witnesses in the eyes of the court. As the prosecution had tried to point to Frenette's personal relationships as a testament of her character, they also tried to argue that the Peters married only because of the trial. Again, the insinuation is that Wobblies had radical beliefs regarding marriage that were threatening to the social order; they were immoral and therefore not to be trusted. Marital status was contested ground, and both the defense and the prosecution tried to use it to their advantage.[32]

During the closing arguments, the same themes were repeated. The prosecution focused on the outsider status of the Wobblies and their lack of stable homes and reliable jobs. Prosecuting attorney Lloyd Black referred to the witnesses for the defense as "wanderers on the face of the earth" and questioned their honesty.[33] Defense attorney Fred Moore instructed the jury to ignore Black's argument about the outsider status of the Wobblies: "In order to measure absolute and complete justice between the warring elements of modern life, you must not allow yourselves to be swerved by the difference in the witness' social positions."[34] The prosecution hoped to convince the jury that respectability—and therefore trustworthiness—was established by a stable home and community ties. The defense argued that this was not the case, but also hedged its bets by focusing on the testimony of reliable and trustworthy Everett citizens and proving that the Wobblies did have respectability on their side. This tactic seemed to have worked, for Tracy was acquitted the next day. The rest of the defendants were released, as the prosecution had no more direct evidence for any of their involvement than it did for Tracy.[35]

As we have seen in Spokane and Seattle, the marital status of men and women associated with the IWW was often questioned during legal proceedings, with prosecutors aiming to connect Wobblies with radical ideas regarding "free love." Individual Wobblies held a variety of beliefs regarding marriage and free love, though the organization itself did not hold any official position on the topic. Elizabeth Gurley Flynn's statement in the IWW's eastern journal *Solidarity* comes closest to a full explanation of Wobbly beliefs regarding women and the home:

> The IWW is at war with the ruthless invasion of family life
> by capitalism. . . . We are determined that industry shall be
> so organized that all adults, men and women, may work and
> receive in return a sufficiency to make child labor a relic of
> barbarism. This does not imply that mothers must work, or
> that women must stay at home, if they prefer otherwise. Either extreme is equally absurd. . . . The free choice of work
> is the IWW ideal—which does not mean to put women
> forcibly back into the home, but certainly does mean to end
> capitalism's forcibly taking her out of the home.[36]

Statements in IWW newspapers tended to be rather vague, usually pointing out that most problems women faced would become obsolete after the coming of the One Big Union, but almost always noting that women should be able to choose whether or not they want to work, get married, or have children.[37]

The IWW believed industrial unionism was the key to women's emancipation. But what would this emancipation entail? Individual Wobblies held a variety of beliefs. One was that the goal of One Big

Union was a "family wage" that would enable men to make enough money so their wives would not have to work and could remain in the domestic sphere of the home. Another view was that women needed to work and make as much money as men, so they could be independent and marry for love rather than for financial support. These two views are expressed in an exchange of letters in the June 1910 issue of *Solidarity*. The first letter, signed, "A Man Toiler," espoused the common Wobbly belief that the vote would not do anything for women and that industrial organization was the only key to emancipation. He finished his letter with, "What we want, girls, is less work and more pay and we want you to keep out of the factory and mill and give us a chance to earn enough money to marry some of you and give you a decent home."[38] The response came a few weeks later from "A Woman Toiler." She believed that by moving into the workplace, women could avoid being forced into marriage in order to survive. She wrote,

> The best thing that ever happened to woman was when she was compelled to leave the narrow limits of the home and enter into the industrial life of the world. This is the only road to our freedom, and to *be free* there is not anything to be desired more than that. . . . In the home she is more apt to become more limited in reasoning power, more bound by religious superstitions, more a slave to social conventions, more petty and gossipy and meddlesome. . . . So we will stay in the factory, mill, or store and organize with you in the IWW for the ownership of the industries, so we can provide ourselves with decent homes, then if we marry you it will be because we love you so well we can't get along without you. . . . We are slaves in revolt against the employing class. We will have none of their religion, their politics, their marriage system. They all work to keep the worker in subjection.[39]

What "Woman Toiler" wanted was to be on an equal playing field with men, making the same wages and organized in the same union. But instead of attacking the male toiler for his views, she puts the blame on the exploitative capitalist system. While this "woman toiler" holds a slightly patronizing view of women's work within the home, she sees industrial unionism as the only avenue toward female equality.

Wobbly views on marriage, not surprisingly, tended to focus on economic arguments. Many radicals of the time followed the line of reasoning that marriage constituted legalized prostitution, a woman giving away her body for a home, money, and protection in return. Others put it more simply, such as in an article in the *Industrial Worker* in 1913, called "On Free Love and the Home," which boiled it down to the phrase "one room is cheaper than two." The author, Ernest Griffeath, pointed out that many members of the working class had no homes of their own, and he knew many couples that lived together out of economic necessity, with no intention of marriage. He concluded, "Whether the monogamous form of marriage would be desirable under a free system is hard to determine."[40]

So although the organization itself held no firm beliefs on the subject of marriage and women's place inside or outside the home, individual Wobblies held views across all parts of the spectrum. Undoubtedly many men in the organization wanted to earn a "family wage" so that they could marry and support a wife and children. Many others held much more radical beliefs, including free love and the abolition of the institution of marriage. The prosecution played on this fear to make their case during the Tracy trial. In return, the defense argued that Wobbly views on marriage were irrelevant to the case at hand, while at the same time minimizing the damage of the prosecution's efforts by downplaying those unconventional beliefs.

The danger of the Wobblies as "outsiders," people with no connection to Everett, was a common theme of the prosecution during the Everett trial. Historians of the IWW, and some Wobblies, have traced the radicalism of migratory workers—like those in the lumber camps— to their lack of family ties.[41] Early histories of the IWW connected the "footloose" nature of the single, male, migrant Wobblies to their belief in industrial unionism and willingness to engage in potentially dangerous activities such as free speech fights. Whether the ideal Wobbly was a migratory worker or someone with a stable home and a family was also debated within the organization. Some praised the flexibility of the migratory workers, whereas others believed that those workers without community ties could easily run away when the going got tough. The latter group argued that workers with families actually sacrificed more and were more radical because they had no other choice. In the IWW paper *Solidarity*, a Wobbly wrote a response to an article praising the radicalism of the footloose western worker:

It was at Lawrence and elsewhere in the East that the workers who were oppressed the most fought the hardest and
stood the brunt of the battle (the women, encumbered with
babes and husbands). I doubt if there ever would have been
a strike in Lawrence if the workers in the mills had been
"wifeless, babeless, vagabond adventurers," whose "mobility is amazing," and had not been "afraid of losing their
jobs." They would have *quit* without disputing the control
of the mill and departed for another job.[42]

Similarly, in her study of two mining strikes in Cripple Creek,
Colorado, Elizabeth Jameson found that, rather than homeownership
and a family making workers more conservative, those who were the
most active were those who had the most to lose: those with homes,
wives, and children. The popular myth that the radicalism of the Wobblies can be tied to their lack of stable homes is false. As was the case
in Spokane, Portland, and Everett, many Wobblies with families were
active in the union's struggles.[43]

The aftermath of the Everett Massacre constituted the highest
point of IWW support nationally. The trial concluded on May 5, 1917,
just a month after the United States entered World War I, and before
the wartime repression of the IWW began in earnest. The violence
against Wobblies, the obvious disregard for First Amendment rights by
Everett authorities, and the fact that the Wobblies, not the vigilantes,
stood trial for murder, aroused popular support nationally for the IWW.
The Wobblies mounted a huge publicity tour to raise money for the
defense of the Everett prisoners and were able to raise a total of $37,825.
Unfortunately, within a few short months, even attending a Wobbly
fund-raiser could be grounds for investigation of seditious and "un-
American" activity.[44]

6

World War I and Its Aftermath, 1917–1920

Repression, Arrests, and Defense Work of Female Wobblies

The spring of 1917 was an optimistic time for the IWW, following its success in the Everett trial. Support for and donations to the organization had poured in from around the country, and the trial gained the Wobblies nationwide publicity. Organizers were optimistic that this publicity would spur organizing drives around the country and lead to the growth of the union. Instead, it coincided with a marked increase in patriotism, antiradical sentiment, and government repression as the United States entered World War I.

Wobblies were at risk of arrest simply for membership in the organization during the repressive years of World War I and the Red Scare that followed. The male leadership was rounded up in raids across the country, and women were arrested for supporting the organization behind the scenes by editing and distributing the *Industrial Worker*, providing support for men in jail, and working with defense organizations to raise money for trial expenses and to support the families of those in jail. While women's work in jail support and defense is important, it was typical for women to be supportive behind the scenes rather than as frontline agitators. The authorities, however, recognized this support, and therefore women were targets of federal surveillance as much as any of the well-known male Wobblies of the period. In this chapter I examines how the massive arrests affected Wobbly communities and how women worked to support those in jail and risked arrest themselves.

When the war began in Europe in 1914, public opinion in the United States was divided on whether the country should intervene, but that quickly changed. Though Woodrow Wilson was reelected in 1916 under the popular slogan, "He kept us out of war," preparedness parades

had become popular in many cities around the country. The preparedness movement had started as early as 1914, advocated most famously
by former president Theodore Roosevelt. The idea behind preparedness
was the belief that the United States would eventually have to join the
European conflict, so the government should build up the military to
be ready when that time came. Preparedness gained traction after the
sinking of the *Lusitania* by the Germans in 1915 and increased again
after the raid on New Mexico by Mexican general Pancho Villa in 1916.
By 1916 preparedness parades were occurring all over the country.

Antiwar radicals often protested preparedness parades or organized competing peace marches. In July of 1916, a bomb exploded
during a preparedness parade in San Francisco, killing ten people, and
labor leaders Tom Mooney and Warren Billings were unjustly arrested
and charged and convicted of setting off the explosive. The Mooney-
Billings case became a popular cause for radicals, and money was raised
for them, often in conjunction with other defense cases, during and
after the war. But the Mooney-Billings case publicly associated labor
and antiwar activism with violence, even though the men were falsely
accused. It fueled resentment toward antiwar activists and led public
officials to more actively persecute them. Mooney and Billings were initially sentenced to death, although they would both later be pardoned.

Patriotism and pro-war feelings surged once the United States entered the war, which led to ostracism and periodic legal action against
those who did not support it. Once the United States had officially declared war, Congress passed laws severely limiting freedom of speech
and dissent. The first was the Espionage Act, passed in June 1917 and
amended in May 1918. Whereas the original act pertained more to actual
spying and giving information to enemy countries, the amended act,
known as the Sedition Act, stated that anyone who, during wartime, willfully incited "insubordination, disloyalty, mutiny, or refusal of duty, in
the military," obstructed enlistment in the military, or was proved to "ut-
ter, print, write, or publish any disloyal, profane, scurrilous, or abusive
language about the form of government of the United States, or the Constitution of the United States, or the military or naval forces of the United
States, or the flag . . . or the uniform of the Army or Navy of the United
States, or any language intended to bring the form of government . . . or
the Constitution . . . or the military or naval forces . . . or the flag . . . of the
United States into contempt, scorn, contumely, or disrepute," or who was

Workers outside Lumber Workers Industrial Union hall in Arlington, Washington, 1917. Walter P. Reuther Library, Archives of Labor and Urban Affairs, Wayne State University, 5006.

known to willfully "urge, incite, or advocate any curtailment of production in this country of any thing or things . . . necessary or essential to the prosecution of the war," or advocated or suggested others do any of those things, should be punished by "a fine of not more than $10,000 or imprisonment for not more than twenty years, or both." In sum, radicals could not say or write anything negative about the government, flag, military, or the draft without risking prosecution.[1]

Thus the wartime government of the United States finally had the legal justification for persecuting radicalism that had been lacking in the prewar years. The IWW as an organization never took an official stand for or against the war or the draft, but IWW strike activity in the vital lumber industry during wartime made it an obvious target of government repression. Although the war was detrimental to Wobbly communities in the cities and towns of the Pacific Northwest, the IWW actually scored one of its biggest successes in the early war years with the strike in the lumber camps. Wartime hysteria limited freedom of speech for labor organizers, but it benefited workers in general by stimulating job growth. Because high production was needed, the workers had more power in their relationships with employers than in earlier times of high unemployment. The lumber industry boomed in the Northwest because of the demand for raw materials for war production. Prior to the war, the Wobblies had been involved in strikes of shingle weavers and lumberyard workers, but had had little success in the camps. Organizers saw their chance in this new wartime environment and successfully executed a strike in 1917–1918, improving hours and conditions in the lumber camps.

IWW leadership of the massive lumber strike during the war led to increased paranoia regarding German influence in the union, and the government stepped up surveillance and coordinated nationally to strike at the heart of the organization. Rumors swirled that the Wobblies were German spies, that the strike was financed by Germany, and that members sabotaged the war effort by setting fires to munitions factories. Arizona senator Henry Ashurst announced to the Senate that IWW stood for "Imperial Wilhelm's Warriors." Newspapers also ramped up anti-Wobbly hysteria with headlines such as "State Unit Forms to Check IWW Activities in Eastern Oregon Menace" and "Overthrow of All Power IWW Aim: Murder Not to Be Avoided," from 1917 issues of the *Oregonian*.[2]

In addition to federal legislation, many states also passed criminal syndicalism laws during the war specifically aimed at the IWW. Subsequent raids on IWW offices and arrests of members drastically curtailed the efficacy of the union in cities during this time, despite its success in the lumber camps. This increased scrutiny put immense pressure on the radical community that the IWW was a part of, and difficult decisions needed to be made about where to focus financial and legal support. Nationally, the organization focused on defense and support of the 113 Wobblies on trial in Chicago for their involvement with the union. Defense work in the Northwest centered on those picked up during raids on Wobbly halls or in lumber camps rather than those who acted individually (such as women like Louise Olivereau and Marie Equi, whom we will learn more about in the chapters that follow).

On September 5, 1917, a coordinated series of federal raids hit Wobbly halls across the nation, arresting members and confiscating property, including valuable subscription and membership lists, as well as innocuous items such as a framed map of the State of Washington taken from the Seattle local. The police extended their raids into the homes of union members. In Portland the police raided the home of

Mr. and Mrs. Harry Lloyd and confiscated Mrs. Lloyd's luggage and the pictures of family and friends from their walls. These raids disrupted the Wobbly community in the Northwest in two ways. Raids on halls and the ensuing arrests of everyone inside meant that Wobbly halls could no longer function as safe spaces for workers to gather with their children for dances, plays, concerts, and other community events as they had for the last decade. Raids on homes put privacy and property at risk for anyone associated with the IWW.[3]

After the raids on Wobbly halls and meetings across the country resulted in the arrests of several prominent Wobblies, the nation watched as 113 members of the IWW stood trial in Chicago in the case of *United States v. William D. Haywood, et al.* The men were tried together and defended by George Vanderveer, who had spearheaded the defense in the Everett Case, arguably the Wobblies' most successful court appearance. Each Wobbly was charged with one hundred different crimes. The prosecution immediately realized the difficulty of proving the guilt of each individual defendant. Instead, it painted the organization itself as seditious. The government used prewar pamphlets, such as *Sabotage*, and songs and articles to argue that the IWW was a seditious organization, and therefore proof of membership in the organization was all that was needed to convict. The trial lasted five months, from April 1 to August 30, 1918. The jury deliberated for only an hour before convicting all the men on all the counts for which they were charged. The men were found guilty and received sentences ranging from one year to twenty, with eighty-eight of the defendants sentenced to at least five years. The convicted men were sent to Leavenworth Penitentiary, many leaving wives and children behind.[4]

As demonstrated by the trial in Chicago, membership and an active role in the IWW carried real risks during this oppressive time. The risk of association with the IWW increased for men and women who were not US citizens. During this period of anti-Wobbly fervor, membership in the organization was reason enough for authorities to start deportation proceedings for alien immigrants. A group of immigrant Wobblies were rounded up and held for deportation in Seattle, some for more than a year, before being sent to Ellis Island on February 7, 1919. But some noncitizens won their cases, and not all were deported. Of the total of 150 Wobblies arrested and headed for deportation during 1918 and 1919, only twenty-seven were actually sent back to Europe.[5]

In 1919 the House Committee on Immigration questioned Byron Uhl, acting commissioner of immigration, about the deportation of alien radicals. The committee wondered why only sixty out of the 691 people arrested for preaching the overthrow of government between February 7, 1917, and November 1, 1919, had been deported. Congressmen Albert Johnson, a representative from Washington State who was chairman of the House Committee on Immigration, referred to the "Red Special" of radical aliens from Seattle as "the most conspicuous instance of the failure of the deportation process." He even accused Wobblies of using the train as a free ride to New York: that they were claiming they were aliens in Seattle but then showing proof of citizenship once they arrived.[6] As this example demonstrates, the federal government attempted to destroy the organization by targeting immigrants, but the very premise that deporting aliens would curtail Wobbly activities was a flawed one. Although there were some cases of deportation (a few of which will be outlined here), a great majority of Wobbly leadership and the rank and file in the Pacific Northwest were citizens.[7]

Among those from the Northwest who were actually deported were a husband and wife, Mr. and Mrs. Peter Williamson Merta (also known as Melta), and a pair of sisters, Margaret and Janet Roy. Peter Merta was secretary of the IWW local in Raymond, Washington; he was arrested in April 1918 for his membership and active role in the organization and scheduled for deportation to Finland. For unknown reasons, the Mertas were initially released, but Peter was arrested again in Duluth, Minnesota, for his work as editor of a Finnish-language Wobbly paper. Else Merta may have come to Ellis Island of her own free will to be deported with her husband, but the commissioner of immigration denied this was the case, and noted that the acting secretary of labor had ordered her to be deported because of her membership in the IWW.[8]

A story of two young women exemplifies the risk associated with IWW membership during this period. Margaret and Janet Roy were sisters who were arrested in Seattle in June 1918. Margaret was about twenty-six years old, and Janet was around twenty-three at the time of their arrest.[9] Hulet Wells, the chairman of the Socialist Party of Washington, who was convicted of sedition in 1918, described the case of the Roy sisters. They were from Scotland and had become interested in the IWW while in Chicago, before they traveled to Seattle in 1918. Wells noted that they were "quiet, demure, refined little Scotch girls, . . . so modest and unassuming that it is hard to imagine them being connected with a revolutionary movement."[10] Upon arrival in Seattle, they looked up Walker Smith, well-known Wobbly and editor of the *Industrial Worker*, for advice on finding a room. That the Roy sisters knew to contact Smith when they arrived in Seattle is an example of how the informal radical community functioned. The police must have followed the Roy sisters, because Smith's house was raided while they were visiting him and his family, and the officers greeted the Roy sisters by name. As was the case in other raids on homes of Wobblies, the officers produced a liquor warrant as a reason to enter the home. Washington State had prohibited the manufacture and sale of liquor as early as 1914, and searching for bootlegging operations was often used as an excuse for searching homes. The officers arrested Smith and the Roy sisters.[11] When the women's trunks were searched, the police found their IWW red cards and a letter of introduction from Chicago headquarters. The women were also described as "well supplied with money."[12] Smith was released after ten days, but the sisters were held in Seattle for over two months.[13] The Roy sisters, by virtue of association with Wobbly leadership and their membership in the organization, were targeted for deportation and charged with "advocating or teaching the unlawful destruction of property."[14] It is unclear on what evidence these charges were based, but it could have been possession of pamphlets such as Smith's *Sabotage: Its History, Philosophy and Function*. The Roy sisters eventually gave up on their appeals and were deported to Scotland on July 22, 1919.[15]

Walker C. Smith, his wife Marie, and daughters Shirley, Enid, and Lois, 1925. Everett Public Library.

Along with the men arrested in Chicago, many lesser-known women were arrested for supporting the IWW during this time. One woman, Nora Fuller of Spokane, was arrested and fined ten dollars for asking a jailer to deliver a basket of fruit along with a note to inmates Donald Sheridan, James Rowan, and W. Moran. She was held incommunicado for thirteen days and then released on a one-hundred-dollar bail. Fuller was fined, refused to pay, and instead took jail time. The *Industrial Worker* sarcastically observed, "Mrs. Fuller's son, who voluntarily enlisted in the army, will be pleased to learn that is mother is now lying in Spokane's filthy jail."[16]

One of the most upsetting arrests for the northwest Wobblies was that of Kate B. MacDonald, or "Mrs. Mac," as she was known to the locals. Mrs. MacDonald was the wife of J. A. MacDonald, editor of the *Industrial Worker* until he was indicted and sent to Chicago for the Haywood trial. Mrs. MacDonald had been the bookkeeper at the paper for a year, and had taken over all the business responsibilities since her husband's arrest two months prior to hers. Her arrest shocked her Fellow Workers:

> Everyone who has had business at the *Worker* office, has
> always been met by Mrs. Mac (the diminutive denoting
> friendliness, not presumptive or coarse familiarity) with
> gentle courteousness, refinement and womanliness, coupled
> with a reserved and firm control that won and retained
> friendship, yet repelled and held in check any who might
> overstep the bounds of decency. She is thoughtful and, at
> times, a little too serious, which however, is compensated
> for by a keen appreciation of humor, which manifests itself
> through merry twinkling eyes and a hearty, wholesome
> laugh.[17]

The description of this "pure, wholesome, womanly woman," as she was described in the paper, was then contrasted with the horrors she faced in jail:

> She had to come in contact with all sorts of unfortunate
> and degraded women—the prostitute; the hopeless, help-
> less dope fiend; the drunkard, screeching vile and filthy

language—all wrecks of women who once were fair and
pure, mayhap had loved and suckled child at breast, had
noble aspirations and high ambition; but now—all is lost,
they are submerged, their habitat the slum. Reeking odors
and no conveniences. None of the privacy that the refined
woman desires even when among her own sex.[18]

But as a true Rebel Girl, she is happy to share in this burden:

Yet the women fellow workers take their stand by the men
in the glorious battle for freedom, and when the heavy hand
of capitalistic laworder grasps and forcibly immures them
in filthy jails, our sisters in the struggle make no complaint,
but take their medicine with a fortitude worthy of the noble
cause in which they fight![19]

The article ends with the loaded question "What are you doing on
the outside?" Mrs. McDonald, charged with disorderly conduct, was
released on a one-thousand-dollar bail, and the charges were eventually
dismissed.[20]

Women also supported the organization by helping sell the *Industrial Worker* in the streets of Seattle. Two women, Mrs. Dessie Hubbard
and Mrs. Clara Alderton, took to the street on January 16, 1918, to sell
copies of the paper. They lasted about fifteen minutes before they were
arrested. In response, two more women and "about fifty lumberjacks"
grabbed papers to sell in a free press version of the previous free speech
fights, an attempt to overwhelm the police and test their commitment to
arresting anyone who distributed the paper. Mrs. Blair Cairns and Mrs.
Edith Osborne were also arrested. When Mr. Alderton and Mr. Hubbard arrived at the station to bail out their wives, they were arrested
as well. The Aldertons were then held by immigration authorities for
possible deportation to England. According to one of the female prisoners, as they were put in the city jail the matron announced, "Some more
IWW girls. I suppose we will get another snotty write-up when they
are released, the same as that one Kate MacDonald gave us. I wish I had
her here now so I could break a chair over her head." Women in the
IWW prided themselves on their exposure, in the *Industrial Worker*
and *Daily Call*, of the filthy conditions in the women's jails.[21]

Mrs. Blair Cairns was arrested again a few months later in a raid on the Spokane IWW hall, along with Mrs. Dorcas Lloyd, wife of Harry Lloyd who was on trial in Chicago, and Mrs. Daughs, the secretary of the Socialist Party of Spokane. Daughs was working as a stenographer for the Lumber Workers Industrial Union; she was immediately released after her arrest. Lloyd, who was working as a copy clerk for the IWW, and Mrs. Cairns were each given thirty days and fined one hundred dollars. In Tacoma, military police, accompanied by a mob, ransacked an IWW hall, destroyed decorations, and burned literature and records in the street. Among the arrests that day were two more Wobbly couples: Mr. and Mrs. A. R. Tucker and Mr. and Mrs. S. Jones. By mid-1918 the *Industrial Worker* had ceased to function, until July 1919, when it was published in Everett. Therefore there was no longer an official Wobbly paper in the Northwest to distribute news about arrests and defense efforts.[22]

The arrests of women and their rough treatment in jails in the Pacific Northwest was part of a larger pattern. In California, the arrest of thirty-eight-year-old Theodora Pollok in Sacramento provides another detailed example of the way even upper-class females were treated by authorities. Pollok was arrested when she arrived at the jail to arrange bail for some of the Wobblies who had previously been rounded up in raids of Wobbly halls. She was a well-educated woman with many respectable supporters petitioning on her behalf after her arrest. Born in Baltimore and educated in New York and Washington, DC, she was described by one of her supporters, J. H. Byrd, as "an exceedingly brilliant girl." Byrd also described Pollok as someone "blessed or cursed with a courageous big heart," who became involved with the IWW "without realizing, in the slightest, what she was being drawn into."[23] Another friend of Pollok's, lawyer Henry Twombly, described her as "a refined, cultured lady of integrity and magnanimous spirit." Similar to what we will see in the case of Louise Olivereau, Pollok's supporters appealed for her release by emphasizing her maternal nature and emotional need to help others that led her to association with the IWW.[24]

The authorities, on the other hand, saw Pollok as a threat. After her arrest, Pollok was subjected to "a medical examination intended for prostitutes." Such treatment of a "respectable" woman was considered so outrageous that even President Woodrow Wilson questioned the need for such an examination. United States attorney John Preston ignorantly replied that "Wobblies, like prostitutes, were notoriously promiscuous sexually, only in their case love was not for sale."[25]

According to authorities, Pollok's alleged sexual promiscuity was matched by her supposed influence in the organization. San Francisco district attorney Charles Fickert called Pollok "the head of the IWW" on the West Coast. Fickert was the prosecutor for the Mooney-Billings preparedness parade bombing case and was extremely antiradical; Pollok was active in the Mooney-Billings Defense Committee and therefore likely familiar to him prior to her arrest. Fickert believed that Pollok's middle-class background was beneficial to the Wobblies and that it allowed her to serve as a liaison between the "direct action anarchists and the 'parlor bolsheviki.'" Fickert also felt that there was a cabal of socialists in DC that were secretly working for her release.[26]

Pollok did have some allies in Washington. Congresswoman Jeanette Rankin wrote to the president regarding Pollok's case, and Wilson then wrote to Attorney General Thomas Gregory requesting that California district attorney Preston dismiss the case. Preston wrote to Gregory laying out the details of the case and Pollok's involvement with the IWW as a member, and as a part of the General Defense Committee, which worked for the release of IWW prisoners. He also noted that although Pollok had not specifically spoken out against the war, she did not publicly support it by writing patriotic articles or buying Liberty bonds.[27]

Unlike the cases of other IWW women arrested on flimsy evidence, Pollok's case was not dropped. The reasons the prosecution did not dismiss her case were fairly simple: they had more evidence on her than on the rest of the less-respectable Wobblies they had arrested.[28] If they dismissed her case for lack of evidence, then what reason would they have for keeping the male Wobblies? Therefore, authorities tried to build a public relations case to justify continuing her prosecution despite weak evidence. Assistant United States attorney Patrick Johnson called her "one of the most dangerous members of the IWW in California."[29] Local newspapers described her as "a college graduate, and art connoisseur, and secretary of the IWW Defense League."[30] Pollok complained about her treatment, saying that she was "vilified and abused" when she testified in front of the grand jury.[31]

The majority of the forty-six Wobblies tried in Sacramento opted for the "silent defense," not hiring lawyers or putting up a defense, in the belief that they would never see true justice in the capitalist courts. Only Pollok and two other defendants who were part of the International Workers Defense League hired lawyers. The defendants were held in jail anywhere from six months to a year before the trial began, with only four having been released on bail in that time, and five died of influenza. On January 19, 1919, the jury deliberated for an hour before returning a verdict of guilty on all counts for all defendants. After several appeals, Pollok secured a letter from a physician stating that jail time would kill her (she had recently been diagnosed with tuberculosis) and her sentence was reduced to a one-hundred-dollar fine. The Pollok case signifies the zeal with which local authorities manufactured cases against anyone with a Wobbly connection, even at the risk of alienating federal officials in Washington. Local officials continued this trend in the Pacific Northwest by spying on and arresting women based on evidence no stronger than that in Pollok's case.[32]

Washington State secret service agents kept very close watch on several women who were connected to the IWW in the Northwest. The secret service suspected that women passed along messages, hid suspects, or helped prisoners escape. If Wobbly women were involved in any of these activities, they were, by necessity, secretive, so evidence other than spy reports is hard to come by. Nevertheless, these cases do help showcase some of the women who were, at the very least, supportive of the organization during this period of repression.

In addition to Washington State agents, federal government agents kept records on other women associated with the IWW in the Northwest. The intelligence officer in Spokane, Washington, wrote in December 1917 that "it is now the policy of the IWW to use women runners in important matters, in the hope of eluding the Federal and Civil Authorities that way." He kept an eye on Clara Irvin, tracking her whereabouts from Spokane to Astoria and Portland, Oregon. The officer noted that her visit in Spokane and her secret departure indicated "that the organization is using her as a runner for messages," which therefore proved to him "that the leaders of the organization are aware that mail, parcel post, and express surveillance is being carried on by the Federal Authorities."[33]

Another federal agent was particularly suspicious of a Mrs. Brown of Everett, Washington, and first reported on her in October of 1917, describing her as a Wobbly. The agent read letters sent to her from imprisoned Wobblies Red Doran and Walter Smith. In those letters,

Smith said how much he loved her pumpkin pie and was hoping she could send some to him in jail. The agent was suspicious of this "pie," thinking that it held some larger significance and was another reason to be suspicious of Wobbly women bearing gifts and food for prisoners. The men addressed Brown as "mother" in the letters, and she referred to them as "her boys." The Wobbly woman as maternal figure, a motif that recurs in the case of Louise Olivereau, was repeated in Mrs. Brown's case. These types of women were more likely to provide food and shelter to Wobblies passing through than to engage in agitation in the streets.[34]

The agents were watching another "mother figure" at that same time in Everett, Mrs. Grant. Grant ran a restaurant in Everett, which the agent referred to as headquarters for all news regarding the arrested men. There was also a hotel upstairs that was frequented by Wobblies—at least by "the better ones." Mrs. Doran came to stay with Grant, and Grant said she would put her up rent-free for the duration of her husband's jail time as a reward for the sacrifice he had made for his fellow workers. Mrs. Grant fed the Wobblies whether or not they could pay, and organized most of their local functions, even though her husband did not support the organization. She even "roughed it" and camped out with the boys. The agent noted that she was "indiscreet," but he had "never heard her moral character assailed." She would have taken out a red card but for the fact that she owned the restaurant and therefore was barred from membership. The agent traveled to Everett from Seattle in May 1918 to investigate the purchase of a large boat by Mrs. Grant. Mrs. Grant had stated that she wanted the boat to fish near Alaska, but the agent was convinced that the actual purpose was to ferry Wobblies under indictment to Siberia. For unknown reasons, by June, Grant had sold her boat and ceased her involvement with the IWW. The surveillance by federal agents and risk of arrest may have been too much for her relationship and her business to bear.[35]

In response to the waves of arrests, the efforts of Wobbly women who had not been arrested, or had been arrested and released, focused on the local and national defense committees. The work of the defense committees had several objectives, but the main task was to raise money and publicity for trial expenses. It also financially supported the men who were in jail and their dependents. For example, in 1918 the Seattle Defense Committee paid relief to the following:

Mrs. J. T. Doran, Seattle, $10/week
Mrs. J. P. Thompson, Seattle, $10/week
Mrs. John M. Foss, $10/week
Mrs. Geo. Hardy, Seattle, $10/week, 3 children
Mrs. E. F. Doree, Rex, OR, $10/week, 1 child

Although the list is rather small, it again reminds us that the men who were jailed were not all "footloose hoboes" with nothing to lose, but men with families, and the organization recognized that.[36]

As arrests continued, the need for a national general defense organization grew stronger. On February 14, 1918, the General Executive Board created one. The committee solicited funds to help with defense and also aid those affected by the arrests. In June 1921 they decreed that relief was to be given first to wives of prisoners who had dependent children, then to prisoners in need of adequate food and clothing, then to others who were in need. An example of these disbursements is as follows:

Disbursements of General Defense Committee July 1921

Mrs. Lucy L. Embree, Relief collected by Butte 50.00
Mrs. John Avila, Relief, two weeks 16.00
Mrs. Etta Reeder, Relief, two weeks 30.00
Mrs. John Avila, Relief, two weeks 16.00
Mrs. Jas. P. Thompson, Relief 2 weeks, 20.00
Mrs. Etta Reeder, Relief, 2 weeks, 30.00
Mrs. E. F. Doree, Relief, 2 wks, 24.00
Mrs. Lucy L. Embree, Relief, 2 wks, 30.00
Mrs. John M. Foss, relief, 2 wks, 20.00
Mrs. Mary Graber, relief, 2 wks, 20.00
Mrs. J. T. Doran, relief, 2 wks, 20.00

Thus the relief given out by the Seattle Defense Committee was part of a larger national effort to support the families of imprisoned Wobblies. As we will see later, in the case of the Doree family, this aid did not always come without strings attached.[37]

Women who supported the organization contributed financially to the defense funds, and they also donated food and clothing to the

IWW Picnic, Seattle, 1919. University of Washington, Special Collections, UW6633.

imprisoned men. A letter of thanks was sent to the *Industrial Worker* in November 1920 by the men in the Montesano county jail for the "large assortment of home-canned fruits, jellies, preserves, honey and smoked salmon" they had recently been sent. It is not surprising or controversial that women contributed food to prisoners, but it is important to remember that many of these women, such as in the cases of Mrs. Brown, Mrs. Grant, or Mrs. Fuller, faced tracking by government agents or even the possibility of their own arrest by supporting jailed Wobblies.[38]

These examples give us a glimpse into the surveillance that Northwest radicals faced during World War I and its immediate aftermath. Women risked arrest stepping in for their jailed male counterparts in tasks such as editing and selling the *Industrial Worker*. They risked arrest working on defense committees. They risked arrest for visiting men in jail. They risked arrest by simply being present at an IWW hall. In spite of this, many women continued to support the IWW. When selling a newspaper or visiting a friend in jail could lead to arrest, women had to make difficult choices about how to support the organization. As persecution persisted and jail sentences wore on, the organization, as it had existed prior to World War I, deteriorated.

The persecution of the organization, its members, officials, halls, mail, and newspapers during the war made it extremely difficult for supporters of the IWW to function as a community. Individuals took action to support those in jail, but they could no longer freely associate, and the days of movie showings and Wobbly concerts were gone. This is not to say that the organization did not continue to function, but the Wobbly Hall as a family-friendly center of the radical community had ceased to exist. The persecution also took its toll on individual activists who were jailed for their antiwar activities and then released to a world where their community had splintered. As we will see, the cases of Louise Olivereau and Marie Equi exemplify the detrimental effects of this mistreatment at the hands of the federal government.

7
Seattle 1917–1920
Anarchism, Antiwar Activism, and the Case of Louise Olivereau

Numerous individuals took actions, big and small, to support the IWW during World War I and the Red Scare that followed. Not all those actions were explicitly antiwar, and the organization as a whole, unlike the Socialist Party, did not take an official stand. But women like Louise Olivereau and Marie Equi acted individually to protest what they felt was an unjust war. Their public actions, whether in speech or writing, made them targets of prosecution under wartime acts aimed at curbing antiwar activity. Their gender and radical political and social views affected the amount of support they received from both their fellow workers and the general public during this challenging time. Their two cases also underscore the tension within the radical community of the Pacific Northwest during a period of severe repression.

On November 30, 1917, Louise Olivereau was convicted of sedition and sentenced to ten years in prison for mailing flyers encouraging young men to resist the draft by becoming conscientious objectors. Olivereau was a stenographer for the IWW and a member of the union. She differed from many Wobblies arrested during the war by openly declaring herself an anarchist. Olivereau was not very well known and had little public support outside of her best friend, Minnie Parkhurst, who worked tirelessly on her behalf. Her case was not widely discussed in IWW newspapers, which were focused more on the tribulations of the union leadership in Chicago and on people who were arrested solely because of their IWW membership. Olivereau ended up serving twenty-eight months in Cañon City jail in Colorado, and retired from activism after her release.

Olivereau's solitary act of defiance and her explanation of anarchist beliefs during her trial separated her from male members of the organization who were also on trial during this period. Her case and ensuing

Louise Olivereau, from the pamphlet *The Louise Olivereau Case*, 1918. University of Washington, Special Collections, UW39282.

appeal sheds light on some of the internal struggles of the organization during the war years, and on the limits of solidarity during a time of immense legal and political pressure. Although she received little support from the IWW, her association with the organization still loomed large at her trial, and with it brought scrutiny of her personal life and beliefs similar to what women in earlier IWW trials, such as Becky Beck and Edith Frenette, had faced.

Louise Olivereau was born in the United States in 1884 to parents who had emigrated from France. Except for her trial, most of her life was spent out of the public spotlight. She attended college in Illinois and worked as a stenographer. She lived in Portland for a few years, and was involved in the Modern School Movement there before moving to Seattle and converting to anarchism.[1] Olivereau's early activism is most evident in a series of letters to the *Oregonian* newspaper starting in 1913.

The first letter advocated teaching sex hygiene in public schools, while later letters denounced the indoctrination of children at the Seventh Annual Purity Congress in Minneapolis, put on by the World's Purity Federation. The federation was founded in 1905 with the goal of combating vice and prostitution, as well as "the promotion of a high and single standard of morals for men and women."[2] Olivereau claimed that at the Purity Congress the schoolchildren of that city were "inoculated with Comstockitis," which she defined as "the most deadly and filthy of moral disorders, to-wit, a morbid pruriency and propensity to meddle in the private affairs of others."[3]

"Comstockitis" referred to Anthony Comstock, a postal inspector obsessed with policing vice and immorality who advocated laws banning obscene materials and censored materials he found objectionable. Olivereau continued her letter castigating so-called morality crusaders who scared children by warning them of the dangers of "nude art, comfortable bathing garments, healthy frankness regarding sex, and finally, against that stupendous fabrication of the moralist's imagination, the white slave trade."[4] While in Portland, Olivereau was also involved in birth control activism, and she gave a lecture about English physician and human sexuality expert Havelock Ellis at a meeting of the Birth Control League in 1915; she was elected secretary when the Portland branch of the league was formed.[5] Olivereau's support of frank discussions of sex and sexuality, as well as access to birth control, were radical for the period and placed her outside the bounds of respectability. But she was not a well-known activist, and there is no evidence of her giving any other public speeches or playing an active role in protests. Olivereau made mention of her lack of notoriety during her trial, stating, "I have never been a public propagandist in Seattle, and to a very limited extent only in any other place."[6] She also noted that her sedition trial was her first time as a defendant in court. So although Olivereau was a Wobbly, she focused more on peace, birth control, and sex education than on labor-specific causes. It was her actions combating the draft during World War I that led to her arrest.[7]

Women constituted a very small portion of those convicted of sedition or espionage during World War I, roughly twenty of eight hundred cases. Historian Kathleen Kennedy argues that the majority of these women fell outside the bounds of what the upper and middle classes deemed appropriate female behavior, either by holding occupations normally held by men, such as doctors or political leaders, or by their status as unmarried women or women without children. Kennedy analyzes these women in relation to appropriate societal roles as mothers, but, as I have argued in previous chapters, they can also be analyzed under the broader scope of respectability. Although respectability was associated with family status, it encompassed more than just motherhood: it included having a legal spouse and a home. Many of the women arrested for acting out against the war were not only childless, but also unmarried and frequently moving or traveling around the country. Subjecting these types of women to interrogation was not new. Prior to the war, prosecutors tried to construe morality laws in a way that would apply to radicals, such as the case of Becky Beck in Seattle. But during the war the government had a very broad legal right to suppress dissent, and nontraditional views on love, sex, or marriage could be questioned in relation to seditious activities.[8]

Olivereau's activities during the war fell under the broad scope of the new sedition laws. Antiwar radicalism took a variety of forms, from protesting preparedness parades to giving speeches and writing articles. Olivereau's particular form of activism was to encourage young men to register as conscientious objectors. The Selective Service Act of 1917 allowed for conscientious objectors (COs) to avoid combat duty, though they were still required to play some kind of noncombatant role in the military. Initially those who could register as an objector to the war were limited to members of a number of religious sects. Conscientious objectors not claiming religious beliefs as their reason for objecting, and instead citing political, social, or moral beliefs, had a much more difficult time achieving CO status. Almost sixty-five thousand people filed as COs. Of that number, almost fifty-seven thousand were recognized as sincere. Nonreligious objectors were initially less likely to be seen as sincere, but by December 1918 they were officially recognized by Secretary of War Newton Baker.[9]

Many radicals felt that conscientious objection was the only morally acceptable reaction to conscription, but they may not have realized the consequences facing registered conscientious objectors. If a potential CO cleared the hurdle of acceptance by the local draft board, he was not completely free of military obligation. Although COs could avoid combat duty, they were still under the control of the military. They had the legal right to object, but the culture of the military was not forgiving to men who chose not to serve. Once COs entered the camps, most were persuaded to accept combat roles through peer pressure, jeering, beatings, or solitary confinement. An estimated four-fifths of those who registered as COs ended up accepting some kind of military duty, an astonishingly high number considering the lengths they had to go to be declared COs in the first place. They were also more likely to be court-martialed for "violation of the articles of war." Among 540 COs court-martialed, there were "17 death sentences, 142 life terms, and 345 cases with average sentences of 16½ years." Most of those sentences were reversed, but they do serve as an example of what COs faced once in the military.[10]

Louise Olivereau was likely ignorant of the harsh conditions that faced the young potential draftees if they were to heed her advice and register as COs. But she spoke out strongly against the war and criticized President Wilson's speeches concerning conscription. In his Proclamation on Conscription on May 18, 1917, Wilson maintained that "it is in no sense a conscription of the unwilling. It is, rather, selection from a nation which has volunteered in mass."[11] Olivereau rejected Wilson's assertion that the nation had volunteered to fight:

> Now the Conscientious Objector is decidedly unwilling
> to render military service; therefore, by the terms of the
> President's explanation of the act, he should be exempt
> from military service without further discussion of the
> matter. . . . Now this nation has not volunteered in mass.
> This nation has not volunteered at all. If the nation had
> volunteered, it would never have been necessary to pass a
> conscription act.[12]

Olivereau then wrote two letters, addressed to "Fellow-Conscript," and sent them to men who were drafted. Olivereau assumed that these young men would be more amenable to her argument since they had not volunteered to serve in the armed forces. The first letter discussed the meaning of patriotism. In it Olivereau argued that

> the present war is clearly a war for financial profit and
> power, unmistakably forced upon the nation by a small
> minority. . . . The great mass of men in this nation believe

the war to be wrong. Shall we then allow ourselves to be
used, not only to our destruction, but to the unspeakable
degradation of the nation as a whole?

Olivereau used "we" repeatedly in the letter, and signed it "Conscientious Objectors," giving the impression that there was more than one
author and that the authors were male.[13]

The next section of the circular focused on alternative service
and advocated that men resist serving even in a noncombat position.
Olivereau argued that "it is as wrong to help in the destruction of life
as it is to destroy life." Indeed, she argued, it was more ethical for a CO
to risk his life in combat than to hide from hazardous duty by accepting something more removed from the violence of war. But the only
irreproachable option was to resist the draft openly, refuse alternate
service, and face prison. Thus while Olivereau initially advised the men
to become COs, she switched tactics and ultimately advised they resist
the draft altogether.[14]

The second circular argued that government existed only to protect property:

Government means nothing to the workers (I assume you are
of this class) except a method of oppression by which he is
made to work for the benefit of another class, from which
he receives nothing, not even protection and an adequate
living. It is this thing which you are asked to protect with
your life, for which you are ordered to go into the worst hell
imaginable.

This circular did not discuss becoming a conscientious objector, but
instead more directly advocated that draftees "Resist: Refuse To Go:
Stay Away."[15]

Olivereau mailed the circulars on August 28 or 29, 1917. On September 5 the police raided the IWW hall in Seattle, seizing records and
pamphlets, including copies of Olivereau's letters. She went to the police
station two days later to request that pamphlets that were her personal
property be returned. It was then that she was questioned about the letters. She stated that she produced and financed them herself, and that
they had no connection to the IWW, even though at that time she was

employed by the organization as a stenographer. She had been at that job for seven or eight weeks, earning eighteen dollars per week. She admitted to preparing and mailing out roughly two thousand circulars and claimed her only hope was to make a few people rethink their position in the war. After questioning by the police she was held for arrest. Later it was revealed that local agents had been watching her house as early as August 24. Olivereau surmised that the delay in her arrest was so that the raids on the Wobbly halls could be finished, and some evidence would be found connecting the organization to her circulars. No such evidence was found.[16]

Since Olivereau worked alone to write, print, and distribute the fliers, she stood trial alone. Olivereau faced the decision that confronted other antiwar radicals: whether or not to hire legal counsel to present a legalistic defense of the charges. Anarchist Emma Goldman tackled the same issue after her arrest for sedition and came to the conclusion that her "trial would have meaning only if we could turn the court-room into a forum for the presentation of the ideas we had been fighting for throughout all of our conscious years." This was the model Olivereau followed. She opted to not have counsel and to use her trial to explain her anarchist beliefs and antiwar position.[17]

During her trial, Olivereau explained the reasoning behind her decision. At the outset she declared herself a "direct actionist," stating that she believed "in keeping the relations between individuals and groups on a simple fundamental human basis whenever it is possible to do so." She then questioned potential jurors about whether they held any prejudice against self-identified anarchists. Olivereau planned to explain her beliefs as motivation for her actions; therefore, allowing prejudiced jurors would make it difficult for her to make her case. When one of the potential jurors answered in the affirmative, Olivereau moved to have him dismissed. The judge then notified Olivereau that whether she was an avowed anarchist had nothing to do with the case, and therefore the juror would be allowed.[18] The mainstream press, however, felt that Olivereau's political beliefs were central to the case, with headlines that read "Girl Says 'I Am an Anarchist.'" The accompanying article also referred to Olivereau as an "anarchist leader." The paper noted that Olivereau was well known in Portland for being active in birth control activism and "radical social reform work" in the city.[19]

Aware of the stereotype of the bomb-throwing, immigrant anarchists popularized in the press, Olivereau took pains to explain the jurors what she believed anarchism to be and how it inspired her actions.
She delivered this eloquent definition of anarchism:

> Anarchism is the working philosophy of those who desire
> to bring about a condition of society in which force and
> violence will have no place. As a social student, I am con-
> vinced that violence breeds violence, war breeds hatreds
> and fears and revengeful desires which lead to other wars;
> suppression within a nation or a community results in
> rebellion, insurrection, revolution. A thoughtful survey of
> the evolution of life, whether from the point of physical or
> social development, leads inevitably to the conclusion that
> mutual aid, the communal sense, the social sense, recogni-
> tion of common interest among individuals, is the greatest
> factor in the world's progress, and always has been.[20]

She then insisted that in order for society to progress, freedom of
speech, opinion, and assembly must be maintained. Pointing out that
these were the ideals that the United States was founded on, she also
noted that they had always been constrained to "'freedom within the
law,' which is not freedom at all," for the law sought to limit those freedoms when it finds necessary, often during wartime. Olivereau saw her
case as directly tied to the First Amendment, and maintained that those
rights must be protected, especially during times of war:

> The real issue in this case is, have citizens of these United
> States the right to confer together on the subject of war,
> and upon other closely related subjects? Have citizens who
> have been drafted, or may be drafted, the right to think
> of their relation to the war and to the government, and of
> the relation of this government to other governments of the
> world, in any terms except those of complete acceptance of
> orders which may be issued to them by the Government?
> Are the laws of this country at the present time such as to
> demand for their obedience that citizens resign rights that
> we have been accustomed to consider fundamental in a

democracy—namely, the rights of free speech, free press,
and free assemblage?[21]

Olivereau reasoned that her right to free speech was outlined in the
Constitution, as had Elizabeth Gurley Flynn during the Spokane free
speech fight. And, similar to Flynn, she believed that she had the right
to interpret the Constitution and disobey laws that she believed vio-
lated those rights.[22]

Pacifists of many different political and religious backgrounds
advocated that draftees register as conscientious objectors. Olivereau
came to her trial espousing objection to the war as a tenet of her anarchist beliefs, which she believed she was, under the Constitution,
entitled to hold. The mainstream press and political conservatives often
used the terms "anarchist," "IWW," "Wobbly," and "Bolshevik" inter-
changeably, but among the radicals these labels had precise meanings
and took on a much larger importance. The IWW often felt the need
to proclaim that it was not an anarchist organization. Whereas the
focus on direct action and disavowal of political means of revolution
are often associated with anarchist beliefs, the union is often characterized as anarcho-syndicalist. Many anarchists were Wobblies, but the
organization as a whole never espoused such a label, and articles in
IWW newspapers often declared emphatically that members were not
anarchists. Anarchism, as a philosophy, appealed to some upper-class
or wealthy individuals, but the IWW constitution proclaimed that the
working class and the employing class had nothing in common, and the
organization did not officially welcome cross-class allies.[23] From the anarchist perspective, Emma Goldman felt that the IWW did not give her
the credit she deserved for helping out in free speech fights. She noted
in her autobiography that "not one of the IWW papers had protested
against our arrest and conviction" during the war.[24] Olivereau was clear
to make sure that people knew she was an anarchist, and that the ideals
she spoke of in her trial were anarchist in nature. At one point after
her trial, Olivereau found out that socialist-leaning Seattle *Daily Call*
newspaper published parts of her opening speech. While Olivereau was
appreciative of their support, she emphasized that "the speech is *not*
socialistic propaganda, but most decidedly anarchistic."[25]

Her anarchism distanced Olivereau from the IWW, despite being
a member and an employee. When the *Industrial Worker* reported on

her arrest and trial in December 1917, the editors kept a measured tone and were sure to detach the IWW from her efforts. The article praised the "considerable force and logic" of her opening speech before going on to write,

> Louise Olivereau is an anarchist. She is also a member of the IWW. Recently she was a stenographer in one branch of the union in Seattle. From her wages, after paying for her own support, she paid for the anti-draft literature which she publicly and proudly admits having circulated after her work day had ended. While her activities in this direction have no more connection with the IWW than have the affairs of the Birth Control League and similar organizations whose membership rolls include, among others, the names of IWW members, we can, without either condemning or commending her anti-conscription work, yield an ungrudging admiration for the brave stand she has made in defense of the principles which she holds dear.

Although this article showed some support for Olivereau, the tone and the relative lack of attention signified that the union wanted to separate itself from this case.[26]

In the October 1919 issue of the IWW paper *One Big Union Monthly*, Anne Gallagher wrote about Olivereau's case. Although the article is in support of Olivereau, Gallagher takes pains to point out that Olivereau's anarchist politics were not in agreement with hers. "Her position, viewed from the standpoint of the Class Conscious Mass Actionist, is not without it [*sic*] illogicality, for after all, it is the extreme individualism of capital society that is responsible for so much of its injustice. . . . The real conflict, then, is between classes, not individuals, so an appeal to the individual conscience to right social wrongs, is based on a misconception of society." Although dismissing Olivereau's beliefs, the article did say that she took a heroic stand and that "her able defense of her principles and ideals, have won her the admiration of all who are familiar with the case." The article ended by proclaiming Olivereau one of "our" class war prisoners. The IWW's minimal support during Olivereau's trial and appeal was less the result of her gender than of her anarchist belief system.[27]

The lack of support that Olivereau received from her fellow workers is demonstrated most directly in the correspondence between then-jailed Olivereau and her steadfast ally Minnie Parkhurst.[28] The two had become friends while living in Portland. They then moved to Seattle, where Olivereau became an anarchist. Parkhurst and Olivereau wrote back and forth, working through two critical issues. The first controversial decision was whether to appeal her case, which led to the second and more vital issue: how to fund the appeals process once it began. This is where Olivereau would need the most help from her fellow radicals and Wobblies, help that was not forthcoming. Olivereau and Parkhurst refer often to Fellow Workers Hays and Harvey (full names unknown), who were against the appeal, wanting to focus efforts on the Wobblies on trial in Chicago. Olivereau wrote that she wished she could speak to "the boys," believing if she did they would surely change their minds. Walker Smith was also critical of the appeal, but Olivereau did not want his help in the case, stating, "As for Walker Smith and the other critics, I want nothing from them except that they should attend strictly to the IWW cases. I thought I had made that plain before I left." Olivereau wrote again two weeks later: "As for my boys, who don't approve of the appeal—they are young and have no experience. Were our positions reversed, I fancy their views would change." She seemed hurt by the lack of support from Hays and Harvey most of all, and surprised by their lack of encouragement.[29]

Anna Louise Strong was another Seattle friend whose support wavered after Olivereau's trial. Strong was a progressive journalist and supporter of the local labor movement. She had previously reported on the Tracy trial after the Everett Massacre for the New York *Evening Post*. She then became involved in antiwar activities and started writing for the Seattle *Daily Call*. Strong testified on behalf of Hulet Wells, former president of the Seattle Labor Council and chairman of the Socialist Party of Washington, during his sedition trial in 1918. She testified that the anti-conscription leaflet that the men were arrested for was funded with help from such well-known and respected reformers as Jane Addams and Lillian Wald.

Strong's testimony on behalf of Wells led to a campaign to recall Strong from her position on the Seattle School Board, though it did not achieve much popularity at first. Strong later noted in her autobiography that because she "'befriended' an anarchist, Louise Olivereau," the recall effort was revived and was ultimately successful. Association with a well-known anarchist was enough to undermine Strong's status as a respected member of the community. She could no longer be trusted with the welfare of Seattle's schoolchildren. This exemplifies the stress that members of the radical community in the region faced during this period. They had to make careful decisions about how vocal they could be in support of those arrested for antiwar beliefs.[30]

Strong attended Olivereau's trial, at the request of the defendant. She described Olivereau's response to war as emotional: "She was one of those poetic souls to whom war never became a statistical movement of forces, but always vividly remained torn flesh, scattered brains and blood. She heard in her soul the shrieks of each murdered victim and hated war with emotion." Strong judged Olivereau's actions to be based on emotion, not reason, and later wrote of their futility: "The mimeographing was so badly done [on the anti-conscription letter] that one could hardly read it; there was nothing to prove that a single drafted soldier had been influenced from his allegiance."[31]

Strong also questioned Olivereau's decision to not have an attorney: "She rushed on jail as a moth to a flame. Nothing that we of the *Call* could say could dissuade her from this demonstration."[32] Strong was apparently not alone in this opinion, and Olivereau herself was aware that others felt this way. In a letter to Parkhurst, Olivereau wrote, "I'm sorry Anna thinks and has been saying that I was anxious to come to prison. The Paas boys thought I wanted to be a martyr too I believe. Such misconceptions can't be helped, when people can't distinguish between duty and desire." Olivereau felt that she never really had a choice in her actions if she wanted to stay true to her beliefs. This is a huge dividing point that came during the war between Progressives and radicals, and among radicals themselves. The "you could do much better work on the outside" argument swayed some, but others felt it would be hypocritical to do so.[33]

While Olivereau adjusted to prison life, on the outside Minnie Parkhurst continued to try to raise funds for an appeal, despite the lack of support from the radical community. In a letter to Ed Nolan, she wrote,

> The radicals here have been most contemptible about her
> case. It was the old story, "thou shalt have no Gods beside

me." In other words all gods must be the Old recognized gods—with such titles as Socialist, IWW, etc. after their names and never such a rash name as Anarchist. Only three or four understood and was sensible about her case. I could not get support for her appeal and so had to drop it. . . . However, the atmosphere is changing some here now in regard to her case. And I now and then hear such remarks as this which I heard in the Longshoremen's hall the other day. "I have more respect for that woman than the whole dam bunch Kate Sadler included."[34]

Even though they were not initially supportive, Parkhurst would not let the Seattle radicals forget about Olivereau:

Some of the radicals are getting ashamed apparently of their attitude I have rubbed it in so much and so strong. I believe it is having some effect at last, and they hate me most of them yes, because they know I am right about some things they will confess it when I am alone with them but they wouldn't give me that much satisfaction in the presence of half a dozen people. And then most of them are cowards after all. I am sorry to have to say it but I do believe it yes, I know it.[35]

This letter points to the difficulty historians have understanding how a radical community like this one functioned during times of extreme duress. We have hints from Parkhurst that people privately supported Olivereau but would not publicly comment on her actions. The IWW was not publicly critical either, but Olivereau certainly never received much attention or support from the organization. What becomes clear from both public Wobbly pronouncements and private conversations reported by Parkhurst is that Olivereau's anarchist belief system caused other radicals to shy away from supporting her.[36]

Regardless of their lack of support, Olivereau found solace in the idea her comrades were also imprisoned. When she found out that many of the "Chicago boys" were going to Leavenworth, she wrote, "I feel my isolation pretty keenly at times; but it's only a bodily isolation after all: the spiritual solidarity cannot be broken, tho each of us were put into a separate prison. Perhaps the Fellow Workers wouldn't like the term 'spiritual'; they can substitute any other they like; the fact remains the same—we are One." She still felt a strong connection with her Fellow Workers in the IWW, even though they may not have agreed with her actions or supported her appeal.[37]

The letters between Olivereau and Parkhurst do mention support from various friends in Seattle and around the country. She still maintained correspondence with Fellow Worker Harvey, who ended up enlisting in the army, and Hays, and wrote that she "loves them almost to death." She also received gifts from comrades: Brown bought her a dress, the "Tacoma boys" sent a box of candy, and Vilma Walden in Seattle sent seven dollars. She even made a favorable comment about Walker C. Smith: "Am much interested in all this publicity my child [her pamphlet *The Louise Olivereau Case*] is receiving. Hooray for Walker C.! He will be a good fellow yet, by the time he grows up if he keeps on improving at this rate."[38]

Former Wobbly Harvey O'Connor's memoir, *Revolution in Seattle*, includes an appendix by his wife Jessie Lloyd O'Connor on Louise Olivereau. Lloyd and O'Connor both describe Olivereau as a maternal figure. It is possible that O'Connor is the Harvey that Olivereau referred to in her letters. Lloyd notes that Olivereau had "long taken a motherly interest in the high school youngsters who sought out the Wobbly hall for adventure in the great task of improving conditions." O'Connor referred to Olivereau as a "motherly kind of woman." While Olivereau was emotional about her cause, she also provided intellectual grounds for her actions in her trial testimony. Parkhurst took pains to advertise this in publishing the trial transcripts in her pamphlet. This information seemed to have fallen on deaf ears, for in the writings of other radicals about Olivereau, her political beliefs are rarely mentioned. Although she was close to the Wobblies, as both an employee and a member of the organization, her political beliefs strayed from what even the most anti-centralization Wobblies espoused.[39]

The radical community of the Northwest, especially the IWW, was torn apart during the war. The Northwest Defense Committee chose to focus on those accused in big trials, arrested under criminal syndicalism laws, or threatened with deportation. How much money and effort to put into other cases, especially for those who had willfully broken the law, was a subject of debate. Olivereau demanded neither help nor funds from anyone, though privately she was obviously upset about the lack of support from her Fellow Workers.

Olivereau's Wobbly comrades had sympathy for her case, but felt, in the long run, it was not important enough to expend the time, money, and manpower that the other cases warranted. This is not to say that her fellow Wobblies should be blamed for this. She took actions that she knew could lead to her arrest, and she did it willingly, out of what she felt was her duty. The Wobblies who were being rounded up merely for carrying a red card took priority, because their arrests meant that merely being a member in the organization was an illegal act. To tie the IWW to anarchism at that point would have made fighting those arrests that much more difficult.

Olivereau's sentence was commuted in June 1919, and after her release she returned to Portland, where she spoke to members of the Prison Reform League about prison conditions, the most pressing of which was the lack of preparation for a productive life once released.[40] Once again, as we found in the Spokane and Portland cases, women connected with the IWW who had spent time in prisons had an avenue for speaking publicly about their experiences and advocated prison reform. After this point, though, Olivereau faded from the spotlight. In the 1960s, Jessie Lloyd O'Connor reported that a friend remembered seeing Olivereau in California in the early 1920s, where she was married to a conservative and had cut all ties to her radical friends. Another friend noted, "What hurt Louise the most after she came out of prison . . . was the bitter divisions she found among men and women who had been so united in working for a better world for labor when she was taken away in 1917."[41] In 1922 Olivereau wrote to Parkhurst,

> As for my place in the radical movement—that seems to be
> a good deal of a dream, or joke, or something. In the first
> place, I can't find any radical movement....The California
> jails and prisons are full of reds convicted under the anti-
> syndicalist laws, but I can't do anything about it and don't
> see the use of going to jail in protest.[42]

The unity of the past is often idealized: by 1920 new parties had arisen, old alliances were broken, and the radical community looked very different. Olivereau, who faced difficulty getting full support from her community while in prison, left prison and entered a very different world. The conservative climate of the 1920s, herself growing older, and the splintered movement all played a part in Olivereau's decision to retire from politics, but one cannot help but wonder if she felt that the sacrifice of her freedom had not been appreciated by her fellow radicals, and that it had done nothing to stop the war in the long run. Her case sheds light on internal conflicts in the movement that rarely make their way into the official records and demonstrates the messiness that occurred in response to legal and tactical disputes. But Olivereau was not the only woman associated with the IWW who was jailed for antiwar activities in the Northwest. We now turn to a case that received much more publicity, that of a woman reviled in the papers and beloved by her supporters, Dr. Marie Equi.

8
Portland 1916–1920
Birth Control, Antiwar Activism, and the Case of Marie Equi

One year after Louise Olivereau's sentencing in November of 1918, Marie Equi was also convicted of sedition and sentenced to three years in prison, serving ten months. Equi was a self-employed physician and, as such, was ineligible for membership in the IWW. Despite this, she was a vocal supporter of the union from the 1913 Oregon Packing Company Strike through her time in jail. As a doctor and notable public personality, Equi was widely known in Portland and had a much broader base of support than Olivereau. Her supporters included such diverse parties as the former governor of Oregon and the Oregon State Federation of Labor. She also had much more public support from the IWW itself, and hired IWW lawyer George Vanderveer to represent her. Equi and Olivereau differed in their personalities and belief systems, but they both acted independently in their antiwar actions, and therefore neither was arrested solely for membership in the IWW.

Equi and Olivereau both served time in jail, but their cases, trials, and appeals were very different. As explained in the previous chapter, Olivereau was an anarchist, and although she was a Wobbly, she explained her antiwar actions as being a result of her anarchist beliefs. Equi's arrest came from a speech that she gave at the IWW hall. She was publicly associated with the organization and did not stray far from popular Wobbly talking points about the necessity of the One Big Union. Equi was a firebrand, but she was also a respected physician, and had both working-class supporters and middle- and upper-class allies. Unlike Olivereau's philosophical statements about the nature of war and government, Equi brought something more concrete to the working men and women of Portland: knowledge of birth control and abortion. She also enjoyed the spotlight and was notorious for her outspoken behavior. She was a local celebrity, appreciated by the working class and often feared by city leaders, and that notoriety translated into a broad base of support during her trial.

Far more historical research has been done on Marie Equi's life than on that of Olivereau. Equi was an anomaly of the early twentieth century as a female physician and an open lesbian. She was born on April 7, 1872, and was raised in New Bedford, Massachusetts. Her mother, Sarah Mullins, had immigrated to the United States from Ireland and her father, Giovanni Equi, from Italy. One of eleven children, Equi dropped out of high school in her first year to work in the local textile mills. With the help of an older high school friend, Bessie Holcomb, Equi was able to leave the mills to enter Northfield Seminary for Young Ladies to resume her education. Unfortunately, she could not finance a second year on her own; with the help of her father she spent two years with family in Italy before returning to the United States in 1892. Before long she followed Holcomb out west, to The Dalles, Oregon, where they proceeded to live together for the next five years.[1]

Marie Equi first attracted public attention in 1893 when, at the age of twenty-one, she threatened to horsewhip a man accused of owing money to Holcomb, an incident that was reported in the local paper, as well in as the larger *Oregonian* and the San Francisco *Examiner*. After leaving The Dalles for San Francisco in 1897, Equi enrolled at the College of Physicians and Surgeons in the city, joining the two to three women registered in each freshman class. By 1901 she had moved to Portland, and she graduated from the University of Oregon's medical branch there, where women made up about 15 percent of the student body, in 1903.[2] In the ensuing decade, Equi practiced medicine in the Portland area. Her most notorious actions prior to the war years occurred during the strike at the Oregon Packing Company in 1913.[3]

Equi's political leanings prior to the 1913 strike could best be described as Progressive. She had previously volunteered with a group of physicians who traveled to San Francisco to help out after the 1906 earthquake. She was also active in the women's suffrage movement in Oregon, which earned women the right to vote in 1912. She was radicalized during the 1913 Oregon Packing Company strike and remained devoted to the IWW after the strike ended. She often spoke at IWW halls and raised money for the Everett Defense Fund in 1916. Equi was also the Oregon delegate chosen to distribute a portion of Joe Hill's ashes after his execution in November 1915, which shows how well she was regarded

Marie Equi, Oregon Historical
Society, bb002610.

by the organization despite her status as a self-employed professional.
Equi worked with men and women of all stripes and provided abortions
to the women of Portland. She charged on a sliding scale, depending
on the wealth of the patient, although some former comrades recalled
that she would provide procedures for no charge if the woman couldn't
pay. She was never arrested for this work, as the authorities in Portland
tended to turn a blind eye to the procedure during this period.[4]

    As a radical and a physician, Equi took a leading role in the move-
ment in Portland to provide access to information about birth control
to working-class women. Radicals, including the IWW, dominated the
push for wider access to information about birth control during the
early stages of the movement. Activists specifically tied birth control
to economic issues and advocated its necessity if the working class was
ever to be emancipated. Historian Linda Gordon has argued that early
advocates believed "that birth control could alleviate much human misery and fundamentally alter social and political power relations, thereby

creating greater sexual and class equality." Equi, Emma Goldman, and Margaret Sanger are all examples of women who advanced this argument. Sanger organized for the IWW in the Paterson strike of 1913, and Wobblies helped distribute *Family Limitation*, her first pamphlet to give explicit information on birth control methods.[5]

Equi's birth control advocacy was inseparable from her support of the IWW. The IWW, like Equi, advocated birth control as a class issue. Well-planned families would reduce the number of people in the working population, lead to healthier and more well-cared-for children, and free women from the burden of a large family. An article in the *Industrial Worker* in 1911 argued, "Many women are 'stuffed' with the 'dope' that it is God's will to have all the children possible. If God wants them he should have sense enough to tell them where to find employment and where to decently live." The author then linked the issue to economics: "Large families are good things for the boss as they give him a surplus of starving slaves to draw on in case of strikes besides furnishing the army with targets to be shot at."[6] Restricting access to birth control information was, in this view, a tool of the employing class to keep the working class down.[7]

Although more male voices could be heard proclaiming the economic benefits of birth control in IWW newspapers, female agitators were more interested in women's emancipation. Margaret Sanger, Caroline Nelson, and Elizabeth Gurley Flynn all promoted birth control education in speeches in Wobbly halls all over the country. Margaret Sanger's earliest publication advocating birth control, a journal called *The Woman Rebel*, printed the preamble to the IWW constitution in every issue. According to Linda Gordon, *The Woman Rebel* was an attempt by Sanger "to combine her IWW-influenced commitment to direct action with her deepened feminism and sense of the radical potential of birth control." After the journal was suppressed in 1915, Sanger wrote *Family Limitation*, which, unlike *The Woman Rebel*, gave specific information on how to prevent pregnancy instead of just advocating that the information should be available. *Family Limitation* did not as explicitly tie birth control to economic emancipation in the way that the earlier journal had, but by providing detailed information about preventing contraception, it was much more useful to working-class women. IWW member Bill Shatoff printed one hundred thousand copies to be distributed by IWW locals across the country.[8]

Elizabeth Gurley Flynn wrote frequently about birth control in IWW journals. She lectured throughout the country, and one of her most popular talks was titled, "Small Families—A Working-Class Necessity." In an article on the case of Margaret Sanger, Flynn praised Sanger's work for birth control education and asked for contributions to her defense fund. Flynn advocated and explained Sanger's view:

> [Sanger] urges the women of the working-class to decide the conditions of their maternity and to refuse to bring more children into the world than can be properly fed, clothed, housed and educated. She advises the workers to cease hampering themselves in strikes and class battles, with a large number of helpless, hungry children and to refuse to furnish an overproduction of slaves—food for mine and loom, prostitution, prison and cannon.[9]

Wobbly women's support for birth control was in evidence during the Paterson strike in 1913. Almost two thousand silk workers in Paterson, New Jersey, the majority of them female, were on strike for better wages and conditions. As in the Lawrence textile strike of 1912, the IWW helped connect and encourage grassroots leadership of the strike. Italian Wobbly organizer Carlo Tresca addressed a crowd of strikers and made a comment about shorter hours, and husbands and wives being able to spend more time together, and jokingly said, "More babies." The crowd was not amused, and Bill Haywood stepped in and said, "No, Carlo, we believe in birth control—a few babies, well cared for!" To that the crowd responded with cheers.[10]

Marie Equi met Margaret Sanger when Sanger came to visit Portland, a city that Linda Gordon described as "a strong IWW city that was a veritable hotbed of birth-control fervor."[11] Equi was at the center of this agitation. When Sanger visited in June 1916, Equi used her medical knowledge to revise Sanger's *Family Limitation* pamphlet for accuracy.[12] Equi also directed this message to the working class in her inscription for the Portland version: "This edition is made chiefly for union men and women. It is placed in their hands with the sincere wish that it may help in realizing the ideals of union labor. We believe it will aid in the emancipation of women and help to bring better working class conditions."[13] Equi tied the aims of the pamphlet to those of the IWW, and to the broader labor movement.

But despite Portland's reputation as a center of birth control activism, distributing "obscene" material was still illegal. While Sanger was visiting the city, three men were arrested for selling *Family Limitation*: Carl Rave, C. L. Jenkins, and Ralph Chervin. A rally took place in their defense, and at that time Equi, Sanger, and several other Portland women were arrested. The arrests for distributing birth control information caused nationwide controversy. Angry letters poured in from around the country vilifying Portland mayor H. Russell Albee for the arrests. Albee's reply noted that he had nothing against birth control itself, but that the pamphlet being passed out in Portland contained "paragraphs presenting matters concerning sex relations in a manner which makes said relations appear to the young as not only necessary, but beautifying to a young woman" and that it gave "entire pages to explanation of the joy and pleasure of cohabitation, its beautifying effect and pleasant result on women, explanation as to how to increase the pleasure and enjoyment of same, etc."[14] The ruling of the City of Portland echoed Albee's viewpoint:

> Personally I am not opposed to the so-called family limita-
> tion or birth control. . . . But because pages 5, 11, and 13
> of the pamphlet sold and distributed by the defendants,
> contain matter wholly foreign to the question of birth
> control, but deal with the act of copulation in such a man-
> ner as to be offensive to the chastity and modesty of the
> average man or woman, and this pamphlet containing the
> objectionable matter just above referred to, if falling into
> the hands of the young of either sex, or even into the hands
> of persons of more advanced years, produces thoughts
> of impure and libidinous character, and would have the
> tendency to deprave and corrupt those minds that would be
> open to immoral influences, and might easily be calculated
> to excite impure desires.[15]

Thus according to Albee and the court, the problem was not birth control, but that the pamphlet encouraged women to take control of their own sex lives. Authorities were aware of the popularity of birth control and that denying access to information was a losing battle. They could still, however, defer to public morality where matters of sex education were concerned. The defendants were all found guilty, but only the men were fined, and that fine was waived.

The radical push for birth control peaked in 1916, for during the war years many radicals, such as Equi, focused on antiwar activities instead. The information espoused by Sanger and Equi no doubt continued to make the rounds among women, but the public speeches and massive pamphlet distribution were limited. Equi continued to provide access to abortion and birth control for the next decade, though her ability to do so was restricted by her legal troubles stemming from her political and antiwar beliefs. Margaret Sanger continued to push for access to birth control information, but began to work more with professional physicians, no longer advocating birth control as a tool of working-class emancipation.

Equi's antiwar beliefs led her to join the American Union Against Militarism. When the city of Portland held a Preparedness Day Parade on June 3, 1916, Equi drove her car to the parade route with a banner that read "Prepare to Die, Workingmen, J.P. Morgan & Co. Want Preparedness for Profit, 'Thou Shalt Not Kill.'" The pro-preparedness marchers rushed the car, tore down the banner, and used it to attack Equi. The altercation between Equi and the men from the parade led to her arrest, as well as the arrest of two of the men she was arguing with. She was released later that day. She was involved in many other antiwar actions, including protesting a group of wealthy women who were campaigning around the country in 1916 for Republican presidential candidate Charles Evans Hughes on the basis of his pro-suffrage beliefs. Hughes was also pro-war, which Equi felt made Wilson the lesser of two evils as a presidential candidate.[16]

What led to her eventual imprisonment, however, was a speech Equi made at the Portland IWW hall on June 27, 1918. Officials alleged that during her speech Equi argued that

> it was against the IWW platform . . . to injure or kill another fellow worker but if it was necessary to do this, to gain their rights that she for one and every man or woman packing a red card . . . would be willing to sacrifice all they had, their life if need be, for the cause of industrial freedom.[17]

Equi continued that "the Irish Revolutionists now had a chance to throw off their master . . . while he was weak and unable to stop them, and that the Irish were taking advantage of this condition and were asserting their rights, and that the IWWs . . . should do likewise."[18] Employees of the Military Intelligence Bureau testified that they heard Equi speak these words, and accused her of calling members of the military "scum," which she denied.[19]

After Equi's arrest on June 30, 1918, her ten-thousand-dollar bail was furnished by local friends. Equi's supporters were much wealthier than Olivereau's, and this sum was not difficult to come by. She did not even spend a night in jail before her release. She then began a long road of a trial and ensuing appeals and requests for commutations of her sentence. From the day of her arrest, over two years and three months elapsed before Equi began serving her sentence. During that time the war ended and the hysteria of the Red Scare had begun to die down.[20]

Equi's personal life has always been fodder for speculation by both her allies and detractors, and this continued during her trial. She was rumored to be linked romantically to many different women she had been friends with in her lifetime. Many of these relationships were mutually shared affections, and some were platonic friendships. Equi's longest-lasting and most well-documented relationship was with Harriet Speckart. In 1915 Equi and Speckart adopted a girl, whom they named Mary, though she was raised primarily by Harriet. Harriet had moved to Seaside, Oregon, by the late teens and was raising Mary there, although she still made appearances during Equi's trial and corresponded regularly with her during her imprisonment. Speckart and Equi continued their relationship for twenty years, despite the other women in Equi's life, until 1927, when Speckart died after a cerebral hemorrhage.[21]

In addition to her long-term relationship with Speckart, several other notable women were important figures in Equi's life. She was rumored to have been intimate with Margaret Sanger, lived with Elizabeth Gurley Flynn for a number of years in the 1920s, and, during the war years, developed a romantic relationship with Kathleen O'Brennan, who ended up playing an important role during Equi's trial and subsequent appeals.[22] O'Brennan was an Irish nationalist, born in Ireland in 1886, and a well-known speaker for the cause; she had come to the United States in October 1914. She arrived in Portland in July 1918, where federal agent William Bryon put her on watch at the request of the FBI in Seattle, where she had previously been living. Bryon believed that O'Brennan's "alleged interest in the freedom of Ireland [was] merely a subterfuge to permit her to go about the country, living off the misguided contributions of others."[23] O'Brennan was well known for supporting the Irish cause, but a spy, later revealed to be Margaret Paul, a friend of O'Brennan and Equi, reported that Equi radicalized O'Brennan and that, as their relationship developed, O'Brennan started focusing more and more on the labor question. Equi and O'Brennan spent a significant amount of time together during Equi's trial, and O'Brennan organized much of her support and publicity.[24]

Whereas Louise Olivereau defended herself, Marie Equi had IWW attorney George Vanderveer presenting her case. Vanderveer had defended the Wobblies on trial in Chicago and so had considerable experience in cases of this nature. Equi's defense argued that she had not used the words ascribed to her and that her speech had not intended to cause harm. Vanderveer instructed the jury to ignore whether she had spoken at IWW halls or spoken to audiences that consisted primarily of Wobblies, because such an act was not illegal and so was irrelevant to her case. The defense also argued that Equi's actions at the preparedness parade occurred before the United States joined the war, and therefore were not illegal. The prosecution argued that Equi's statements were made with the intent "to interfere with the operation and success of the military and naval forces of the United States." The prosecution would therefore have to prove that those eligible for the draft or already drafted had been present at her speech. While Olivereau's trial focused on philosophical issues and freedom of speech, Equi's defense team wanted to prove that she had not said anything seditious.[25]

Department of Justice special agent William Bryon was in charge of building the prosecution's case against Equi, and he did not take pains to hide his contempt for her. In his reports he accused Equi of being possessed "with a criminal paranoia for martyrdom" and in other instances referred to her as a vampire sucking money away from the AFL and IWW. In one of his reports Bryon observed that Equi's plea for executive clemency held signatures of several physicians whose loyalty to the government had never been questioned. He could not comprehend that they might support Equi's case on its own merit, and reasoned that blackmail could be the only explanation. He concluded,

"These signatures are attached through no reason in the world only fear of knowledge in the possession of this woman, direct or indirect, of violations of law or ethics in the medical profession. There can to the mind of this agent be no other solution or explanation."[26] It is possible that Bryon could have been referencing the practice of providing abortions to patients.

The bad blood between Bryon and Equi was so deep that it led to a physical altercation after her initial sentencing in December 1918. Equi claimed that Bryon struck her with his fist, and witnesses reported, "Bryon pushed Dr. Equi out of his way when she attempted to intercept him and that he threw his hand back and as vigorously shoved Mrs. Speckart to the floor when she tried to pull him from Equi." Bryon made no apologies for his actions, and said that Equi had previously threatened him so he was justified in believing she meant to do him harm. After the shove, Equi "heaped her vituperation on Bryon in torrents" and allegedly threatened that her brother would be in town soon and he would kill Bryon. During Equi's subsequent appeal for clemency, Bryon reported that if she did not go to prison "the result would sow one of the worst seeds, if not the very worst seed of anarchy that has ever been sown on the Pacific Coast."[27]

The federal authorities were determined to convict Equi, and her Department of Justice files are filled with reports after her arrest and before her imprisonment. One set of reports was made by Margaret Lowell Paul, who posed as a friend of Equi and whom she met through Kathleen O'Brennan. Paul, listed as "Informant #53" in her reports, seemed to be close to the two women. She was often in Equi's hotel room or taking meals with the two of them, mostly around October of 1918. According to Agent Bryon, Paul was a supporter of Irish freedom and was introduced to O'Brennan by fellow Irish nationalist Thomas Mannix, an attorney in Portland. Paul and O'Brennan discussed the Irish situation for a few days, and O'Brennan eventually introduced her to Equi.[28]

By December 1918, Equi and O'Brennan were aware that Paul was employed by the government. O'Brennan announced that Equi had suspected all along that Paul was with the secret service, but O'Brennan had not believed her. O'Brennan asserted that when Paul became ill and was nursed back to health by Equi, Paul "was so affected by Dr. Equi's kind treatment that she broke down and cried, and confessed that she was in the employ of the Department of Justice; that Dr. Equi had no chance of a fair trial and that she was bound to be convicted." Paul then told Equi that if Equi gave her two thousand dollars, Paul would take it to Haney [the district attorney] and the charges would be dropped.[29] According to Paul's reports, Vanderveer called her out as an agent on November 18, though she suspected they had known for a few days prior. Paul sat through the whole trial, and reported that Equi and Vanderveer were both friendly. Equi boasted that she knew all along Paul was an agent, but "of course from the evidence she gave to me against herself, there seems little likelihood of the truth of this statement." Even if Equi had known all along, it was not apparent to everyone in Equi's circle that Paul was a spy, an example of how well government agents could blend in to radical circles.[30]

Although O'Brennan was the friend who brought the spy into Equi's inner circle, she was also Equi's biggest public proponent. While facing deportation for her radical activities, she still came to Equi's aid and, in 1919, distributed a pamphlet titled *Workers Unite* that outlined Equi's case. The pamphlet was released in the summer of 1919 to gain support for the appeals in her case. In the pamphlet, O'Brennan denounced Paul as a "second rate actress" who was "lazy and luxurious of the truly parasitical type." O'Brennan stated that, after the defendant became aware Paul was a spy, Paul "broke down, confessed, and begged for mercy." The pamphlet accused the government of using additional underhanded methods to get evidence of sedition by Equi. O'Brennan alleged that the two men who gave evidence of Equi's seditious statements at the Wobbly hall, Sitton Linville and James P. Brady, were "employees of the Military Intelligence Bureau at Portland, Oregon and evidently tools of the lumber interests." She charged that they were ordered to "get" Equi and find, or make up, evidence against her. The two men dressed as workingmen and "carried cards in a working-class organization."[31]

Equi's supporters and the authorities told conflicting tales of a young woman who tried to discredit Linville and Brady's testimony against Equi. According to O'Brennan, Linville told a young Portland woman that he and Brady had orders to "get the doctor," and if it would not be for her speech at the hall, they would get her on something else. "Outraged at this method of hunting and downing 'selected' victims, this young woman voluntarily went on the stand and testified to the statements of Linville." After her testimony against the two agents, the woman was arrested and held for sixty-five days. After release "she was practically hounded out of Portland by secret service agents."[32]

Agent Bryon told a very different version of these events. He claimed a twenty-two- or twenty-three-year-old woman named Llewellen, "a reform school girl and natural outlaw," waited outside his office and "made it her business to be friendly with this agent."[33] He was suspicious of the woman's intentions and asked Brady and Linville if they had any association with her. When Brady took the witness stand, the prosecution asked if he was "clear of any entanglement," romantic or personal, to which he replied in the affirmative but then, under cross-examination by George Vanderveer, "admitted the contrary when confronted by the Llewellen woman."[34] Bryon reported that Llewellen was also known by the name Beryl Grayson, and he accused O'Brennan of paying Grayson to discredit the witnesses in Equi's case and that the payment was authorized during a recent IWW meeting. Bryon and the federal government clearly went to great lengths to discredit Equi and anyone around her. Evidently something was fishy about Agent Bryon, for he was asked to resign in August of 1921. The official report listed lack of funds for his position, but the *Oregonian* surmised that it was because of the unpopularity of decisions in several high profile Espionage Act cases during the war.[35]

Against the power of the state and overzealous agents like Bryon, Equi had the support of the IWW and O'Brennan. In addition, she drew on a much broader base than many other Wobblies during this period. Former Oregon governor Oswald West even testified on her behalf. Federal agent no. 18 reported in July of 1918 that "from present indications, the AFL Unions will come to the assistance of Dr. Equi (IWW) as she had given a great deal of her time to collecting funds for the Mooney defense and Pres. Hartwig of the State Federation of Labor has promised to get the different organizations to assist her."[36] In October of that year, the Equi Defense Committee, authorized by the State Federation of Labor and the Central Labor Council, visited various AFL locals to give details on her case and try to raise funds. During her trial Vanderveer noted that most of her expenses were paid by the AFL, and only partly by the IWW. The Oregon State Federation of Labor passed a resolution condemning Special Agent William Bryon and calling for an investigation into Equi's case. The resolution pointed to the altercation between Equi and Byron after her sentencing as evidence of his prejudice in the case. Not long after its convention, the Pacific Coast Metal

Trades Association also condemned Byron's actions. While Olivereau had trouble securing even local Wobbly support, Equi received funds and publicity from the IWW and AFL-affiliated unions.[37]

Although Equi's trial was not a rallying point for the IWW nationally, locally the organization did help her cause. According to Charles Reams, an informant who was undercover as a member of the organization, handbills advertising meetings in support of Equi were funded and organized by the IWW, even though they were published under the name of the Socialist Party. Joe Thornton, a Wobbly, was the chairman of the Dr. Equi Defense Committee.[38]

As Minnie Parkhurst had done for Olivereau, O'Brennan organized a publicity campaign in support of Equi. Unlike Olivereau, O'Brennan and Equi had much more powerful connections, and O'Brennan was able to gather Equi's middle- and upper-class allies in support of the case. Equi's status in Portland meant that her backers had more access to funds and publicity. In 1918, while advertising mass meetings to raise funds for her defense, supporters were able to take out large ads in the *Oregonian*, the Portland *Evening Journal*, and the Portland *Daily News*. Paul reported that she and O'Brennan purchased the ad in the *Oregonian* for forty-two dollars—which is highly likely much more than Parkhurst had to spend on advertising meetings in support of Olivereau. Equi told Paul contradictory stories about who paid for the *Journal* and *News* advertisements, once stating that it was the State Federation of Labor, and another time saying it was the IWW. Although the IWW was supportive of Equi, it is likely that the AFL had much more funding available to help pay for things like publicity expenses.[39]

The mass meeting that they were advertising took place on December 5, 1918, at Arion Hall. The speakers were Dr. C. H. Chapman, Kathleen O'Brennan, H. M. Wicks, and James Robinson. Secret service agent W. E. Hudson described the attendees with disgust as "men with ill-smelling breaths; foreigners, cripples and degenerates." This was the same meeting in which O'Brennan outed Paul as an informant. It is quite possible that Equi helped many of these men's wives or girlfriends at some point, which could explain their loyalty to "Doc," as many of them called Equi.[40]

After a lengthy wait, Equi's appeal was heard in San Francisco circuit appeals court in June 1919. During her appeal, prominent Portland attorney and radical C. E. S. Wood argued that the sedition laws

Marie Equi, while imprisoned
at San Quentin, 1921. Oregon
Historical Society, bb013178.

were unconstitutional. Equi was out on bond at the time of her appeal
and was "accompanied by six women said to be prominent in IWW
activities in the Pacific Northwest."[41] Her sentence of three years and a
five-hundred-dollar fine was upheld on October 27. The Supreme Court
of the United States upheld the lower court's decision on January 26,
1920. At that point, Senator James D. Phelan of California delivered a
petition to President Wilson asking for a presidential pardon for Equi.
Wilson granted her two stays of execution of her sentence; both were
protested by the American Legion in Oregon. Wilson finally commuted
her sentence October 13, 1920, reducing it from three years to one year
and one day. She was originally ordered to serve her sentence on Mc-
Neil's Island in Washington, but because of the lack of accommodations
there for women, she was sent to San Quentin in northern California
instead. She surrendered herself to the court in Portland on October 15,
1920, amid several friends and photographers, to await transportation

to California. A mass meeting was held at the Machinist's Hall on October 17 to discuss her case, and a resolution protesting her conviction was sent to President Wilson.[42]

Equi entered San Quentin on October 19, 1920, more than two years after her original arrest, and was released on August 9, 1921. She continued to reside in San Francisco for a few weeks after her sentence ended in order to take care of some of the prisoners at San Quentin with whom she had become acquainted during her stay. As did Olivereau, Equi spoke on prison reform and continued to support her fellow San Quentin prisoners shortly after her release, and moved back to Portland.[43]

Unlike Olivereau, Equi did maintain some ties with the radical community after her release. Elizabeth Gurley Flynn moved in with Equi in Portland in 1926 to recuperate after a mental and physical breakdown. She stayed for ten years. Flynn had several relationships with men throughout her life, but during this period, according to Flynn's biographer, Rosalynn Baxandall, Flynn's family thought Flynn and Equi were lovers and tried to separate the two. Equi's biographer, Michael Helquist, found no direct evidence of a sexual relationship between the two and writes that "Flynn's feelings for Equi, at least those evidenced in her journal and correspondence with others, suggest more of a respectful collaboration, a sense of obligation, and an appreciation for her care and assistance rather than a romantic or sexual attraction."[44] Regardless of its nature, the relationship was a difficult one for both women, and Flynn finally left in the 1930s. The two did not keep in touch after that point. Baxandall writes that Flynn found the Portland years with Equi some of the most difficult of her life.[45] This was not made public, as Flynn's first autobiography, which was written in the 1950s but only covered her life until the early 1920s, did not mention her tumultuous relationship with Equi. She had only kind words to say about Equi and how Equi had helped her and other radicals who came to Portland. She wrote that Equi "was among the most feared and hated women in the Northwest because of her outspoken criticisms of politicians, industrialists, so-called civic leaders and all who oppressed the poor. She was loved and cherished by masses of plain people."[46] Equi's forceful personality was well-documented, so it is likely that there was some difficulty during their time together, although Flynn would not have wanted to make that public.

Despite living with one of the most famous female agitators of the 1910s, Equi's public life was fairly quiet through the 1920s. Nancy

Krieger attributes Equi's lack of political activity after her release to her age, health, and the conservative climate of the time. Similar to Olivereau, Equi reentered a world where the friendships and camaraderie she had known within the radical community of the Pacific Northwest had largely vanished. Equi suffered a heart attack in 1930, which severely limited her mobility, though she did make a few public appearances in the 1930s to support the striking waterfront workers. She died in Portland on July 12, 1952, at the age of eighty.[47]

Marie Equi denied until the end of her life that she had called men serving in the military "scum," but she did not deny her role denouncing the war in the preparedness parade and the later meeting at the Wobbly hall. Equi was confrontational and controversial. Accustomed to and fortified by the public spotlight, she had many loyal followers, and many friends in high places. Her trial, rather than focusing on her philosophy or issues of free speech, instead became as dramatic as Equi herself, denouncing people as spies and accusing government agents of framing her.

Equi had many Progressive allies, and she received more help from the Wobblies than Olivereau. Equi, as a physician, was useful to the IWW. She examined the bodies of the Everett victims, provided information about birth control, and provided care to working-class patients. From working-class men to the Oregon State Federation of Labor to wealthy Portlanders, Equi had a cross-class appeal that Olivereau did not. Despite her transgressive sexuality and radical politics, the practical nature of her support for working-class men and women by providing medical care endeared her to both Wobblies and members of the AFL, who supported her throughout her trial. Middle- and upperclass women also likely utilized Equi's services, and knew the value of a physician willing to break the law to serve her patients. Though not a Wobbly herself, Marie Equi symbolized the organization for many people in Portland, and she was one its most steadfast allies. That she also retired from activism shortly after her imprisonment is testament to the difficulties the radical community faced during and after the war as it lost many of its loudest voices to prison.

Conclusion
The Decline of the Wobbly Community in the Pacific Northwest,
1920–1924

In this book I have shown that although the single, male, migratory workers of the lumber camps and harvest fields made up the majority of IWW membership in the Pacific Northwest, to focus entirely on their experiences ignores the male and female Wobblies in the cities and towns of the Pacific Northwest who had homes and families. They too were attracted to the IWW and played an essential role in the functioning of a radical community in the region. The division between the "hobo" Wobblies and the "family" Wobblies comes into stark relief when examining how each group fared during the difficult war years. Although the Wobblies as a labor union gained one of their biggest successes in the lumber strike during the war and were successful in organizing agricultural workers in the early 1920s, the Wobblies working in cities and small towns lost Wobbly halls that had previously functioned as community centers. Those Wobblies with families, both male and female, faced a much bigger risk in breaking the law, and some found that the Wobbly leadership did not prioritize supporting the families of those sentenced to prison.

Two events in the postwar years that were paramount for Northwest radicals were the Seattle General Strike and the Centralia Massacre. On February 6, 1919, workers in Seattle went on strike. The strike involved about 60,000 workers out of a total population of 315,000. Strikers organized to serve food, staff hospitals, and keep peace in the streets during the week-long strike. In Harvey O'Connor's memoir, *Revolution in Seattle*, he noted that although newspapers across the country blamed Wobblies and Bolsheviks for the insurgence, "their only participation, besides sympathetic support, occurred when IWW members also held AFL cards." Nonetheless, IWW halls were again raided in the aftermath of the strike.[1]

More directly affecting the union was the Centralia Massacre. The IWW first opened a hall in Centralia, a small logging town between Portland and Seattle, in the spring of 1918. As happened elsewhere, the hall was raided by a mob during a Red Cross parade in May 1918. Windows were smashed, records destroyed, and Wobblies beaten. The Wobblies were then driven out of town and warned not to return. They left Centralia for more than a year, until Britt Smith opened a new hall in September 1919. Smith was a local, born in a town not far from Centralia, and had worked in logging camps for twenty years. He found space to rent on the ground floor of the Roderick Hotel—frequented by loggers—and moved in on September 1.[2]

The first annual celebration of the armistice, on November 11, 1919, was filled with patriotic celebrations in cities and towns throughout the country. A parade was planned for Centralia, which included the American Legion, veterans, Boy Scouts, Red Cross, Salvation Army, and Elks Lodges. The Armistice Day parade was scheduled to march directly past the IWW hall. The Wobblies, worried that something might happen, sought assurance from local law officials that the hall would be protected. When no law officials came, they decided to defend it on their own. The Wobblies issued a circular to the "law-abiding citizens of Centralia and to the working class in general" to denounce those who planned to raid the hall and proclaim their innocence of any wrongdoing. They also visited a lawyer, Elmer Smith, and asked what their legal rights were if there was an attack on the hall. He told them they had the legal right to defend themselves with force if under attack with no protection from the law.[3]

The Centralia Wobblies then formulated a plan to defend themselves and procured weapons. On the day of the parade, seven men were stationed in the hall, four of them armed. Others were stationed in hotels near the hall. Several hundred marchers walked by the hall, but as the final group of uniformed veterans approached, the man leading them called for them to halt and close up ranks. A moment later, a small contingent of veterans marched on the hall and broke down the door. That's when the shooting started, with three legionnaires fatally wounded.

When the Wobblies inside the hall realized that their gunfire was not deterring those attacking the hall, they fled. Most of them hid in the hall or nearby, but Wesley Everest made his way out into an alley and shot at two veterans who started to follow him. He continued to shoot at his pursuers, though he was eventually captured when he tried to reload. A mob followed Everest to the jail, where a rope was tied around his neck and hung to a pole before one prominent citizen talked the crowd out of lynching him. Everest was then put in a cell. But the mob was not entirely quelled. Later that night, men surrounded the jail, and someone shut off power to the town. They broke into the jail, grabbed Everest, and put him a car waiting outside. The took him to a bridge that crossed the Chehalis River and hung him, shooting the body roughly twenty times once the deed was done.[4]

All the Wobblies associated with the Centralia hall were arrested during the week following the massacre, and eleven were finally indicted for the murder of Warren Grimm, the American Legion post commander killed in the initial shoot-out. Those indicted included Elmer Smith, the Wobbly lawyer, who had not been involved in the actual confrontation at the hall. George Vanderveer was secured as council. The courthouse was packed with armed Legionnaires, who were paid four dollars a day to attend. There was even a troop of federal soldiers stationed on the front lawn of the courthouse, to "protect" the court and jury from a Wobbly invasion. Vanderveer argued that the Wobblies were victims of a conspiracy among business interests in Centralia and had fired in self-defense, after requesting—and not receiving—protection from the police. The prosecution argued that the Wobblies fired on a peaceful march and that there had been no attack on the hall. While Vanderveer produced several witnesses stating that the hall had been attacked, and that they had heard discussions of a plan to wreck the hall, the judge ruled that the defense could not try to prove a business conspiracy to prove the homicide justifiable unless they could tie Grimm directly to the conspiracy.[5]

The judge did not give the jury the option of finding the men innocent. He argued that since some of the men were stationed outside of the hall, they could not be acting in self-defense. The jury had the choice of murder in the first or murder in the second degree for all the defendants with the exception of Elmer Smith, the lawyer. The jury ignored his orders and found two of the men not guilty, one insane, two guilty of manslaughter, and the rest of murder in the second degree. The judge didn't accept it, and they came back with a new verdict: one defendant insane, two not guilty, and the rest guilty of murder in the second degree. The jury also recommended leniency, which the judge ignored, giving them all the maximum sentence, twenty-five to forty years. The men remained in prison until 1933.[6]

As the Wobblies dealt locally with the Centralia case and continued arrests of members, appeals continued in the Chicago and Sacramento cases, though they ended in April 1921, when the United States Supreme Court refused to look at the cases. Forty-six Wobblies were released on bail during the appeals process, the foremost being Big Bill Haywood. Instead of returning to prison, Haywood jumped bail and headed for Soviet Russia. This was a shock to many of his supporters. Mary Marcy, a Socialist intellectual, editor of the *International Socialist Review*, and member of the IWW, put up her home as guarantee and lost it when Haywood fled to Russia, which was reportedly the cause of her suicide in 1922. Some viewed Haywood's escape to Russia as the betrayal of those who put in their hard-earned money and property for his bail. This could have led some to become frustrated with Wobbly leadership and disengage themselves from the union, even if they still supported the Wobblies in workplace issues.[7]

Early historians of the IWW pointed to the postwar period as the demise of the organization. More recently Greg Hall has successfully argued that the immediate postwar years did not destroy the IWW entirely, but led to increases in membership of agricultural workers. But a marked decline occurred in 1924, caused by conflicts within the organization around three major debates: centralization versus decentralization, what kind of relationship the IWW should have with the Communist Party in the United States and the Third Communist International (established by Lenin and headquartered in Moscow, also known as the Comintern), and the issue of executive clemency for those imprisoned during the war.[8]

The three issues were actually intertwined. The union members known as centralists wanted more centralized power for the General Executive Board in Chicago. The decentralists thought the power should reside at each individual union local. Many of the centralists were jailed during the war, as the government targeted the national leadership. This left the decentralists the majority on the outside. The Third International existed to foment worldwide Communist revolution. The centralist Wobblies tended to be friendlier to the Third International.

The decentralists wanted nothing to do with them, and so the question of the relationship with Russia, and with the newfound Communist Party in the United States, led to a split in the organization. The anti-Bolshevik group was headed by C. E. Payne and headquartered in Everett, Washington. Personal antagonisms deepened the antipathy on both sides and resulted in the 1924 split of the IWW into two groups.[9]

Historians have argued that, in addition to disagreements within the organization, the Wobbly decline after WWI was also a result of changing social status of workers. Workers in lumber and agriculture became more stable, more "home guard" than "hobo," and thus the Wobbly life did not appeal to them. Greg Hall blames the decline of the IWW as less a result of that disillusionment after the split and more of the Wobblies' inability to recognize and adapt to the changing migrant workforce. Hall argues that the harvest Wobblies "could not or would not break free of their own worklife culture to articulate a meaningful message" to the newer groups of workers that, in California especially, included Latino workers and families. In the Northwest, more and more agricultural workers were single women and families working for summer to supplement their income. The Wobbly organizer who had focused on hobo jungles and riding the rails to draw single male workers into the union in the beginning had no resonance with these new workers. More and more workers traveled to job sites in cars, and therefore did not need a red card to ride the rails. According to Hall, the union's inability to adapt to this changing workforce, combined with continued repression and changing agricultural technology, led to the decline of the IWW in the 1920s.[10]

The changing nature of the workforce may have played a role in the organization's decline, but as I have shown in previous chapters, the IWW did appeal to many "home guard" family men and women before the war, and so we must also look at other explanations. Foremost among these must be the repression during wartime, which made attending meetings or social gatherings a dangerous activity. The Wobbly hall ceased to function as a family-friendly center that built solidarity in the cities and towns of the Northwest. The repression may have also led to a sense of disillusionment, as male and female Wobblies who were subject to arrest and long-term imprisonment during the war often felt that their actions had little effect in changing the outcome of the war, and some felt betrayed by IWW leadership that did not appreciate their sacrifice. Therefore the lessons of the family-friendly prewar organization were lost. With few exceptions, such as the Finnish Wobblies in Grays Harbor, although the organization continued to survive, the "family-friendly" aspect of the IWW community suffered a marked decline during this period.[11]

The case of Pacific Northwest Wobbly organizer E. F. Doree provides one example of how his frustration with IWW leadership mounted during his long imprisonment, caused by what he perceived as the lack of concern over the well-being of his wife and child. Doree's disillusionment hinged on the issue of commutation of the jail sentences for imprisoned Wobblies. Each individual Wobbly, in jail or out, faced tough decisions during the years following the raids and repression of 1917. Although official reports, newspaper articles, and spy reports can give us part of the story, we are left guessing what many individuals and their families felt about these circumstances. Fortunately, Ellen Doree Rosen, Doree's daughter, compiled and published the letters her father wrote to her mother, Ida, during his stay in Leavenworth Penitentiary in Kansas. The letters paint a picture of a very committed and equal partnership between husband and wife, and also divulge some of the internal struggles of the organization during this period.

Edwin F. Doree was born in Philadelphia in 1889, though his family moved to the Northwest not long after. At the age of sixteen he lost two fingers on his left hand in an industrial accident working on the railroad and was promptly fired from his job. His daughter later surmised that this event radicalized him, and he joined the IWW in 1906 in Spokane, just a year after the accident. He left the organization after a few months, dreaming of a career as a professional baseball player. After another injury forced him to abandon that idea, he joined the IWW again in 1910 and became an organizer shortly after. He met his wife Ida in 1914 while organizing textile workers, of which she was one, in New York. They had their first child, Frederick, referred to by Doree as "Bucky Boy," in Philadelphia in 1916.[12]

The letters between Ed and Ida amplify what is hinted at when reading newspaper reports of Wobbly husband and wife teams organizing, street speaking, and getting arrested together: that they were in a committed, loving, and respectful relationship. Barring a few stray remarks warning Ida to watch her weight, Ed constantly wrote about how much he loved and missed his wife and son during their years apart and told her to do what she thought was right in regard to publicity for his case. He undertook an informal study of his fellow prisoners and found that "rebel wives" were more loyal than average:

> I was informed by those who are in a position to know that 81 percent of the prisoners who come here with sentence of three years or more, lost their wives by divorce or desertion. These figures struck me as a poor average for love. Then I set to gather the data on so-called "reds" and find that of the 64 married ones located, who had three years' sentence or more (and most of whom had been in confinement more than three years already) that only four had their wives desert them, or, that is less than 6 ½ percent of their wives had proved lacking in that love that lives.[13]

He then turned his study toward a critique of those who feared Wobbly morality was a threat to "American values":

> And I must say again that we have wonderful little women, the best on earth. And, they say that we would break up their homes, and they are afraid. They have tried their darndest to break up ours, and can't. They say we would break up the family and we have builded [sic] unbreakable families. Separate the average couple today and in three years time, nearly all love has flown, but separate the "despised red" couples and they move heaven and earth to come together, contemplating a greater love.[14]

For all the attention paid to unconventional Wobbly views on love and marriage, in trials from Spokane onward to Doree and his fellow inmates, a commitment to the free choice of association did not lead to desertion or to weaker families but instead strengthened the bond of committed Wobbly partnerships.[15]

Doree was one of the imprisoned Wobblies hoping for his sentence to be commuted on an individual basis, as opposed to those who felt that no Wobbly should be released until they were all set free. From his letters, it is evident that he was more concerned about taking care of his family than in showing solidarity with the other jailed Wobblies. By June 1921, Doree was discussing in his letters the split between prisoners over which course of action to take. The "resolutionist" group favored a proposal that resolved that no Wobbly should accept commutation unless all were free. Doree also referred to this group as "die-hards," "irreconcilables," or the "hard-liners." The rest of the jailed Wobblies, referred to by the resolutionists as "clemency hounds," wanted to work on a case-by-case basis, believing that each successful commutation paved the way for the next. Doree told his wife,

> [The] resolution adopted here was . . . a lie on the face of
> it. . . . That is why I did not sign it. It is a negative resolu-
> tion in that it suggests no line of action, it merely condemns
> a particular method. . . . None of those who refused to sign
> would ever ask for their personal freedom at the cost of
> others. To infer that, as the resolution does, is really rotten.[16]

The conflict continued to brew for those still in jail, and some of those released at the end of their five-year sentences campaigned against the "clemency hounds" from the outside. Doree referred to "bitter attacks" of the resolutionists against Roger Baldwin, founder of the American Civil Liberties Union, Elizabeth Gurley Flynn, and other supporters of the clemency cause in Philadelphia. He also noted that the General Membership Board threatened to expel all those asking for clemency and tried to break up defense groups working for the release of individuals.[17]

This controversy turned Doree bitterly against the IWW General Membership Board. Beyond tarnishing the names and reputations of those in jail waiting for clemency, the board also either refused support for their wives or made that financial support difficult. Doree warned Ida to think twice before writing to Chicago for financial aid, for "what they give in cash they collect from one's soul and spirits."[18] The General Defense Committee and Prisoner Comfort Committees throughout the country supplied money to the resolutionists in prison and outfitted them with fifty dollars and a new suit upon release. This support was denied those who applied for clemency.[19] The month before his release, Ed made his feelings clear to Ida:

> You may rest assured that I am done with the IWW. After
> their treatment of you and me, do you think I would so

much as walk across the street to do them a favor? So far
as I am concerned, they can go to hell. . . . Any movement
that becomes dead to human emotions, is dead as it can ever
become.[20]

Although Ed made his contempt open to Ida, he kept it between the
two of them. He did not want to make any public statements denouncing the IWW while he was still imprisoned for fear that he would look
like a coward who was only renouncing the organization for a better
chance at a pardon.[21]

Doree was, in a sense, vindicated in his view by the 1924 IWW
convention, when, after all the sentences had been commuted, hard
feelings still erupted. James P. Cannon, who reported on the proceedings, noted that fifteen of the twenty-six Wobblies still imprisoned in
Leavenworth in 1923 accepted the clemency. At that point the eleven
who did not accept clemency demanded that none of those who did be
allowed to do any work on behalf of class war prisoners. Ralph Chaplin
was the particular target of this group. According to Cannon,

The excellent standing and long-proven revolutionary
integrity of the men involved made their case of concern
to the entire radical labor movement. Any official action to
discredit them and to exclude them from activity would
have been a decidedly reactionary step and would have
produced a most unfavorable impression.[22]

The rest of the convention agreed. Those who accepted commutation
were exonerated, and those who attacked them were condemned. Nonetheless, the harm was done, and neither Doree nor his wife returned to
the IWW.[23]

As my research has shown, women were crucial to the existence and
success of the IWW in the Northwest. The triumphs and failures of the
IWW cannot continue to be judged by the experience of men alone.
Women actively participated in Wobbly issues that reflected the radical
ideals of the organization, such as free speech fights and birth control
agitation. Women interacted with the IWW as a social organization in
the cities, rather than in the lumber camps or agricultural fields where

the migratory male workers were often introduced to the organization. Wobbly halls that had previously functioned as community centers became targets of government officials during the war years. Despite this loss, women continued to support jailed Wobblies and risk arrest themselves. But the continual arrests and repression took its toll. Some members, such as the Doree family, felt that their sacrifices were not appreciated by the national leadership, or even by their friends and fellow workers. Although the Wobbly community continued to exist in pockets of the Northwest, in cities such as Portland, Everett, Seattle, and Spokane the camaraderie and community that existed prior to the war had disappeared.

This is not to say that it disappeared forever. Whereas the decade of the 1920s was a conservative one in the United States, the 1930s proved that radicalism was alive and well. The industrial unionism favored by the IWW was popularized with the formation of the Congress of Industrial Organizations (CIO). The work that women, including Elizabeth Gurley Flynn, did with the Communist Party and individual unions in the 1930s was tremendously important in the tide of unionization sweeping the country. The IWW as an organization did not play a prominent role in the 1930s, but many former Wobblies were involved in different organizations during that time. The existence of the Junior Wobblies, a group of working-class children, complete with their own paper, *The New Recruit*, shows that Wobbly family life was alive and well in some circles during this time. The Junior Wobblies Union was an organization of children of the working class, "learning the rudiments of unionism and disciplining themselves for the final struggle with capitalism." But they also "know how to have good times" while learning to grow up to be good union men and women. The idea of having a good time while waging a war against capitalism was undoubtedly what drew many people to join the IWW. But the solidarity, the sense of community, and the place for women to play active roles in the organization kept them there, until repression and long jail sentences strained those community ties to a breaking point. The spirit of that movement did not die, but hibernated to emerge in a new form in the 1930s, and the contribution of women, begun and exemplified by women in the IWW, was essential to its success.[24]

Acknowledgments

This book has been over a decade in the making, and I have been supported by numerous individuals and organizations along the way.

I would like to thank the archivists and librarians at the archives big and small that I visited during the course of my research, including the Washington State Archives, in Olympia and Cheney, the National Archives in Seattle, the Oregon Historical Society Research Library, City of Portland Archives and Records Center, Special Collections at the Watzek Library at Lewis & Clark College, Special Collections at the University of Washington, and Special Collections at the Water P. Reuther Library at Wayne State University.

I would also like to thank my professors, fellow students, and colleagues at the University of California, Riverside, Simon Fraser University, and Portland Community College. Special thanks goes to my advisor at SFU, Mark Leier, for sticking with me and providing encouragement and advice through a dissertation process that lasted much longer than either of us expected. His critiques and suggestions have been invaluable.

Several of the subjects of this book have been topic of presentations at conferences for the last decade, and I am thankful to the thoughtful comments and encouragement I have received, particularly from members of the Pacific Northwest Labor History Association, and the Labor and Working Class History Association. I am also thankful to my frequent co-presenter and fellow SFU alumni Aaron Goings for his feedback and for having someone to share with this particular obsession with Northwest Wobblies.

This book owes its existence to Mary Elizabeth Braun, the Acquisitions Editor at Oregon State University Press, who expressed interest in the early stages of my research, and has been supportive and encouraging as the book moved towards reality. I would also like to thank the two anonymous reviewers for their thoughtful comments, as well as my copyeditor Susan Campbell for her helpful changes and suggestions. Everyone at OSU Press has been a pleasure to work with.

I would have not been able to see this project to fruition without the tremendous support of my family and friends. My mother Patty, my father Larry, and my brother Tristan supported me (with words and sometimes a place to live) in the early stages of my PhD research. Although my dad is no longer around to see the final version, I know he would be proud.

My husband Tayo has been my rock in the final stages of the dissertation and through all parts of the book. From defending my thesis while pregnant with our son Cameron, to finishing up the book while pregnant with our daughter Maya, I could never have done this without his support and advice. He has been an amazing partner, husband, and father, and Cameron, Maya and I are lucky to have him in our lives.

Notes

INTRODUCTION

1 *Industrial Worker*, July 15, 1909; also cited in Greg Hall, *Harvest Wobblies* (Corvallis: Oregon State University Press, 2001), 46.

2 *Industrial Worker*, July 7, 1917. For a detailed analysis of the radical community in the Grays Harbor area, see Aaron Goings, "Red Harbor: Class, Violence, and Community in Grays Harbor, Washington" (PhD diss., Simon Fraser University, 2011).

3 For examples of works on women and the IWW, see Philip Foner, *Women and the American Labor Movement* (New York: Free Press, 1979); Meredith Tax, *The Rising of the Women* (Urbana: University of Illinois Press, 1980); Ann Schofield, "Rebel Girls and Union Maids," *Feminist Studies* 9, no. 2 (Summer 1983). Local and regional studies include Nigel Sellars, *Oil, Wheat, and Wobblies* (Norman: University of Oklahoma Press, 1998); Peter Cole, *Wobblies on the Waterfront* (Chicago: University of Illinois Press, 2007); Verity Bergmann, *Revolutionary Industrial Unionism* (Cambridge, UK: Cambridge University Press, 1995); and Ardis Cameron, *Radicals of the Worst Sort* (Urbana: University of Illinois Press, 1995). For studies on masculinity and the IWW, see Francis Shor, "'Virile Syndicalism' in Comparative Perspective: A Gender Analysis of the IWW in the United States and Australia," *International Labor and Working-Class History* 56 (1999); Todd Depastino, *Citizen Hobo* (Chicago: University of Chicago Press, 2003); Frank Tobias Higbie, *Indispensable Outcasts* (Urbana: University of Illinois Press, 2003); and Hall, *Harvest Wobblies*.

4 *Industrial Worker*, November 10, 1909.

5 Two great examples are Laurie Mercier, "Reworking Race, Class, and Gender into Pacific Northwest History," *Frontiers* 22, no. 3 (2001); and Elizabeth Jameson, *All That Glitters* (Urbana: University of Illinois Press, 1998).

6 *Industrial Union Bulletin*, April 9, 1907.

7 Mari Jo Buhle, *Women and American Socialism, 1870–1920* (Urbana: University of Illinois Press, 1983), 228.

8 Historians and social scientists often refer to the "politics of respectability" as the movement by African Americans in the early twentieth century to counteract racist stereotypes by promoting "respectable" behavior in areas such as language, dress, and sexuality.

9 For more on this, see David Goodhew, "Working-Class Respectability: The Example of the Western Areas of Johannesburg, 1930–1955," *Journal of African History* 41, no. 2 (2000). Mark Leier makes a similar point in *Red Flags and Red Tape* (Toronto: University of Toronto Press, 1995), and in *Rebel Life* (Vancouver: New Star Books, 1999).

10 Candace Kruttschnitt, "Respectable Women and the Law," *Sociological Quarterly* 23 (Spring 1982): 221.

11 *Industrial Union Bulletin*, April 25, 1908.
12 Tax, *Rising of the Women*, 131.
13 Historian Alice Kessler-Harris advocated this approach and points out that
     "the broader conception of economic activity encompasses the workplace and
     the household/community in a reciprocal and changing relationship where
     each participates in shaping the other. Part of the shaping process involves the
     subjective experiences, understandings, and expectations of men and women for
     whom gender *may* be the most salient part of their sense of social order." Alice
     Kessler-Harris, *Gendering Labor History* (Urbana: University of Illinois Press,
     2007), 150. Italics added.

CHAPTER 1

 1 Carlos A. Schwantes, *Radical Heritage: Labor, Socialism, and Reform in
    Washington and British Columbia, 1885–1917* (Seattle: University of Washington
    Press, 1979), 6–11.
 2 Carlos A. Schwantes, *The Pacific Northwest: An Interpretive History*, Rev. and
    enl. ed. (Lincoln: University of Nebraska Press, 1996), 294, 329.
 3 Tom Fuller and Art Ayre, *Oregon at Work: 1859–2009* (Portland: Ooligan Press,
    2009), 81.
 4 Fuller and Ayre, *Oregon at Work*, 81. Janet Rasmussen, *New Land, New Lives:
    Scandinavian Immigrants to the Pacific Northwest* (Seattle: University of
    Washington Press, 1998), 170, 180–184.
 5 Schwantes, *The Pacific Northwest*, 202.
 6 Hall, *Harvest Wobblies*, 40–47.
 7 Schwantes, *The Pacific Northwest*, 218–221. Cloice Howd, *Industrial Relations in
    the West Coast Lumber Industry* (Washington: Government Printing Office, 1924),
    5.
 8 Ralph Hidy, *Timber and Men: The Weyerhaeuser Story* (New York: Macmillan,
    1963), 212–224. Note that the Northern Pacific Railway Company was renamed
    the Northern Pacific Railroad in 1896.
 9 Howd, *Industrial Relations*, 18–27.
10 Ibid., 40–45; *Oregonian*, March 4, 1907.
11 Howd, *Industrial Relations*, 45.
12 This was one of the successes of the 1917 strike, which mandated the camps
    provide blankets. This, however, did nothing to improve the infestations of lice
    (Howd, *Industrial Relations*, 38–44).
13 *The Socialist* (Seattle), March 16, 1907; Industrial Workers of the World, *The
    Lumber Industry and Its Workers* (Chicago: IWW Press, c. 1920), 58; Andrew
    Mason Prouty, *More Deadly Than War: Pacific Coast Logging, 1827–1981* (New
    York: Garland Publishing, 1985), 121,124.
14 *Industrial Worker* (Spokane) July 2, 1910, as quoted in Joyce Kornbluh, ed.,
    Rebel Voices: An IWW Anthology (Ann Arbor: University of Michigan Press,
    1964), 257–259; Industrial Workers of the World, *Lumber Industry*, 56–57;
    John Clendenin Townsend, *Running the Gauntlet: Cultural Sources of Violence
    Against the I.W.W.* (New York: Garland Publishing, 1986), 147; Howd, *Industrial
    Relation*, 38.
15 Howd, *Industrial Relations*, 44.
16 For a detailed discussion of homosexuality within the logging camps and the ur-
    ban areas of the Pacific Northwest, see Peter Boag, *Same-Sex Affairs: Constructing*

and Controlling Homosexuality in the Pacific Northwest (Berkeley: University of California Press, 2003).

17 Schwantes, *Radical Heritage*, 24.

18 Howd, *Industrial Relations*, 55–69.

19 For a more thorough examination of socialist politics in the NW see Jeffrey Johnson, *"They Are All Red Out Here"* (Norman: University of Oklahoma Press, 2008); Charles LeWarne, *Utopias on Puget Sound, 1885–1915* (Seattle: University of Washington Press, 1975); Schwantes, *Radical Heritage.*

20 For more on Home Colony see Gregory Hall's MA thesis "The Theory and Practice of Anarchism at Home Colony, 1896–1912" (Washington State University, 1994); and LeWarne's *Utopias on Puget Sound* and "The Anarchist Colony at Home, Washington, 1901–1902," *Arizona and the West* 14, no. 2 (July 1, 1972): 157, 167.

21 Paul Avrich, ed., *Anarchist Voices* (Oakland: AK Press, 2005).

22 Johnson, *They Are All Red Out Here*, 59.

23 Ibid., 166.

24 Ibid., 160–161.

CHAPTER 2

1 In addition to those in the northwest, outlined here, free speech fights also occurred in Fresno, California, in 1911; in San Diego in 1912–1913; in Denver, Colorado, in 1914; and Sioux City, Iowa, in 1914. Some remained small, local affairs, while others, like those in San Diego, drew national attention.

2 Jacqueline Jones, *The Life and Times of Lucy Parsons, American Radical* (New York: Basic Books, 2017).

3 Proceedings of the Founding Convention of the Industrial Workers of the World, 1905, https://www.iww.org/history/founding.

4 Foner, ed., *Women and the American Labor Movement*, 393–394.

5 Carolyn Ashbaugh, *Lucy Parsons* (Chicago: Charles H. Kerr, 1976), 217.

6 J. H. Walsh, "IWW Red Special Overall Brigade," *Industrial Worker*, September 19, 1908, as quoted in Kornbluh, *Rebel Voices*, 41. Walsh's first name has been listed in different sources as John, Jack, or James. He usually signed his correspondence in the industrial worker as "JH Walsh."

7 Depastino, *Citizen Hobo*, 96.

8 *Industrial Worker*, January 18, 1912.

9 Green et al., *The Big Red Songbook* (Chicago: Charles H. Kerr, 2007), 117.

10 Johnson, *They Are All Red Out Here*, 111, 134–135.

11 *Industrial Worker*, November 2, 1910.

12 1910 United States Census; *Industrial Worker*, April 29, 1909.

13 *Industrial Worker*, June 17, 1909.

14 For more about Flynn's life, see Elizabeth Gurley Flynn, *I Speak My Own Piece* (New York: International Publishers, 1973); Rosalyn Baxandall, *Words on Fire* (New Brunswick, NJ: Rutgers University Press, 1987); and Helen Camp, *Iron in Her Soul* (Pullman: Washington State University Press, 1995).

15 1910 United States Census; 1911 British Columbia Census; ancestry.com.

16 Letters between W. H. Westman and W. F. Moudy, February 1945, IWW Records, box 91, IWW Collection, Walter P. Reuther Library, Wayne State University; Franklin Rosemont, *Joe Hill* (Chicago: Charles H. Kerr, 2003), 289.

17 I have seen her name also spelled Agnes Thesla Fair and Agnes Thesia Fair. *Industrial Worker*, January 11, 1917. The article was reprinted from the *Oregonian*. Rosemont, *Joe Hill*, 299–304.

18 *Industrial Worker*, October 20, 1909; Philip Foner, ed., *Fellow Workers and Friends* (Westport, CT: Greenwood Press, 1981), 28; Elizabeth Flynn, *The Rebel Girl* (New York: International Publishers, 1973), 104.

19 Flynn, *The Rebel Girl*, 105.

20 "Synopsis: Spokane Free Speech Fight," *Industrial Worker*, March 19 and 26, 1910, as reprinted in John Duda, *Wanted* (Chicago: Charles H Kerr, 2009), 111–125; Glen Broyles, "The Spokane Free Speech Fight, 1909–1910," *Labor History* 19, no. 2 (1978): 240.

21 IWW Executive Council Minutes, Spokane City Clerk, 1909, Washington State Archives, Eastern Region Branch.

22 Ibid.

23 IWW Statements—Douglass, Spokane City Clerk, 1909, Washington State Archives, Eastern Region Branch.

24 Kornbluh, *Rebel Voices*, 95.

25 Elizabeth Gurle y Flynn, "The Free-Speech Fight at Spokane," *International Socialist Review*, December 1909, reprinted in Duda, *Wanted*, 56.

26 Elizabeth Gurley Flynn file, Spokane City Clerk, 1909, Washington State Archives, Eastern Region Branch.

27 Ibid.

28 *Industrial Worker*, November 10, 1909; also similar report in December 1909 issue of *International Socialist Review*, reprinted in Duda, *Wanted*, 55–59.

29 *Industrial Worker*, November 10, 1909; Melvyn Dubofsky, *We Shall Be All* (Chicago: Quadrangle Books, 1969), 182; *Industrial Worker*, November 24, 1909.

30 Green et al., *The Big Red Songbook* (Charles H. Kerr: Chicago, 2007), 37–39.

31 Ibid.

32 Elizabeth Gurley Flynn, "The Shame of Spokane," *International Socialist Review*, January 1910, reprinted in Duda, *Wanted*, 62.

33 Ibid., 64.

34 Evidence Folder, Spokane City Clerk, 1910, Washington State Archives, Eastern Region Branch.

35 Flynn, "Shame of Spokane," in Duda, *Wanted*, 64–65.

36 *Spokesman-Review*, February 19, 1910.

37 The Spokane *Press*, February 25, 1910, http://chroniclingamerica.loc.gov/.

38 Flynn, "The Free Speech Fight at Spokane," in Duda, *Wanted*, 56–57; Dubofsky, *We Shall Be All*, 179.

39 Elizabeth Gurley Flynn, "Call to Action," *Industrial Worker*, November 10, 1909, in Duda, *Wanted*, 47.

40 Flynn, *The Rebel Girl*, 108.

41 Agnes Thecla Fair, "Miss Fair's Letter," *Workingman's Paper*, November 20, 1909, in Duda, *Wanted*, 85–86.

42 Spokane *Spokesman-Review*, November 3, 1909, copy found in Frederick W. Thompson Papers, Walter P. Reuther Library, Wayne State University.

43 Elizabeth Gurley Flynn, "Story of My Arrest and Imprisonment," *Workingman's Paper*, December 11, 1909, in Duda, *Wanted*, 50–53.

44 Ibid.

45 Ibid.

46 The Spokane *Press*, January 15, 1910, http://chroniclingamerica.loc.gov/lccn/sn88085947/1910-01-15/ed-1/seq-1/.

47 Flynn "Latest News from Spokane," *International Socialist Review*, March 1910, in Duda, *Wanted*, 72. It is not clear what the results of the suit were. Most likely it was dropped.

48 Spokane *Daily Chronicle*, January 21, 1927; *Spokesman-Review*, April 22, 1914; American National Red Cross, *A Record of the Red Cross Work on the Pacific Slope* (Oakland, CA: Pacific Press Publishing Company, 1902).

49 *Industrial Worker*, January 15, 1910; *Spokesman-Review*, May 10, 2012.

50 Report, "In the Matter of the Investigation of the Police Department of the City of Spokane by A Committee Consisting of Dr. Thomas L. Catterson, and Others," Spokane City Clerk, 1910, Washington State Archives, Eastern Region Branch, 17, 26.

51 Ibid., 44–47.

52 Ibid., 179–180.

53 Ibid., 211.

54 *Solidarity*, July 31, 1915.

55 Ibid.

56 The Spokane *Press*, March 5, 1910.

CHAPTER 3

1 I use the term "strike" (singular) to denote this series of somewhat coordinated efforts in tailor shops during this two-month period (*Industrial Worker*, October 17, 1912). It's unclear which one was considered unsuccessful.

2 1910 United States Census. For an example of coordinated efforts, in 1910 the Seattle IWW local organized a Ferrer remembrance celebration along with the Workingmen's Circle, Russian Workingmen's Association, Radical Library Association, and Socialist Party (*Industrial Worker*, November 2, 1910). In February 1912, the Seattle local held a large meeting in support of the Lawrence strikers (*Industrial Worker*, February 22, 1912).

3 Seattle *Union Record*, April 27 and May 4 and 11, 1912.

4 *Oregonian*, April 3, 1912. The letter was reportedly seized in a raid in Raymond, Washington, and then printed in the *Oregonian*.

5 Seattle *Post-Intelligencer*, May 16, 1912.

6 Examination of Jack Solomon, Seattle, Washington, May 25, 1912, Records of the Immigration and Naturalization Service Series A: Subject Correspondence Files Part 6: Suppression of Aliens, 1906–1930, Microfilm, Reel 2.

7 Avrich, *Anarchist Voices* (Oakland: AK Press, 2005), 332.

8 Examination of Becky Beck, Seattle, Washington, June 5, 1912, Records of the Immigration and Naturalization Service; Avrich, *Anarchist Voices*, 332. This interview, done while Beck was ninety, may have downplayed her relationship with the IWW. It is likely that she was already affiliated with the organization, considering that both she and Solomon were organizers of strike activity.

9 Examination of Becky Beck, Seattle, Washington, June 5, 1912, Records of the Immigration and Naturalization Service; Seattle *Daily Times*, May 14, 1912. Beck was found not guilty on May 28. Seattle *Star*, May 18, 1912. Interview with Rebecca Beck, August 1973, http://symposia.library.csulb.edu/iii/cpro/DigitalItemViewPage.external?lang=eng&sp=1001918&sp=T&sp=1&suite=def.

10 Seattle *Daily Times*, May 15, 1912.

11 Seattle *Post-Intelligencer*, May 16, 1912.

12 "An Act to Regulate the Immigration of Aliens into the United States."

13 Matthew Frye Jacobson, *Barbarian Virtues* (New York: Hill and Wang, 2001), 93.

14 Ellis Butler to Commissioner General of Immigration, July 5, 1912; Selma Rosenthal to Mrs. Harris, March 11, 1912. Records of the Immigration and Naturalization Service.

15 Examination of Jack Solomon, Seattle, Washington, May 25, 1912, Records of the Immigration and Naturalization Service.

16 Examination of Becky Beck, Records of the Immigration and Naturalization Service.

17 David Langum, *Crossing Over the Line* (Chicago: University of Chicago Press, 1994), 46. Langum also covers the case of *Caminetti v. United States*, in which the Supreme Court decided that the law was upheld even in cases where the immorality was noncommercial.

18 Langum, *Crossing Over the Line*, 46.

19 Examination of Jack Solomon, Seattle, Washington, May 25, 1912, Records of the Immigration and Naturalization Service.

20 Unfortunately, some of the transcripts for this interview are illegible. Examination of Becky Beck, Records of the Immigration and Naturalization Service.

21 Emma Goldman, *Anarchism and Other Essays* (New York: Dover Publications, 1969), 227.

22 Ibid.; Avrich, *Anarchist Voices*, 332.

23 Candace Falk, *Love, Anarchy and Emma Goldman* (New Brunswick, NJ: Rutgers University Press, 1990).

24 Examination of Becky Beck, Records of the Immigration and Naturalization Service.

25 Ibid.

26 DeBruler to Cable, July 5, 1912, Records of the Immigration and Naturalization Service.

27 Coleman to Cable, n.d., Records of the Immigration and Naturalization Service.

28 Petition to Release Solomon and Beck, n.d., Records of the Immigration and Naturalization Service.

29 Cable to DeBruler, July 11, 1912; Cable to Gompers, July 16, 1912; Records of the Immigration and Naturalization Service.

30 Beck, August interview.

31 Avrich, *Anarchist Voices*, 333.

CHAPTER 4

1 The strike has been the subject of several important articles. For more detail on the strike and its implications in Portland, see Janice Dilg, "By Proceeding in an Orderly and Lawful Manner" (MA thesis, Portland State University, 2005); and Adam Hodges, "The Industrial Workers of the World and the Oregon Packing Company Strike of July 1913" (MA thesis, Portland State University, 1996). For more on Marie Equi's life and her role in the strike, see Michael Helquist, *Marie Equi* (Corvallis: Oregon State University Press, 2015). For more background on Progressive Era Portland, see Robert Johnson's *The Radical Middle-Class* (Princeton, NJ: Princeton University Press, 2003). Johnson argues that Portland, which was seen as conservative by many by the early twentieth century, actually possessed a "democratic populist, and even anticapitalist," spirit.

2   Women made up 43 percent of the population (1910 United States Census); Greg
    Hall, "The Fruits of Her Labor," *Oregon Historical Quarterly* 109, no. 2 (Summer
    2008); Janice Dilg, "For Working Women in Oregon," *Oregon Historical Quarterly*
    110, no. 1 (Spring 2009).

3   *Industrial Worker*, May 11, 1911.

4   Janice Dilg suggests that the Consumer's League of Oregon was initially in favor
    of proposing a minimum wage bill that covered all workers, but for several
    reasons (most notably that most thought a gender-neutral bill could not pass
    in the political climate of the time), it was changed to cover only women and
    minors. Janice Dilg, "For Working Women in Oregon"; "Harry Albee to Portland
    Non-Partisan League," July 31, 1913, Albee Subject Files, box 3, file 27, City
    of Portland Archives and Records Center (hereafter PARC). The platform of
    the Portland Non-Partisan League explained that its central purpose was to
    "investigate records and standing of candidates for municipal, county and state
    offices" and "to do all things necessary and proper towards insuring to the city
    and state an honest, economical, and efficient administration of state, county and
    municipal affairs." Although it was formed under the guise of nonpartisanship,
    the very first resolution the group passed endorsed the actions of city officials
    "in their efforts to enforce the law against the order of Industrial Workers of
    the World and other disturbers of the peace, and heartily approve of the action
    to prevent anarchistic abuse of the American flag and American Government
    under the guise of 'free speech.'" *Oregonian*, August 3, 1913; Press Committee of
    Strikers, "On the Job in Oregon," *International Socialist Review*, August 1913,
    164.

5   Here are a few choice headlines from the 354 that resulted from a search of the
    term "white slavery" in the *Oregonian* from 1907 to 1913: "Victim of White
    Slavery: Seattle Woman Tells Chicago Police of Agent's Methods," *Oregonian*,
    February 29, 1908; "Women Rally to Edna Gingles' Aid: Pretty Irish Girl
    Says White Slavers Tried to Lure Her to Their Dens," *Oregonian*, July 2, 1909;
    "Disgraced Tutor Indicted: Charge of White Slavery Is Placed Against Joseph
    Hidalgo," *Oregonian*, June 25, 1910; Langum, *Crossing Over the Line*, 35.

6   Michael E. McGerr, *A Fierce Discontent* (New York: Free Press, 2003), 90. For a
    complete history of the Mann Act, see Langum, *Crossing Over the Line*.

7   Joanne J. Meyerowitz, *Women Adrift* (Chicago: University of Chicago Press,
    1988).

8   Mary Odem, *Delinquent Daughters* (Chapel Hill: University of North Carolina
    Press, 1995), 4–5.

9   Oregon State Board of Control, *Biennial Report* (Salem, OR: State Printing
    Department, 1914), 210.

10 Frank Welles, "Our Oregon State Institutions," *Oregon Teachers' Monthly* (1915):
    270–272.

11 Ruth Rosen, *The Lost Sisterhood* (Baltimore, MD: Johns Hopkins University
    Press, 1982), 22–23. As Mary Odem points out in *Delinquent Daughters*, feeble-
    mindedness was also a target for eugenicists, who believed it was passed on
    genetically.

12 *First Report of the Portland Vice Commission to the Mayor and City Council,
    January 1912* (Portland: 1912), 3, 7; E. Kimbark MacColl, *Merchants, Money, and
    Power* (Portland: Georgian Press, 1988), 438.

13 Hall, "The Fruits of Her Labor," 239; "Oregon Packing Plant Strike Narrative"
    [1913], Albee Subject Files, box 1, file 66, PARC.

14 Ibid.

15 Portland *News*, July 2, 1913.

16 "Oregon Packing Company Strike Narrative."

17 Portland *News*, July 4, 1913.

18 Press Committee of Strikers, "On the Job in Oregon," 164.

19 *Oregonian*, July 9, 1913.

20 *Portland News*, July 12, 1913.

21 Press Committee on Strikers, "On the Job in Oregon," 164. For more on Tom Burns, see Peter Sleeth, "Read You Mutt! The Life and Times of Tom Burns, The Most Arrested Man in Portland," *Oregon Historical Quarterly* 112, no. 1 (Spring 2011).

22 "Oregon Packing Plant Strike Narrative."

23 Portland *News*, July 5, 1913.

24 Ibid.

25 *Oregonian*, July 9, 1913.

26 Portland *News*, July 8, 1913.

27 Avrich, *Anarchist Voices*, 21.

28 Portland *News*, July 9–12, 1913.

29 Press Committee on Strikers, "On the Job in Oregon," 166.

30 Portland *Evening Telegram*, July 12, 1913.

31 Press Committee on Strikers, "On the Job in Oregon," 166; Portland *News*, July 14, 1913.

32 Press Committee on Strikers, "On the Job in Oregon," 166; quote from *Oregonian*, July 16, 1913.

33 *Oregonian*, July 18, 1913.

34 "Multnomah County Court Records #53974" (Portland, Oregon), Multnomah County Courthouse.

35 *Oregonian*, July 18, 1913.

36 Portland *News*, July 18, 1913.

37 Ibid.

38 Ibid., July 24 and 29, 1913.

39 Ibid.; *Oregonian*, August 14, 1913.

40 Portland *News*, July 30, 1913.

41 *Industrial Worker*, July 29, 1909.

42 Melvyn Dubofsky, *We Shall Be All*, 129; Philip Foner, *Women and the American Labor Movement*; *Industrial Worker*, January 26, 1911.

43 Industrial Workers of the World, *Little Red Songbook* (Chicago: Charles H. Kerr, 2003).

44 "Letter from Elmer Buse to Congressman Lafferty," August 19, 1913, Albee Subject Files, box 1, file 25, PARC.

45 "Letter from Mayor Albee to Clarence Reames," September 19, 1913, Albee Subject Files, box 3, file 60, PARC.

46 "Oregon Packing Plant Strike Narrative," *Oregon Daily Journal*, July 10, 1913.

47 *Oregonian*, July 18, 1913

48 Portland *News*, August 8, 1913.

49 Baldwin was hired by the Portland Police Bureau in 1908, expressly to look out for young women and girls. Baldwin's biographer notes that Baldwin and others like her "targeted the female 'sexual delinquent' as the antithesis of their ideal of a standardized social morality ethic." For more on Baldwin's life, see Gloria E. Myers, *A Municipal Mother* (Corvallis: Oregon State University Press, 1995), 3.

50 "Lola Baldwin to Albee," November 11, 1913, Albee Subject Files, box 3, file 8, PARC.
51 Ibid.
52 Baldwin included a handwritten postscript to the mayor: "As Mr. Swett is asking of you some favors can you not persuade him to let my cases alone." "Lola Baldwin to Albee," November 11, 1913, Albee Subject Files, box 3, file 8, PARC.
53 "Petition to Remove Lola Baldwin," December 15, 1913, Albee Subject Files, box 3, file 6, PARC.
54 *Oregonian*, November 22, 1913.
55 Ibid., November 23 and 25, 1913; Portland *News*, November 25, 1913.
56 Oregon Board of Control, *Biennial Report*, 1914, 210.
57 *Oregonian*, November 23, 1913.
58 Meyerowitz, *Women Adrift*; Kathy Peiss, *Cheap Amusements* (Philadelphia: Temple University Press, 1986); Elizabeth Alice Clement, *Love for Sale* (Chapel Hill: University of North Carolina Press, 2006), 17.

CHAPTER 5

1 Walker C. Smith, *The Everett Massacre* (Chicago: IWW Publishing, 1918), 291. I rely heavily on Smith's book for the narrative of events in Everett. I was unable to locate transcripts of the trial.
2 Ibid., 24; Norman H. Clark, *Mill Town* (Seattle: University of Washington Press, 1970), 91.
3 Smith, *The Everett Massacre*, 24; Norman H. Clark, *Mill Town* (Seattle: University of Washington Press, 1970), 92.
4 Smith, *The Everett Massacre*, 29–32.
5 Clark, *Mill Town*, 179–180.
6 Smith, *The Everett Massacre*, 34–38; *Industrial Worker* (Seattle), August 26, 1916.
7 Anna Louise Strong, "Week 5 Report," Anna Louise Strong Papers, University of Washington Special Collections; Smith, *The Everett Massacre*, 38.
8 Everett *Tribune*, September 8–9, 1916.
9 Smith, *Everett Massacre*, 49; *Industrial Worker*, September 30, 1916.
10 Everett *Tribune*, September 9, 1916.
11 Smith, *The Everett Massacre*, 50–56.
12 Ibid., 61.
13 Ibid.
14 Ibid., 74.
15 Clark, *Mill Town*, 125, 185.
16 Everett *Tribune*, November 5, 1916.
17 Ibid.
18 Smith, *The Everett Massacre*, 84–88.
19 Ibid., 88, 89, 114.
20 Ibid., 92.
21 Seattle *Union Record*, November 11, 1916.
22 Smith, *The Everett Massacre*, 92; Seattle *Union Record*, November 11, 1916.
23 Smith, *The Everett Massacre*, 106–108; *Industrial Worker*, November 19, 1916.
24 Smith, *The Everett Massacre*, 123, 138, 277.
25 Seattle *Union Record*, March 10, 1917.
26 Smith, *The Everett Massacre*, 151–153, 156.

27 Ibid., 185.

28 Since Frenette was not on the *Verona* on November 5, her arrest and trial were separate from those who were (Smith, *The Everett Massacre*, 155, 194; *Industrial Worker*, December 2, 1916). Mahler and Peters were released on November 14 (Seattle *Post-Intelligencer*, November 6 and 9, 1916).

29 Seattle *Union Record*, November 11, 1916, and April 14, 1917.

30 Everett *Tribune*, April 13, 1917.

31 Ibid.

32 Everett *Daily Herald*, April 29, 1917. This same tactic was used during the testimony of James P. Thompson during the Chicago trial of Wobblies arrested during World War I. Thompson was asked about Wobbly beliefs regarding love and marriage. *US v. Haywood, et al., 1918*, IWW Collection, Reuther Library.

33 Everett *Daily Herald*, May 3, 1917.

34 Ibid., May 4, 1917.

35 Smith, *The Everett Massacre*, 289.

36 *Solidarity*, July 15, 1915.

37 Ibid.

38 "The Brain Boilers Academy," *Solidarity*, June 1, 1910.

39 "From a Woman Toiler," *Solidarity*, June 25, 1910.

40 *Industrial Worker*, June 5, 1913.

41 See, for example, Richard Rajala's article, "A Dandy Bunch of Wobblies: Pacific Northwest Loggers and the Industrial Workers of the World, 1900–1930," *Labor History* 37 (Spring 1996).

42 "Some Weaknesses of the Western Wobbly," *Solidarity*, January 16, 1915.

43 Jameson, *All That Glitters*, 238.

44 "Financial Statement of Everett Prisoners Defense Committee," pamphlet (Seattle, Washington, June 1917), 1, Industrial Workers of the World Collection, University of Washington Special Collections.

CHAPTER 6

1 http://wwi.lib.byu.edu/index.php/The_U.S._Sedition_Act.

2 *Oregonian*, July 13, 1917, August 18, 1917, and October 3, 1917.

3 Letter from C. H. Libby to George Vanderveer, September 5, 1917, IWW Collection, Reuther Library; *Industrial Worker*, September 19, 1917.

4 Dubofsky, *We Shall Be All*, 436–437.

5 William Preston, *Aliens and Dissenters* (Urbana: University of Illinois Press, 1994), 206.

6 *New York Times*, November 23, 1919.

7 Preston, *Aliens and Dissenters*, 206; *New York Times*, November 23, 1919.

8 United States Congress House Committee on Immigration and Naturalization, *IWW Deportation Cases* (Washington, DC: Government Printing Office, 1920), 23–26.

9 Ship Manifest, October 27, 1917, Ellis Island Records, https://www.ellisisland.org/.

10 Hulet M. Wells, *Wilson and the Issues of To-Day* (Seattle: The Socialist Party, 1918), 68–69.

11 Ibid.

12 June 22, 1918, Governor Ernest Lister, State Secret Service Reports, Washington State Archive.

13 Frances H. Early, *A World without War* (Syracuse, NY: Syracuse University
     Press, 1997), 169. Early notes that the sisters first came to the United States in
     1911 and were involved in the 1912 Bread and Roses strike in Spokane. The only
     arrival record I could find was in 1916.
14 *IWW Deportation Cases*, 64.
15 Ibid.
16 *Industrial Worker*, November 24, 1917.
17 Ibid., January 5 and 12, 1918.
18 Ibid.
19 Ibid.
20 Ibid.
21 Ibid., January 26, 1918.
22 Ibid., April 27 and May 4, 1918.
23 Letter to Thomas Gregory from J. H. Byrd, August 22, 1918, Department of
     Justice Investigative Files. Byrd described himself as a friend of Pollok's brother.
24 Letter to Assistant Attorney General O'Brien from Henry Twombly, January
     1919, Department of Justice Investigative Files.
25 Dubofsky, *We Shall Be All*, 439.
26 Letter to Francis Welsh from Charles Fickert, October 26, 1918, Department of
     Justice Investigative Files.
27 Letter to Gregory from Woodrow Wilson, August 4, 1918, Department of Justice
     Investigative Files; Letter from Preston to Gregory, April 29, 1919, Department of
     Justice Investigative Files.
28 Dubofsky, *We Shall Be All*, 440.
29 Oakland *Tribune*, January 14, 1918.
30 Ibid.
31 Ibid., February 3, 1918.
32 *The Nation*, January 25, 1919; Dubofsky, *We Shall Be All*, 441.
33 "IWW Activities Weekly Reports," December 7 and December 14, 1917, US
     Military Intelligence Reports: Surveillance of Radicals in the United States,
     1917–1941, Reel 12.
34 October 6, 1917, Governor Ernest Lister, State Secret Service Reports,
     Washington State Archives.
35 Governor Ernest Lister, State Secret Service Reports, Washington State Archives.
36 Prison Relief, 1918, IWW Collection, Reuther Library.
37 General Office Bulletin, February 14, 1918, June 1918, and July 1921, IWW
     Collection, Reuther Library.
38 *Industrial Worker*, November 13, 1920.

CHAPTER 7

1 Kathleen Kennedy, *Disloyal Mothers and Scurrilous Citizens* (Bloomington:
    Indiana University Press, 1999), 71.
2 *Meriden Morning Record* (Meriden, CT), November 8, 1918.
3 *Oregonian*, November 18, 1913.
4 Ibid.
5 *Oregonian*, April 30 and December 15, 1915.
6 "The Case of Louise Olivereau," pamphlet, 1918, Minnie Parkhurst Papers,
    University of Washington Special Collections, 20 (hereafter UWSC).

7 For more on Olivereau, see also Sarah Ellen Sharbach, "Louise Olivereau and the Seattle Radical Community, 1917–1923" (MA thesis, University of Washington, 1986).

8 Kennedy, *Disloyal Mothers and Scurrilous Citizens*, xv.

9 Anne Cipriano Venzon, *The United States in the First World War* (Abingdon, UK: Routledge, 1999), 169; Gilbert Fite and H. Peterson, *Opponents of War* (Westport, CT: Greenwood Press, 1986), 123–124.

10 Fite and Peterson, *Opponents*, 125–131.

11 "Woodrow Wilson: Proclamation 1370—Conscription."

12 "The Case of Louise Olivereau: Trial and Speech to the Jury in Federal Court of Seattle, Wash., November 1917," Minnie Parkhurst Papers, UWSC, 24–25.

13 Ibid., 48.

14 Ibid., 49.

15 Ibid., 54.

16 *United States v. Louise Olivereau*, US District Courts, Western District of Washington, Northern Division, Seattle, Admiralty, Civil and Criminal, 1912–1928, NARA-Pacific Alaska Region; "The Case of Louise Olivereau," 15.

17 Goldman, *Living My Life* (New York: Dover, 1970), 614.

18 "The Case of Louise Olivereau," 7–10, 12.

19 *Oregonian*, September 9, 1917, November 29, 1917.

20 "The Case of Louise Olivereau," 23–25.

21 Ibid.

22 Ibid.

23 The current IWW website has two questions about anarchism in their "Myths about the IWW" section. Salvatore Salerno has the biggest discussion of the influence of anarchism in the organization in his book *Red November, Black November: Culture and Community in the Industrial Workers of the World* (Albany: University of New York Press, 1989).

24 Goldman, *Living My Life*, 642.

25 Olivereau simply refers to the "the *Call*"; she is most likely referencing the Seattle *Daily Call*. The speech, as well as an introduction and court records, were finally published by Parkhurst as a pamphlet titled, "The Louise Olivereau Case." Olivereau referred to the pamphlet as her "child" during their correspondence (Letter, Olivereau to Parkhurst, December 19, 1917, Minnie Parkhurst Papers, UWSC).

26 *Industrial Worker*, December 8, 1917.

27 Although the IWW distanced itself from Olivereau's anarchist beliefs, it was not as dismissive as historians have previously claimed. In *Disloyal Mothers and Scurrilous Citizens*, Kathleen Kennedy maintains that while the *Industrial Worker* expressed support for Olivereau, "as time went on members of the IWW distanced themselves from [her], apparently angry that the government used its case against her to attack their organization." As evidence of this, Kennedy quotes Robert Friedheim's *The Seattle General Strike*: Friedheim wrote that the IWW "were indignant that anyone would think they would trust an emotional, irresponsible girl" to do something as important as anti-conscription flyers. Friedheim cites Anne Gallagher, "The Case of Louise Olivereau." *One Big Union Monthly*, October 1919.

28 Parkhurst is sometimes referred to under her married name, Minnie Rimer (Kennedy, *Disloyal Mothers*, 71).

29 Letter, Olivereau to Parkhurst, January 24 and February 2, 1918, Minnie Parkhurst Papers, UWSC. I have been unable to find evidence of Smith's criticism of Olivereau.

30 Anna Louise Strong, *I Change Worlds* (Berkeley: Seal Press, 1980), 63.

31 Ibid., 63–64.

32 Ibid., 64.

33 Letter, Olivereau to Parkhurst, August 23, 1919, Minnie Parkhurst Papers, UWSC.

34 Kate Sadler was a Seattle-area Socialist who, along with her husband Sam, was also arrested for antiwar activities during this period (Letter, Parkhurst to Ed Nolan, August 31, 1919, Minnie Parkhurst Papers, UWSC).

35 Letter, Parkhurst to Olivereau, February 27, 1919, Minnie Parkhurst Papers, UWSC.

36 Ibid.

37 Letter, Olivereau to Parkhurst, June 13, 1918, Minnie Parkhurst Papers, UWSC.

38 Ibid., September 4, 1919, Minnie Parkhurst Papers, UWSC.

39 Harvey O'Connor, *Revolution in Seattle* (Chicago: Haymarket Books, 2009), 99, 248.

40 *Oregonian*, May 5, 1920.

41 O'Connor, *Revolution in Seattle*, 261.

42 Olivereau's letter to Parkhurst, quoted in Sharbach, "Louise Olivereau."

CHAPTER 8

1 For a more detailed analysis of Equi's life, see Michael Helquist, *Marie Equi* (Corvallis: Oregon State University Press, 2015).

2 Helquist, *Marie Equi*, 44, 49.

3 Tom Cook, "Radical Politics, Radical Love: The Life of Dr. Marie Equi," *Northwest Gay and Lesbian Historian* 1, no. 3 (Summer/Fall 1996), and 1, no. 4 (June 1997), http://theanarchistlibrary.org/library/tom-cook-radical-politics-radical-love. Again, for details on these years and Equi's personal life, see Helquist, *Marie Equi*.

4 Nancy Krieger, *Queen of the Bolsheviks* (Montreal: Kersplebedeb, 2009), 17; Rickie Solinger, *The Abortionist* (Berkeley: University of California Press, 1996), 26–28; Helquist, *Marie Equi*, 95.

5 Linda Gordon, *Woman's Body Woman's Right* (New York: Grossman, 1976), 207, 222.

6 "Large Families," *Industrial Worker*, June 1, 1911.

7 Louis Duchez, "Suffering in Silence," *Solidarity*, January 8, 1910; "Phyllis and Her Babies," *Industrial Union Bulletin*, January 4, 1908; *The New Solidarity*, February 1, 1919; *Industrial Worker*, May 8, 1913; *Industrial Worker*, April 25, 1912; Elizabeth Gurley Flynn, "The I.W.W. Call to Women," *Solidarity*, July 15, 1915.

8 Gordon, *Woman's Body*, 276–277.

9 Elizabeth Gurley Flynn, "The Case of Margaret Sanger," *Solidarity*, January 22, 1916.

10 Elizabeth Gurley Flynn, *The Rebel Girl*, 166.

11 Gordon, *Woman's Body*, 227.

12 Krieger, *Queen of the Bolsheviks*, 15.

13 Michael Helquist, "'Lewd, Obscene, and Indecent': The 1916 Portland Edition of *Family Limitation*," *Oregon Historical Quarterly* 117, no. 2 (Summer 2016): 281.

14 "Albee Reply to Elbert Hubbard," July 6, 1916, Albee Subject Files, box 13, file 40, PARC.

15 "City of Portland Ruling" [1916], Albee Subject Files, box 4, file 3, PARC.

16 Krieger, *Queen of the Bolsheviks*, 14–16; Helquist, *Marie Equi*, 143.

17 *United States v. Marie Equi*, US District Courts, District of Oregon, Portland, Civ. Crim. and Admir. Case File 1911–1922, NARA-Pacific Alaska Region.

18 Ibid.

19 Krieger, *Queen of the Bolsheviks*, 19.

20 *Oregonian*, July 1, 1918.

21 Although some have suggested (as I did in a previous work) that Mary was the daughter of IWW member Wesley Everest, who was later killed in Centralia, Washington, Michael Helquist has found that not to be the case (Helquist, *Marie Equi*, 217, 266n5).

22 Sanger described Equi thusly: "A rebellious soul, generous kind, brave, but so radical in her thinking that she was almost an outcast. Upon arrival she captured every well-known woman who comes to Portland. Her reputation is Lesbian, but to me she was like a crushed falcon which had braved the storm and winds of time and needed tenderness and love. I liked Marie always." Cited in Ellen Chesler, *Women of Valor* (New York: Simon and Schuster, 1992), 526, n20.

23 Adam Hodges, "At War over the Espionage Act in Portland: Dueling Perspectives from Agent William Bryon and Kathleen O'Brennan," *Oregon Historical Quarterly* 108 (Fall 2007): 483.

24 Ibid., 476.

25 According to a government informant, Equi said after a meeting with Vanderveer that she was not happy with him as her lawyer "because then she would be identified solely with IWW propaganda, whereas her case rested upon an entirely different issue." Report of Informant no. 53, October 25, 1918, Department of Justice Files on Marie Equi, Lewis and Clark College Special Collections; *United States v Marie Equi*.

26 Report of Agent Bryon, April 27, 1920, Department of Justice Files.

27 The Portland *Telegram*, December 31, 1918; Report of Agent Bryon, April 27 and 30, 1918, Department of Justice Files.

28 Hodges, "At War," 482.

29 Report made by Agent W. E. Hudson, December 6, 1918, Department of Justice Files.

30 Report of Informant no. 53, November 21, 1918, Department of Justice Files. By December Agent Bryon was requesting Paul be transferred to New York or Washington, DC, because she was facing harassment in Portland (Letter, Byron to A. Bruce Bielaski, December 14, 1918, Department of Justice Files).

31 Hodges, "At War," 478–482.

32 Ibid., 479–480.

33 Ibid., 484.

34 Ibid.

35 *Oregonian*, August 31, 1921.

36 Report of Agent no. 18, July 20 and 26, 1918, NARA-Pacific Alaska Region.

37 Report of Agent Bryon, November 29, 1918, Department of Justice Files; *Oregonian*, January 9 and February 26, 1919.

38 Report of Agent Bryon, December 4, 1918, Department of Justice Files; Letter from Agent Bryon to Lewis Baley, October 22, 1920, Department of Justice Files.

39 For example of an ad, see *Oregonian*, December 5, 1918; Report of Informant no. 53, October 25 and 30, 1918, Department of Justice Files.

40 Report of W. E. Hudson, December 6, 1918, Department of Justice Files.

41 *Oregonian*, June 7, 1919.

42 Ibid., October 28, 1919; June 11, 22, and 23, 1920; October 14, 16, and 18, 1920.

43 Ibid., August 14, 1921.

44 Helquist, *Marie Equi*, 222.

45 Rosalyn Baxandall, *Words on Fire* (New Brunswick, NJ: Rutgers University Press, 1987).

46 Flynn, *The Rebel Girl*, 198.

47 Krieger, *Queen of the Bolsheviks*, 23.

CONCLUSION

1 O'Connor, *Revolution in Seattle*, 146.

2 Tyler, *Rebels of the Woods* (Eugene: University of Oregon Press, 1967), 155–156; John McClelland Jr., *Wobbly War: The Centralia Story* (Tacoma: Washington State Historical Society, 1987), 58.

3 Tyler, *Rebels of the Woods*, 159.

4 Ibid.; McClelland, *Wobbly War*.

5 Tyler, *Rebels of the Woods*, 165–174.

6 Ibid., 175–176.

7 Melvyn Dubofsky, *"Big Bill" Haywood* (Manchester, UK: Manchester University Press, 1987), 178n9.

8 The older works include Patrick Renshaw, *The Wobblies* (Garden City, NY: Doubleday, 1967); Dubofsky, *We Shall Be All*; and Tyler, *Rebels of the Woods*. Newer work includes Greg Hall, *Harvest Wobblies*; and Peter Cole, *Wobblies on the Waterfront*.

9 Renshaw, *The Wobblies*, 257.

10 Tyler, *Rebels of the Woods*, 186; Greg Hall, *Harvest Wobblies*, 214.

11 For more on the Grays Harbor radicals in the 1920s and 1930s, see Aaron Goings, "Red Harbor."

12 Ellen Doree Rosen, *A Wobbly Life* (Detroit: Wayne State University Press, 2004).

13 Letter, E. F. Doree to Ida Doree, September 8, 1921, in Rosen, *A Wobbly Life*, 138.

14 Ibid.

15 Ibid.

16 Letter, Ed Doree to Ida Doree, August 18, 1921, in Rosen, *A Wobbly Life*, 132.

17 Letter E. F. Doree to Rebecca Evans, June 1, 1922; and E. F. Doree to Ida Doree, June 2, 1922, in Rosen, *A Wobbly Life*, 200–201.

18 Letter, E. F. Doree to Ida Doree, April 20, 1922, in Rosen, *A Wobbly Life*, 188.

19 Ibid., 214

20 Ibid., 216.

21 It is impossible to judge from these personal letters how many of his fellow Wobblies who supported clemency agreed with Doree. I have tried to ascertain if married men were more or less likely to support clemency, but I have been unable to obtain records on enough of the members to prove whether or not this was the case. It is possible that those who were against individual clemency were less likely to have a family waiting for them on the outside and more interested in maintaining solidarity among the "family" of Wobblies in prison.

22 Cannon, "The IWW Convention," http://www.marxists.org/archive/cannon/
    works/1924/iwwconv.htm.
23 Ibid.
24 *The New Recruit* (Chicago), June 1, 1930.

Bibliography

MANUSCRIPT COLLECTIONS

Anna Louise Strong Papers. University of Washington Special Collections. Seattle, Washington.

Department of Justice Files on Marie Equi. Lewis and Clark College Special Collections. Portland, Oregon.

Frederick W. Thompson Papers. Walter P. Reuther Library, Wayne State University. Detroit, Michigan.

Governor Ernest Lister Papers. Washington State Archives. Olympia, Washington.

Harry Albee Subject Files. City of Portland Archives and Records Center. Portland, Oregon.

Industrial Workers of the World Collection. University of Washington Special Collections. Seattle, Washington.

Industrial Workers of the World Collection. Walter P. Reuther Library, Wayne State University. Detroit, Michigan.

Marie Equi Vertical File. Oregon Historical Society Research Library. Portland, Oregon.

Minnie Parkhurst Papers. University of Washington Special Collections. Seattle, Washington.

Spokane City Clerk Records. Washington State Archives, Eastern Region Branch. Spokane, Washington.

US District Court Records. National Archives, Pacific Alaska Region. Seattle, Washington.

NEWSPAPERS

Industrial Union Bulletin (Chicago)
Industrial Worker (Spokane, Everett, and Seattle, WA)
International Socialist Review
Meriden *Morning Record* (Meriden, CT)
Oregon Daily Journal (Portland)
Portland *Evening Telegram*
Seattle *Daily Times*
Seattle *Post-Intelligencer*
Seattle *Star*
Seattle *Union Record*
Solidarity
Spokane *Spokesman-Review*
Everett *Daily Herald*
Everett *Tribune*

The Nation
New Recruit (Chicago)
New Solidarity
New York Times
Oregonian (Portland)
Portland *News*
Spokane *Press*
The Tailor
Weekly People (New York)

BOOKS AND PERIODICALS

Ashbaugh, Carolyn. *Lucy Parsons: American Revolutionary*. Chicago: Charles H. Kerr, 1976.

Avrich, Paul, ed. *Anarchist Voices*. Oakland, CA: AK Press, 2005.

Baron, Ava, ed. *Work Engendered: Toward a New History of American Labor*. Ithaca, NY: Cornell University Press, 1991.

Baxandall, Rosalyn. *Words on Fire: The Life and Writing of Elizabeth Gurley Flynn*. New Brunswick, NJ: Rutgers University Press, 1987.

Beloso, Brook Meredith. "Sex, Work, and the Feminist Erasure of Class." *Signs* 38, no. 1 (2012).

Bengston, Henry. *On the Left in America: Memoirs of the Scandinavian-American Labor Movement*. Translated by Kermit B. Westerberg. Carbondale: Southern Illinois University Press, 1999.

Bergmann, Verity. *Revolutionary Industrial Unionism: The Industrial Workers of the World in Australia*. Cambridge, UK: Cambridge University Press, 1995.

Black, Robert. "Beautiful Losers: The Historiography of the Industrial Workers of the World." March 1998. http://www.infoshop.org/texts/iww.html.

Blair, Karen. "The State of Research on Pacific Northwest Women." *Frontiers* 22 (2001).

———, ed. *Women in Pacific Northwest History*. Seattle: University of Washington Press, 1988.

Boag, Peter. *Same-Sex Affairs: Constructing and Controlling Homosexuality in the Pacific Northwest*. Berkeley: University of California Press, 2003.

Broder, Sherri. *Tramps, Unfit Mothers, and Neglected Children: Negotiating the Family in Nineteenth-Century Philadelphia*. Philadelphia: University of Pennsylvania Press, 2002.

Broyles, Glen. "The Spokane Free Speech Fight, 1909–1910." *Labor History* 19, no. 2 (1978).

Buhle, Mari Jo. *Women and American Socialism, 1870–1920*. Urbana: University of Illinois Press, 1983.

Cameron, Ardis. *Radicals of the Worst Sort: Laboring Women in Lawrence, Massachusetts, 1860–1912*. Urbana: University of Illinois Press, 1993.

Camp, Helen. *Iron in Her Soul: Elizabeth Gurley Flynn and the American Left*. Pullman: Washington State University Press, 1995.

Chateauvert, Melinda. *Marching Together: Women of the Brotherhood of Sleeping Car Porters*. Urbana: University of Illinois Press, 1998.

Chesler, Ellen. *Women of Valor: Margaret Sanger and the Birth Control Movement in America*. New York: Simon and Schuster, 1992.

Clark, Norman H. *Mill Town: A Social History of Everett, Washington, from Its Earliest Beginnings on the Shores of the Puget Sound to the Tragic and Infamous Event Known as the Everett Massacre*. Seattle: University of Washington Press, 1970.

Clement, Elizabeth Alice. *Love for Sale: Courting, Treating, and Prostitution in New York City, 1900–1945*. Chapel Hill: University of North Carolina Press, 2006.

Cobble, Dorothy Sue, ed. *Women and Unions: Forging a Partnership*. Ithaca, NY: IRL Press, 1993.

Cole, Peter. *Wobblies on the Waterfront: Interracial Unionism in Progressive-Era Philadelphia*. Chicago: University of Illinois Press, 2007.

Cook, Tom. "Radical Politics, Radical Love: The Life of Dr. Marie Equi." *Northwest Gay and Lesbian Historian* 1, no. 3 (Summer/Fall 1996), and no. 4 (June 1997).

Cordery, Simon. "Friendly Societies and the Discourse of Respectability in Britain, 1825–1875." *Journal of British Studies* 34, no. 1 (January 1995).

Depastino, Todd. *Citizen Hobo: How a Century of Homelessness Shaped America*. Chicago: University of Chicago Press, 2003.

DeVault, Ileen. *United Apart: Gender and the Rise of Craft Unionism, 1887–1903*. Ithaca, NY: Cornell University Press, 2004.

Dilg, Janice. "By Proceeding in an Orderly and Lawful Manner." Master's thesis, Portland State University, 2005.

———. "'For Working Women in Oregon': Caroline Gleason/Sister Miriam Theresa and Oregon's Minimum Wage Law." *Oregon Historical Quarterly* 110, no. 1 (Spring 2009).

Dreyfus, Philip. "The IWW and the Limits of Inter-Ethnic Organizing: Reds, Whites, and Greeks in Grays Harbor Washington, 1912." *Labor History* 38 (Fall 1997).

Dubofsky, Melvyn. *We Shall Be All: A History of the Industrial Workers of the World*. Chicago: Quadrangle Books, 1969.

Duda, John. *Wanted: Men to Fill the Jails of Spokane: Fighting for Free Speech with the Hobo Agitators of the IWW*. Chicago: Charles H. Kerr, 2009.

Early, Frances H. *A World without War: How US Feminists and Pacifists Resisted World War I*. Syracuse, NY: Syracuse University Press, 1997.

Fite, Gilbert, and H. Peterson. *Opponents of War, 1917–1918*. Westport, CT: Greenwood Press, 1986.

Flynn, Elizabeth Gurley. *I Speak My Own Piece*. New York: International Publishers, 1973.

———. *The Rebel Girl: An Autobiography, My First Life (1906–1926)*. New York: International Publishers, 1981.

Foner, Philip. *Women and the American Labor Movement: From Colonial Times to the Eve of World War I*. New York: Free Press, 1979.

———, ed. *Fellow Workers and Friends: IWW Free Speech Fights as Told by Participants*. Westport, CT: Greenwood Press, 1981.

Fonow, Mary Margaret. *Union Women: Forging Feminism in the United Steel Workers of America*. Minneapolis: University of Minnesota Press, 2003.

Frank, Dana. *Purchasing Power: Consumer Organizing, Gender, and the Seattle Labor Movement, 1919–1929*. Cambridge, UK: Cambridge University Press, 1994.

Fuller, Tom, and Art Ayre. *Oregon at Work: 1859–2009*. Portland: Ooligan Press, 2009.

Gabin, Nancy. *Feminism in the Labor Movement: Women and the United Auto Workers 1935–1975*. Ithaca, NY: Cornell University Press, 1990.

Goings, Aaron. "Red Harbor: Class, Violence, and Community in Grays Harbor, Washington." PhD diss., Simon Fraser University, 2011.

Goldman, Emma. *Living My Life*. New York: Dover, 1970.

Goodhew, David. "Working-Class Respectability: The Example of the Western Areas of Johannesburg, 1930–1955." *Journal of African History* 41, no. 2 (2000).

Gordon, Linda. *Woman's Body, Woman's Right: A Social History*. New York: Grossman, 1976.

Green, Archie, David Roediger, Franklin Rosemont, and Salvatore Salerno, eds. *The Big Red Songbook*. Chicago: Charles H. Kerr, 2007.

Greenwald, Maureen. "Working-Class Feminism and the Family Wage Ideal: The Seattle Debate on Married Women's Right to Work, 1914–1920." *Journal of American History* 76 (June 1989).

Griffin, Farah Jasmine. "Black Feminists and DuBois: Respectability, Protection, and Beyond." *Annals of the American Academy of Political and Social Science* 568 (March 2000).

Guglielmo, Jennifer. "Transnational Feminism's Radical Past: Lessons from Italian Immigrant Women Anarchists in Industrializing America." *Journal of Women's History* 22, no. 1 (2010).

Hall, Greg. "'The Fruits of Her Labor': Women, Children, and Progressive Era Reformers in the Pacific Northwest Canning Industry." *Oregon Historical Quarterly* 109, no. 2 (Summer 2008).

———. *Harvest Wobblies: The Industrial Workers of the World and Agricultural Workers in the American West, 1905–1930*. Corvallis: Oregon State University Press, 2001.

———. "The Theory and Practice of Anarchism at Home Colony, 1896–1912." Master's thesis, Washington State University, 1994.

Helquist, Michael. "'Lewd, Obscene, and Indecent': The 1916 Portland Edition of *Family Limitation*." *Oregon Historical Quarterly* 117, no. 2 (Summer 2016): 274–287.

———. *Marie Equi: Radical Politics and Outlaw Passions*. Corvallis: Oregon State University Press, 2015.

Hidy, Ralph. *Timber and Men: The Weyerhaeuser Story*. New York: Macmillan, 1963.

Higbie, Frank Tobias. *Indispensable Outcasts: Hobo Workers and Community in the American Midwest, 1880–1930*. Urbana: University of Illinois Press, 2003.

Hodges, Adam. "At War over the Espionage Act in Portland: Dueling Perspectives from Agent William Bryon and Kathleen O'Brennan." *Oregon Historical Quarterly* 108 (Fall 2007).

Howd, Cloice. *Industrial Relations in the West Coast Lumber Industry*. Washington: Government Printing Office, 1924.

Hummasti, Paul George. *Finnish Radicals in Astoria, Oregon, 1904–1940: A Study in Immigrant Socialism*. New York: Arno Press, 1970.

Industrial Workers of the World. *Little Red Songbook*. Chicago: Charles H. Kerr Press, 2003.

Jacobson, Matthew Frye. *Barbarian Virtues: The United States Encounters Foreign Peoples and Home and Abroad, 1876–1917*. New York: Hill and Wang, 2001.

Jameson, Elizabeth. *All That Glitters: Class, Conflict, and Community in Cripple Creek*. Urbana: University of Illinois Press, 1998.

Johnson, Jeffrey A. *They Are All Red Out Here: Socialist Politics in the Pacific Northwest, 1895–1925*. Norman: University of Oklahoma Press, 2008.

Johnson, Robert. *The Radical Middle-Class: Populist Democracy and the Questions of Capitalism in Progressive Era Portland, Oregon*. Princeton, NJ: Princeton University Press, 2003.

Jones, Jacqueline. *The Life and Times of Lucy Parsons, American Radical.* New York: Basic Books, 2017.

Kennedy, Kathleen. *Disloyal Mothers and Scurrilous Citizens: Women and Subversion during World War I.* Bloomington: Indiana University Press, 1999.

Kessler-Harris, Alice. *Gendering Labor History.* Urbana: University of Illinois Press, 2007.

Kornbluh, Joyce L., ed. *Rebel Voices: An IWW Anthology.* Ann Arbor: University of Michigan Press, 1964.

Krieger, Nancy. *Queen of the Bolsheviks: The Hidden History of Dr. Marie Equi.* Montreal: Kersplebedeb, 2009.

Kruttschnitt, Candace. "Respectable Women and the Law." *Sociological Quarterly* 23 (Spring 1982).

Langum, David. *Crossing Over the Line: Legislating Morality and the Mann Act.* Chicago: University of Chicago Press, 1994.

Leier, Mark. *Rebel Life: The Life and Times of Robert Gosden: Revolutionary, Mystic, Labor Spy.* Vancouver: New Star Books, 1999.

———. *Red Flags and Red Tape: The Making of a Labor Bureaucracy.* Toronto: University of Toronto Press, 1995.

LeWarne, Charles. "The Anarchist Colony at Home, Washington, 1901–1902." *Arizona and the West* 14, no. 2 (July 1, 1972): 157, 167.

———. *Utopias on Puget Sound, 1885–1915.* Seattle: University of Washington Press, 1975.

MacColl, E. Kimbark. *Merchants, Money, and Power: The Portland Establishment, 1843–1913.* Portland: Georgian Press, 1988.

McGerr, Michael E. *A Fierce Discontent: The Rise and Fall of the Progressive Movement in America, 1870–1920.* New York: Free Press, 2003.

Mercier, Laurie. "Reworking Race, Class, and Gender into Pacific Northwest History." *Frontiers: A Journal of Women's Studies* 22, no. 3 (2001).

Meyerowitz, Joanne J. *Women Adrift: Independent Wage Earners in Chicago, 1880–1930.* Chicago: University of Chicago Press, 1988.

Morgan, Sue, ed. *The Feminist History Reader.* New York: Routledge, 2006.

Myers, Gloria. *A Municipal Mother: Portland's Lola Greene Baldwin, America's First Policewoman.* Corvallis: Oregon State University Press, 1995.

O'Connor, Harvey. *Revolution in Seattle: A Memoir.* Chicago: Haymarket Books, 2009.

Odem, Mary. *Delinquent Daughters: Protecting and Policing Adolescent Female Sexuality in the United States, 1885–1920.* Chapel Hill: University of North Carolina Press, 1995.

O'Neill, Colleen. "Domesticity Deployed: Gender, Race, and the Construction of Class Struggle in the Bisbee Deportation." *Labor History* 34 (Spring/Summer 1993).

Oregon State Board of Control et al. *Biennial Report.* Salem, OR: State Printing Office, 1915.

Overall, Christine. "What's Wrong with Prostitution? Evaluating Sex Work." *Signs* 17, no. 4 (1992).

Peiss, Kathy. *Cheap Amusements: Working Women and Leisure in Turn-of-the-Century New York.* Philadelphia: Temple University Press, 1986.

Portland Vice Commission. *First Report of the Portland Vice Commission to the Mayor and the City Council.* Portland: Portland Vice Commission, 1912.

Preston, William. *Aliens and Dissenters: Federal Repression of Radicals, 1903–1933.* Chicago: University of Illinois Press, 1994.

Prouty, Andrew Mason. *More Deadly Than War: Pacific Coast Logging, 1827–1981*. New York: Garland Publishing, 1985.

Rajala, Richard. "A Dandy Bunch of Wobblies: Pacific Northwest Loggers and the Industrial Workers of the World, 1900–1930." *Labor History* 37 (Spring 1996), 205–234.

Rasmussen, Janet. *New Land, New Lives: Scandinavian Immigrants to the Pacific Northwest*. Seattle: University of Washington Press, 1998.

Records of the Immigration and Naturalization Service. *Series A: Subject Correspondence Files, Part 6: Suppression of Aliens, 1906–1930*. Microfilm, Reel 2.

Reiter, Rayna R., ed. *Toward an Anthropology of Women*. New York: Monthly Review Press, 1975.

Renshaw, Patrick: *The Wobblies: The Story of Syndicalism in the United States*. Garden City, NY: Doubleday, 1967.

Rosemont, Franklin. *Joe Hill: The IWW and the Making of a Revolutionary Working-Class Counterculture*. Chicago: Charles H. Kerr, 2003.

Rosen, Ellen Doree. *A Wobbly Life: IWW Organizer E. F. Doree*. Detroit: Wayne State University Press, 2004.

Rosen, Ruth. *The Lost Sisterhood: Prostitution in America, 1900–1918*. Baltimore, MD: Johns Hopkins University Press, 1982.

Salerno, Salvatore. *Red November, Black November: Culture and Community in the Industrial Workers of the World*. Albany: University of New York Press, 1989.

Sangster, Joan. *Earning Respect: The Lives of Working Women in Small-Town Ontario, 1920–1960*. Toronto: University of Toronto Press, 1995.

Schofield, Ann. "Rebel Girls and Union Maids: The Woman Question in the Journals of the AFL and IWW, 1905–1920." *Feminist Studies* 9, no. 2 (Summer 1983).

Schwantes, Carlos A. *The Pacific Northwest: An Interpretive History*. Rev. and enl. ed. Lincoln: University of Nebraska Press, 1996.

———. *Radical Heritage: Labor, Socialism, and Reform in Washington and British Columbia, 1885–1917*. Seattle: University of Washington Press, 1979.

Sellars, Nigel. *Oil, Wheat, and Wobblies: The Industrial Workers of the World in Oklahoma, 1905–1930*. Norman: University of Oklahoma Press, 1998.

Sharbach, Sarah Ellen. "Louise Olivereau and the Seattle Radical Community, 1917–1923." Master's thesis, University of Washington, 1986.

Shor, Francis. "'Virile Syndicalism' in Comparative Perspective: A Gender Analysis of the IWW in the United States and Australia." *International Labor and Working-Class History* 56 (1999).

Smith, Walker C. *The Everett Massacre: A History of the Class Struggle in the Lumber Industry*. Chicago: IWW Publishing, 1918.

Solinger, Rickie. *The Abortionist: A Woman against the Law*. Berkeley: University of California Press, 1996.

Strong, Anna Louise. *I Change Worlds*. Berkeley: Seal Press, 1980.

Taillon, Paul Michel. "'What We Want Is Good, Sober Men': Masculinity, Respectability, and Temperance in the Railroad Brotherhoods, c. 1870–1910." *Journal of Social History* 36, no. 2 (Winter 2002).

Tax, Meredith. *The Rising of the Women: Feminist Solidarity and Class Conflict, 1880–1917*. Urbana: University of Illinois Press, 1980.

Townsend, John Clendenin. *Running the Gauntlet: Cultural Sources of Violence against the I.W.W.* New York: Garland, 1986.

Tyler, Robert. *Rebels of the Woods: The IWW in the Pacific Northwest*. Eugene: University of Oregon Press, 1967.

United States Congress House Committee on Immigration and Naturalization. *IWW Deportation Cases*. Washington, DC: Government Printing Office, 1920.

Venzon, Anne Cipriano. *The United States in the First World War: An Encyclopedia*. New York: Routledge, 1999.

Weigand, Kate. "Reply to Critics." *Science and Society* 66, no. 4 (Winter 2002/2003).

Welles, Frank. "Our Oregon State Institutions." *Oregon Teachers' Monthly,* 1915.

Wells, Hulet M. *Wilson and the Issues of To-Day: A Socialist Revision of George Creel's Famous Book*. Seattle, WA: The Socialist Party, 1918.

Zatz, Noah. "Sex Work/Sex Act: Law, Labor, and Desire in Constructions of Prostitution." *Signs* 22, no. 2 (1997).

Index

Page numbers with an *f* refer to a figure; *n* refers to an endnote.